ROSE REISMAN

··· BRINGS HOME ···

LIGHT

COOKING

ROSE REISMAN
BRINGS HOME
LIGHT
COOKING

MACMILLAN CANADA
TORONTO

Rose Reisman Brings Home Light Cooking

Copyright © 1993 Rose Reisman

Canadian Cataloguing in Publication Data

Reisman, Rose, 1953–
    Rose Reisman brings home light cooking

Includes index.
ISBN 0-7715-9000-8

1. Cookery. 2. Low-fat diet – recipes.
3. Nutrition.   I. Title.

RM237.7.R45 1993   641.5'638   C92-095788-9

PAGE DESIGN AND COMPOSITION:	MATTHEWS COMMUNICATIONS DESIGN
PHOTOGRAPHY:	MARK SHAPIRO/IN CAMERA STUDIO
FOOD STYLIST:	KATE BUSH
RECIPE EDITOR:	BEVERLEY RENAHAN
GENERAL EDITOR:	JENNIFER GLOSSOP

Cover photo: Salmon Fillet with Sesame Seeds and Teriyaki Sauce (page 81)

Macmillan Canada
A Division of Canada Publishing Corporation
Toronto, Ontario, Canada

Printed in Canada

3456 BP 97 96 95 94 93

Contents

To the Canadian Breast Cancer Foundation, in the hope that money raised from the sale of my book will, with other Canadian Breast Cancer Foundation projects, help to eradicate this disease in the future.

Also to my family: my official taste-tester, Sam, who somehow finds time to manage his own business as well as mine; and to my children, Natalie, David, Laura, and Adam — my one-year-old son, who was the impetus behind this book.

ACKNOWLEDGMENTS

My thanks to the many people and groups who contributed to this book:

The Canadian Breast Cancer Foundation for giving me the opportunity to write this book. A special thanks to Carole Grafstein, Nancy Paul and Michele Levy.

The fund raising committee of the Canadian Breast Cancer Foundation, especially Rosanne Cox and Norma Fitzgerald.

Beverly Tobin who acted as an advisory member for the fund-raising committee.

Mary Cousins who wrote the introduction on nutrition and guided in the development of the book according to current nutritional guidelines for Canadians.

Dr. Roy Clark, Chairman of the Medical Advisory Committee (Canadian Breast Cancer Foundation), for his support.

Macmillan Canada, with a special thanks to Robert Dees and Denise Schon.

Matthews Communications Design for a wonderful design, and special thanks to Peter and Sharon Matthews.

Beverley Renahan, the recipe editor, who taught me the basics of excellent cookbook editing.

Jennifer Glossop, the overall editor, who made certain the entire book had continuity.

Mark Shapiro of In-Camera Studio, who made certain each picture was brilliant.

Dianne Hargrave, my publicist, who through her diligence manages to have me appear on all major media.

Kate Bush, the food stylist.

Grant's Fine China and Gifts in Toronto, Junors in Toronto, and the Main Course in Toronto, for donating the tableware. And a very special thanks to Villeroy & Boch Ltd. in Toronto, who generously supplied an abundance of magnificent tableware.

B.B. Bargoon's in Toronto, who donated the fabrics.

Thames Valley Brick and Tile Inc., for donating the glassblock.

Ramca Tiles Ltd. in Toronto, for donating the tiles.

Testing Kitchen, with a special thanks to Allison Southwood, Edit Vendel, and to Kelly, Agnes, Eva and Edel.

Penny Hill - Fairlawn WordPro, for her diligence in the typing and retyping of the manuscript.

Barb Schon, the recipe indexer, who has made each recipe a joy to find.

INTRODUCTION

I think I have really done it! Get ready to change the way you think about light cooking — I have.

This is my fifth cookbook in as many years, and impolitic as it may be to say so, it is my best. For one thing, I have tested, retested, and tested one more time again, over 300 recipes and then picked the 240 best. Although this is my fifth book, it is the first one I have done unencumbered by other chefs. These are my own creations — not theirs — and so, like one's first child, attention, love and careful planning have been lavished on this effort.

For the first little while, back in April when I began testing, my husband thought romance was born anew — a four- or five-course dinner every evening, two or three desserts appearing later on, fresh banana bread the next morning. He only caught on after I began preparing four to six entrées each night and dinners became 15 courses instead of five; and he wasn't permitted to leave the table until he had tasted and provided comments on each course. He looks none the worse for the wear, and your family will be the beneficiary of his imposed indulgence.

This book has been designed to provide you a daily resource for regular meal preparation, as well as special occasions. Appetizers including dips, using chickpeas, blue cheese and artichoke, or tortillas topped with smoked salmon and creamy ricotta cheese, and fabulous pita pizzas with goat cheese and your choice of vegetables.

Concoctions of puréed pumpkin, sweet potato, leeks and asparagus provide the base for rich, creamy soups.

Sublime ingredients, such as bulgur, barley, pasta, wild rice, couscous and goat or feta cheese are combined to provide stimulating, healthy, versatile and low-cost meals targeted to delight family and friends alike.

With three of my five books focused on desserts, I can claim desserts are my forte, and they are all here: brownies, chocolate cakes, coffee cakes, cookies, rich and dense cheesecakes, muffins and loafbreads — the whole mouth-watering lot, prepared on a nutritionally-sound basis. Enjoy sinful desserts without guilt!

Moreover, all of the recipes here have been nutritionally analyzed and conform with the recommendations of the newly revised 1992 Canada's Food Guide to Healthy Eating. I am neither a nutritionist nor a dietician. I have come to this endeavour in the very same way most of you have. I want to provide a sound diet that my family, including my four children, can enjoy and benefit from. For the last seven months, the recipes included here have been the backbone of that diet.

This book was conceived shortly before the birth of my fourth child, Adam. After a difficult pregnancy, my son's difficult start, the value of life and good health were incomparably reinforced. The impetus led me to write this book, in association with the Canadian Breast Cancer Foundation. Part of the proceeds from each and every book purchased will be remitted to the Canadian Breast Cancer Foundation for its use in furthering breast cancer research and education. With these proceeds, and other funds raised by the Canadian Breast Cancer Foundation, this dreaded disease can be contained, and eventually eradicated. Buy this book or not, but please support the Canadian Breast Cancer Foundation.

Now pick out the recipes that most appeal to you, get your ingredients ready, cook, and enjoy!

Rose Reisman

PREFACE

Cancer presents medical science with one of its most difficult challenges. The disease affects the basic unit of life — the cell. Yet, although we know a great deal about the mechanisms by which cell life is maintained, we cannot create a cell, nor do we understand many of the functions that go on inside the cell.

We do know that cancer is produced by cells that become disorganized and develop into masses of tissue that serve no useful purpose and invade other areas of the body. The cells are not foreign to the body, but they are out of control. Breast cancer is one of the most common tumors, and it is the biggest killer of middle-aged women, accounting for 14 per cent of all deaths between the ages of 25 and 49. The risk of developing breast cancer increases dramatically with age.

Although we don't know the exact cause of breast cancer, we have some clues. There is a higher incidence of breast cancer in parts of the world where the people eat a lot of fatty food. Excessive body weight is also associated with an increase in the incidence of breast cancer and with a poorer prognosis for those who have been treated for the disease. Nevertheless, we cannot prove that a low fat diet, or losing weight, will either reduce the incidence of breast cancer or improve the outlook for those who have been affected.

Many women with breast cancer would like to be able to do something positive for themselves and for their daughters. One of the things they can do is to reduce their fat intake and advise their daughters to do the same. A low-fat diet will also help them to lose weight, since there are twice as many calories in fat as in protein or carbohydrates. A low-fat diet has other advantages: it improves body image; it gives a sense of contributing to a healthier lifestyle; and it reduces the body's cholesterol levels, which may in turn lower the risk of coronary artery disease — a condition that manifests itself in women to a greater extent after the menopause.

The question remains — how do you achieve weight control with a low-fat diet and still indulge in tasty, appetizing food? The answer is found in this cookbook, which offers you sensible but tasty — and certainly not boring — recipes, as well as providing funding for breast cancer research.

R.M. Clark MB, BS, FRCR, FRCPC

Chairman, Medical Advisory Committee
Canadian Breast Cancer Foundation

**CANADIAN
BREAST CANCER
FOUNDATION**

Dear Supporter:

The Canadian Breast Cancer Foundation, a nonprofit organization dedicated to the support and funding of breast cancer research, education and awareness, was established in Toronto in 1986 by a group of 10 community leaders. The Foundation was a driving force behind the establishment of the Ontario Breast Cancer Screening Program, a network of standardized breast-screening clinics throughout Ontario. Over the past six years, the Canadian Breast Cancer Foundation has awarded more than $600,000 for breast cancer research projects to hospitals, universities and cancer centres and will allocate more than $300,000 to breast cancer research during 1992.

The Foundation offers sponsorship, donation, membership and in-memorium opportunities to corporations, foundations, organizations, families and individuals.

We are delighted that Rose Reisman, one of Canada's outstanding cookbook authors, has dedicated a portion of the proceeds from the sale of her fifth cookbook to the Foundation. We hope that this book will:

- *Encourage us all to eat healthy food;*

- *Raise funds for breast cancer research; and*

- *Create public awareness.*

Many thanks to the people who worked along with Rose Reisman to make this book a reality. Our sincere appreciation is also extended to the Canadian Breast Cancer Foundation Cookbook Chairman, Norma Fitzgerald, and to our many volunteers for their continuous support.

Carole Grafstein

*Chairman, Ontario Chapter
Canadian Breast Cancer Foundation*

NUTRITIONAL ADVICE

The purpose of this book is to raise awareness for breast cancer and raise funds for breast cancer research. This cookbook is a collection of delicious lower fat recipes and should not be interpreted as a treatment for any type of existing cancers, including breast cancer.

The relationship between diet and cancer is still very new. The results of long-term intervention trials now underway in North America and designed to examine this association are still many years away. Until that time Canadians should follow the Nutrition Guidelines set down in the *Canada's Food Guide to Healthy Eating* released by Health and Welfare Canada, November 1992.

Today's health concerns, as they relate to diet, are very different from deficiency diseases of the past, and include obesity, heart disease, diabetes and cancer. Malnutrition today doesn't refer only to lack of food but often refers to over consumption of food. A few years ago, Health and Welfare Canada began a process of assessing suitability of the nutrient recommendations to determine if they met the needs of changing society. Since 1987, health officials have been reviewing scientific literature and meeting with public health policy makers and members of the food industry in Canada. The efforts of their work resulted in *Canada's Food Guide to Healthy Eating*.

The Food Guide recommendations for Canadians over the age of four years are:

Grain products	Eat 5 to 12 servings per day and choose whole grain and enriched products more often. These products are high in starch and fibre.
Vegetables and Fruit	Eat 5 to 10 servings per day. Choose dark green and orange vegetables and fruits.
Milk products	Choose 2 to 4 servings per day of lower fat milk products.
Meat	Choose 2 to 3 servings per day of fish, lean meat, dried peas, beans and lentils.

Other foods such as potato chips, chocolate candy and alcohol should be consumed in moderation.

Limit your fat intake by steering clear of fried foods, trimming visible fat from meat, taking the skin off chicken, avoiding salads drenched with heavy oily salad dressings, and choosing lower fat milk and milk products.

Take advantage of the wide variety of foods we have in our marketplace and, above all, use meal time to enjoy your loved ones.

The recipes that Rose has painstakingly prepared in this cookbook support the thinking behind the new Food Guide: eat a variety of foods every day; and choose lower fat foods more often.

Mary Cousins

Research Dietitian

PPETIZERS

1. Dips can be prepared up to one day before, but garnishes should not be added until serving time. Mix dips well before serving since excess liquid can separate.

2. Count on 4 to 6 pieces of hors d'oeurves per person.

3. Many of these appetizers can be served as a first course.

• PITA OR TORTILLA PIZZAS • • •

Serves 6 to 8
or makes 16 hors
d'oeuvres.

TIP

Any combination of
vegetables can be used, as
well as any type of cheese.
Goat cheese is exceptional
on pizzas.

•

Try 1/4 cup (50 mL)
chopped sun-dried
tomatoes.

MAKE AHEAD

Prepare pizzas early in day
and refrigerate. Bake just
before serving.

Preheat oven to 400°F (200°C)

3/4 cup	tomato sauce	175 mL
4	flour tortillas or pita breads (preferably whole wheat)	4
8	small mushrooms, thinly sliced	8
1/4 cup	diced sweet red or green pepper	50 mL
1 tbsp	chopped fresh basil (or 1 tsp [5 mL] dried)	15 mL
1/2 tsp	dried oregano	2 mL
1 cup	shredded mozzarella cheese	250 mL
1/4 cup	chopped feta cheese (optional)	50 mL

1. Divide tomato sauce among breads; spread evenly.

2. Top with mushrooms, red pepper, basil and oregano. Sprinkle with cheese.

3. Bake for 12 minutes or until crisp and cheese is melted. Cut each into 4 pieces.

PER 1/8TH SERVING

Calories	180
Protein	9 g
Fat	4 g
Carbohydrates	26 g
Sodium	504 mg
Cholesterol	11 mg
Fibre	4 g

···················· SHRIMP AND SNOW PEA ···· TIDBITS

Serves 4 to 6
or makes 16 hors
d'oeuvres.

TIP

Buy snow peas that are
firm and crisp, and have
no blemishes.

●

Medium-sized scallops
would also be delicious for
this very sophisticated
hors d'oeuvre.

MAKE AHEAD

If serving cold, prepare
and refrigerate early in
day.

16	snow peas	16
2 tsp	vegetable oil	10 mL
1 tsp	crushed garlic	5 mL
1 tbsp	chopped fresh parsley	15 mL
16	medium shrimp, peeled, deveined, tail left on	16

1. Steam or microwave snow peas until barely tender-crisp. Rinse with cold water. Drain and set aside.

2. In nonstick skillet, heat oil; sauté garlic, parsley and shrimp just until shrimp turn pink, 3 to 5 minutes.

3. Wrap each snow pea around shrimp; fasten with tooth-pick. Serve warm or cold.

PER 1/6TH SERVING

Calories	31
Protein	3 g
Fat	1 g
Carbohydrates	1 g
Sodium	31 mg
Cholesterol	26 mg
Fibre	0 g

••••••••••••••••••ORIENTAL CHICKEN WRAPPED •• MUSHROOMS

Serves 4 to 6
or makes 18 hors
d'oeuvres.

TIP

Tender beef is delicious
with this sweet oriental
sauce.

MAKE AHEAD

Refrigerate chicken in
marinade early in day.
Wrap chicken around
mushroom caps and broil
just before serving.

Preheat broiler
Baking sheet sprayed with nonstick vegetable spray

1 tbsp	rice wine vinegar	15 mL
1 tbsp	vegetable oil	15 mL
2 tbsp	soya sauce	25 mL
1 tsp	crushed garlic	5 mL
2 tbsp	finely chopped onion	25 mL
1 tsp	sesame oil	5 mL
2 tbsp	water	25 mL
2 tbsp	brown sugar	25 mL
1/2 tsp	sesame seeds (optional)	2 mL
3/4 lb	boneless skinless chicken breast	375 g
18	medium mushroom caps (without stems)	18

1. In bowl, combine vinegar, oil, soya sauce, garlic, onion, sesame oil, water, sugar, and sesame seeds (if using); mix well.

2. Cut chicken into strips about 3 inches (8 cm) long and 1 inch (2.5 cm) wide to make 18 strips. Add to bowl and marinate for 20 minutes, stirring occasionally.

3. Wrap each chicken strip around mushroom; secure with toothpick. Place on baking sheet. Broil for approximately 5 minutes or until chicken is no longer pink inside. Serve immediately.

PER 1/6TH SERVING
❚❚❚❚❚❚❚❚❚❚❚❚❚❚

Calories	131
Protein	14 g
Fat	5 g
Carbohydrates	8 g
Sodium	376 mg
Cholesterol	31 mg
Fibre	1 g

❚❚❚❚❚❚❚❚❚❚❚❚❚❚

••••••••••••••••••RICOTTA AND SMOKED SALMON•• TORTILLA BITES

Serves 4 to 6
or makes 24 hors
d'oeuvres.

TIP

These are best served at
room temperature.

MAKE AHEAD

Make early in day and
refrigerate. Arrange on
lettuce-lined plate just
before serving.

1 cup	ricotta cheese	250 mL
1 tbsp	light mayonnaise or light sour cream	15 mL
2 tbsp	chopped fresh dill (or 1/2 tsp [2 mL] dried dillweed)	25 mL
2 tbsp	finely chopped chives or green onions	25 mL
2 oz	smoked salmon, diced	50 g
4	flour tortillas	4
	Lettuce leaves	

1. In bowl or food processor, combine ricotta and light mayonnaise until smooth. Gently stir in dill, chives and smoked salmon until combined.

2. Divide filling among tortillas, spreading evenly. Roll up jelly roll style. Cut each tortilla into 6 pieces. Arrange on lettuce-lined plate.

PER 1/6TH SERVING

Calories	160
Protein	8 g
Fat	6 g
Carbohydrates	18 g
Sodium	247 mg
Cholesterol	17 mg
Fibre	1 g

BRUSCHETTA WITH BASIL AND OREGANO

Serves 4 to 6
or makes 12 slices

TIP

Vary the bruschetta by adding 3 tbsp (45 mL) finely diced yellow or red pepper or red onion to mixture.

•

Or sprinkle 2 tbsp (25 mL) diced sun-dried tomatoes over slices just before broiling.

MAKE AHEAD

Prepare tomato mixture early in day and marinate to allow flavors to blend well. Bake just before serving.

Preheat broiler

2	small tomatoes, diced	2
2 tbsp	olive oil	25 mL
1 tsp	crushed garlic	5 mL
2 tbsp	chopped fresh basil (or 1 tsp [5 mL] dried)	25 mL
1 tbsp	chopped fresh oregano (or 1/2 tsp [2 mL] dried)	15 mL
1 tbsp	chopped green onion	15 mL
12	slices (1/2-inch [1cm] thick) French bread	12
1 tbsp	grated Parmesan cheese	15 mL

1. In small bowl, combine tomatoes, oil, garlic, basil, oregano and onion. Let stand for at least 20 minutes.

2. Toast bread on baking sheet under broiler, turning once, until brown on both sides. Divide tomato mixture over bread; sprinkle with cheese. Broil for 2 minutes or until heated through.

PER 1/6TH SERVING

Calories	93
Protein	2 g
Fat	2 g
Carbohydrates	15 g
Sodium	148 mg
Cholesterol	0 mg
Fibre	1 g

FRESH MUSSELS WITH TOMATO SALSA

TIPS

Substitute fresh coriander for the parsley for a change.

●

This recipe can also be made with fresh clams.

●

Serve as a salad over lettuce.

MAKE AHEAD

Prepare and refrigerate mixture early in day to allow flavors to blend. Spoon into shells a couple of hours prior to serving and keep chilled.

PER 1/6TH SERVING

Calories	18
Protein	2 g
Fat	0.5 g
Carbohydrates	1 g
Sodium	47 mg
Cholesterol	5 mg
Fibre	0 g

24	mussels	24
1/2 cup	water or wine	125 mL
3/4 cup	finely chopped onions	175 mL
1 1/2 tsp	crushed garlic	7 mL
1 cup	coarsely chopped tomato	250 mL
4 tsp	chopped fresh basil (or 1/2 tsp [2 mL] dried)	20 mL
2 tbsp	chopped fresh parsley	25 mL
2 tsp	olive oil	10 mL
1/4 tsp	chili powder	1 mL
	Salt and pepper	

1. Scrub mussels under cold running water; remove any beards. Discard any mussels that do not close when tapped.

2. In saucepan, combine mussels, water, 1/4 cup (50 mL) of the onions and 1 tsp (5 mL) of the garlic; cover and steam just until mussels open, approximately 5 minutes. Discard any that do not open. Let cool then remove mussels from shells, reserving half of shall. Place mussels in bowl.

3. In food processor, combine remaining 1/2 cup (125 mL) onions and 1/2 tsp (2 mL) garlic, tomatoes, basil, parsley, oil, chili powder, and salt and pepper to taste; process using on/off motion just until chunky. Do not purée. Add to mussels and stir to mix. Refrigerate until chilled.

4. Divide mussel mixture evenly among reserved shells and arrange on serving plate.

SALMON SWISS CHEESE ENGLISH MUFFINS

Serves 8
or makes 32 wedges.

Preheat broiler

1	can (7 1/2 oz [220 g]) salmon, drained	1
1/4 cup	light mayonnaise	50 mL
2 tbsp	chopped green onion	25 mL
2 tbsp	chopped red onion	25 mL
2 tbsp	diced celery	25 mL
2 tbsp	chopped fresh dill (or 1 tsp [5 mL] dried dillweed)	25 mL
2 tsp	lemon juice	10 mL
4	English muffins, split in half and toasted	4
1/3 cup	shredded Swiss cheese	75 mL

1. In food processor, combine salmon, mayonnaise, green and red onions, celery, dill and lemon juice. Using on/off motion, process just until chunky but not puréed.

2. Divide salmon mixture over muffins and spread evenly. Sprinkle with cheese. Broil just until cheese melts, approximately 2 minutes. To serve, slice each muffin into quarters.

PER SERVING

Calories	145
Protein	9 g
Fat	5 g
Carbohydrates	14 g
Sodium	351 mg
Cholesterol	20 mg
Fibre	1 g

ASPARAGUS WRAPPED WITH RICOTTA CHEESE AND HAM

Serves 4.

TIP

Choose the greenest asparagus with straight firm stalks. The tips should be tightly closed and firm.

Prosciutto, a salt-cured meat, can replace the ham.

MAKE AHEAD

Assemble rolls early in day and refrigerate. Serve cold or hot.

Preheat oven to 400°F (200°C)
Baking sheet sprayed with nonstick vegetable spray

12	medium asparagus, trimmed	12
4 oz	ricotta cheese	125 g
1/4 tsp	crushed garlic	1 mL
1 tbsp	finely chopped green onion or chives	15 mL
	Salt and pepper	
4	thin slices cooked ham (about 4 oz [125 g])	4

1. Steam or microwave asparagus just until tender-crisp; drain and let cool. Set aside.

2. In small bowl, combine cheese, garlic, onion, and salt and pepper to taste; mix well.

3. Spread evenly over each slice of ham. Top each with 3 asparagus and roll up. Place on baking sheet and bake for 3 to 4 minutes or until hot.

PER SERVING

Calories	94
Protein	10 g
Fat	4 g
Carbohydrates	4 g
Sodium	378 mg
Cholesterol	23 mg
Fibre	1 g

CRAB CELERY STICKS

Serves 4 to 6
or makes 24 hors
d'oeuvres.

TIP

For a less expensive
version, use imitation
crab, often called Surimi.

•

Serve as a dip with
vegetables or broiled on
top of pitas or English
muffins.

MAKE AHEAD

Make and refrigerate
filling early in day. Stir
well and pour off any
excess liquid before filling
celery.

PER 1/6TH SERVING

Calories	15
Protein	1 g
Fat	1 g
Carbohydrates	0.6 g
Sodium	35 mg
Cholesterol	5 mg
Fibre	0 g

1	can (4.2 oz [120 g]) crabmeat, well drained	1
1/4 cup	sliced green onions	50 mL
1/4 tsp	crushed garlic	1 mL
3 tbsp	chopped fresh dill (or 1 tsp [5 mL] dried dillweed)	45 mL
1 tbsp	lemon juice	15 mL
1/4 cup	chopped celery	50 mL
1/4 cup	chopped sweet red or green pepper	50 mL
2 tbsp	2% yogurt	25 mL
1/4 cup	light mayonnaise	50 mL
	Salt and pepper	
24	pieces (2-inch [5cm]) celery stalks	24
	Paprika	

1. In food processor, combine crabmeat, onions, garlic, dill, lemon juice, chopped celery, red pepper, yogurt and mayonnaise. Using on/off motion, process just until combined but still chunky. Season with salt and pepper to taste.

2. Stuff each celery stalk evenly with mixture. Sprinkle with paprika to taste.

SEAFOOD SEVICHE

Serves 4.

TIP

Cilantro, a wonderful herb, is also called coriander or Chinese parsley. If unavailable, substitute fresh parsley.

●

If you prefer, use only scallops or only squid.

1/4 lb	scallops, sliced	125 g
1/4 lb	squid, sliced	125 g
1/2 cup	finely chopped red onion	125 mL
1/2 cup	diced sweet red or yellow pepper	125 mL
1/2 cup	diced tomato	125 mL
1 tsp	crushed garlic	5 mL
1/4 cup	fresh lime or lemon juice	50 mL
2 tbsp	chopped fresh cilantro or parsley	25 mL
1 tbsp	olive oil	15 mL
	Lettuce leaves	

1. In bowl, combine scallops, squid, onion, red pepper, tomato, garlic, lime juice, cilantro and oil; stir to combine.

2. Cover and refrigerate for 2 hours to marinate, stirring occasionally. Serve over lettuce-lined plates.

PER SERVING

Calories	111
Protein	11 g
Fat	4 g
Carbohydrates	7 g
Sodium	95 mg
Cholesterol:	76 mg
Fibre	1 g

Warm Cherry Tomatoes Stuffed with Garlic and Cheese

Serves 6 to 8
or makes 24 hors
d'oeuvres.

TIP

This filling can be used to stuff medium mushrooms. Just remove the mushroom stems.

MAKE AHEAD

Make early in day and refrigerate. Bake just before serving.

Preheat oven to 400°F (200°C)

24	cherry tomatoes	24
1/2 cup	dry bread crumbs	125 mL
2 tbsp	chopped green onion	25 mL
1/2 tsp	chopped garlic	2 mL
2 tbsp	chopped fresh parsley	25 mL
1 tbsp	margarine, melted	15 mL
1/3 cup	shredded mozzarella cheese	75 mL
1 tbsp	grated Parmesan cheese	15 mL

1. Cut slice from top of each tomato; carefully scoop out seeds and most of the pulp.

2. In bowl, combine bread crumbs, onion, garlic, parsley, margarine and mozzarella until well mixed.

3. Spoon into tomatoes; sprinkle with Parmesan. Place on baking sheet and bake for approximately 10 minutes or until stuffing is golden.

PER 1/8TH SERVING

Calories	78
Protein	3 g
Fat	3 g
Carbohydrates	9 g
Sodium	133 mg
Cholesterol	4 mg
Fibre	1 g

················· SAUTÉED MUSHROOMS ON ···
TOAST ROUNDS

Serves 4 to 6
or makes 12 hors
d'oeuvres.

TIP

This mixture can also be
served in whole mushroom
caps.

MAKE AHEAD

Prepare mushroom
mixture early in day and
keep at room temperature.
Assemble and broil just
before serving.

Preheat broiler

2 tsp	vegetable oil	10 mL
1 tsp	crushed garlic	5 mL
2 tbsp	finely chopped onions	25 mL
1/2 lb	mushrooms, chopped	250 g
1 tbsp	chopped fresh parsley	15 mL
2 tbsp	white wine	25 mL
2 tbsp	chopped green onions or chives	25 mL
1 tsp	soya sauce	5 mL
2 tbsp	dry bread crumbs	25 mL
2 tbsp	grated Parmesan cheese	25 mL
	Salt and pepper	
16	slices small rye bread or French baguette	16

1. In small nonstick saucepan, heat oil; sauté garlic, onions and mushrooms until softened, approximately 5 minutes.

2. Add parsley, wine, green onions, soya sauce, bread crumbs, 1 tbsp (15 mL) of the Parmesan, and salt and pepper to taste; cook for 2 minutes. Set aside.

3. On baking sheet, toast bread in oven just until browned on both sides, approximately 2 minutes (or brown in toaster). Divide mushroom mixture over bread; sprinkle with remaining Parmesan. Broil for 5 minutes or until hot, being careful not to burn.

PER 1/6TH SERVING
:∎∎∎∎∎∎∎∎∎∎∎∎∎:

Calories	75
Protein	2 g
Fat	2 g
Carbohydrates	11 g
Sodium	193 mg
Cholesterol	1 mg
Fibre	2 g

:∎∎∎∎∎∎∎∎∎∎∎∎∎:

SMOKED SALMON AND GOAT ·· CHEESE CUCUMBER SLICES

**Serves 4 to 6
or makes 25 hors
d'oeuvres.**

TIP

Goat cheese, also known
as chèvre, comes in a
variety of shapes ranging
from logs to pyramids and
discs. Some are sprinkled
with herb and spices
throughout. Use any
variety.

•

Serve also as a dip or
serve on celery sticks or in
hollow cherry tomatoes.

MAKE AHEAD

Prepare and refrigerate
mixture up to a day
before. Place on cucumber
slices just before serving.

3 oz	smoked salmon, diced	75 g
3 oz	goat cheese	75 g
2 tbsp	2% yogurt	25 mL
1/2 tsp	lemon juice	2 mL
4 tsp	chopped fresh dill (or 1/2 tsp [2 mL] dried dillweed)	20 mL
25	slices (1/4-inch [5 mm] thick) cucumber	25

1. Reserve about 25 bits of salmon for garnish.

2. In bowl or using food processor, combine goat cheese, yogurt, remaining salmon, lemon juice and dill; mix with fork or using on/off motion just until combined but not puréed.

3. Place spoonful of filling on each cucumber slice. Garnish with bit of reserved salmon.

PER 1/6TH SERVING

Calories	14
Protein	1 g
Fat	1 g
Carbohydrates	0 g
Sodium	66 mg
Cholesterol	4 mg
Fibre	0 g

●●●●●●●●●●●●●●●●●●●● RICOTTA AND BLUE CHEESE ●●
APPETIZERS

Serves 4 to 6
or makes 25 hors
d'oeuvres.

TIP

For blue cheese lovers,
increase to 3 oz (75 g).

●

Instead of endive leaves,
fill empty mushroom caps,
or serve as a dip with
crackers or vegetables.

MAKE AHEAD

Prepare dip and refrigerate
up to a day before. Spoon
onto endive leaves just
before serving.

2 oz	blue cheese	50 g
1/2 cup	ricotta cheese	125 mL
2 tbsp	2% yogurt	25 mL
2 tbsp	chopped fresh dill (or 1 tsp [5 mL] dried dillweed)	25 mL
2	Belgian endives	2

1. In food processor, combine blue cheese, ricotta, yogurt and dill; process until creamy and smooth.

2. Separate Belgian endive leaves. Spoon 2 tsp (10 mL) cheese mixture onto stem end of each.

PER 1/6TH SERVING

Calories	87
Protein	6 g
Fat	4 g
Carbohydrates	6 g
Sodium	190 mg
Cholesterol	13 mg
Fibre	3 g

PITA OR TORTILLA PIZZA (PAGE 5) ➤

• BAGEL GARLIC BREAD • • • • •

Serves 6
or makes 12 slices.

TIP

Different fresh or dried herbs can be used; basil or oregano are good choices.

●

Break into pieces and serve with any of the dips or on its own.

MAKE AHEAD

Make early in day. Reheat for 10 minutes or until just warm.

Preheat oven to 350°F (180°C)

2	bagels	2
1 tbsp	margarine, melted	15 mL
1/2 tsp	crushed garlic	2 mL
1 1/2 tsp	grated Parmesan cheese	7 mL
1 tbsp	chopped fresh parsley	15 mL

1. Slice each bagel into 6 very thin rounds.

2. In bowl, combine margarine, garlic, cheese and parsley until well mixed. Brush over bagel rounds. Bake on baking sheet until crisp, 10 to 14 minutes.

PER SERVING

Calories	75
Protein	2 g
Fat	2 g
Carbohydrates	10 g
Sodium	109 mg
Cholesterol	0.3 mg
Fibre	1 g

◄ SEAFOOD SEVICHE (PAGE 14)

TORTILLA OR PITA CRACKERS

Serves 4 to 6
or makes 24 crackers.

TIP

Instead of tortillas, you can separate pitas into rounds then cut into wedges, or use mini pitas separated into rounds.

●

Create your own toppings or try a combination of grated Parmesan cheese, dried herbs, sesame or poppy seeds, minced garlic and chili powder.

●

Serve as crackers by themselves or with any of the dips in this section.

MAKE AHEAD

Make these early in day and let stand, uncovered, at room temperature. They will remain crisp.

PER 1/6TH SERVING

Calories	97
Protein	4 g
Fat	4 g
Carbohydrates	12 g
Sodium	152 mg
Cholesterol	4 mg
Fibre	1 g

Preheat oven to 400°F (200°C)

1	egg white	1
2 tbsp	water	25 mL
3	flour tortillas, cut into 8 wedges	3

1. Mix egg white with water; brush over one side of each tortilla wedge. Place on baking sheet.
2. Sprinkle on topping of your choice and bake until crisp, approximately 15 minutes.

Avocado, Tomato and Chili Guacamole

Serves 4 to 6
or makes 3/4 cup
(175 mL)

TIP

Adjust the chili powder,
to your taste.

•

Serve with pita bread,
vegetables or crackers.

MAKE AHEAD

Make early in day and
squeeze more lemon juice
over top to prevent
discoloration. Refrigerate.
Stir just before serving.

Half	avocado, peeled	Half
3/4 tsp	crushed garlic	4 mL
2 tbsp	chopped green onions	25 mL
1 tbsp	lemon juice	15 mL
1/4 cup	finely diced sweet red pepper	50 mL
1/2 cup	chopped tomato	125 mL
Pinch	chili powder	Pinch

1. In bowl, combine avocado, garlic, onions, lemon juice, red pepper, tomato and chili powder; mash with fork, mixing well.

PER 1/6TH SERVING

Calories	30
Protein	0.5 g
Fat	2 g
Carbohydrates	2 g
Sodium	4 mg
Cholesterol	0 mg
Fibre	1 g

HUMMUS

(CHICK-PEA PÂTÉ)

Serves 4 to 6
or makes 1 cup
(250 mL).

TIP

Tahini is a Middle
Eastern condiment found
in the specialty section of
some supermarkets. If
unavailable, use peanut
butter.

•

Surround the dip with
crackers, fresh vegetable
sticks or pita bread pieces.

MAKE AHEAD

Prepare dip up to a day
before. Stir just before
serving and garnish with
parsley.

1/4 cup	water	50 mL
1 cup	drained canned chick-peas	250 mL
3/4 tsp	crushed garlic	4 mL
2 tbsp	lemon juice	25 mL
4 tsp	olive oil	20 mL
1/4 cup	tahini	50 mL
1 tbsp	chopped fresh parsley	15 mL

1. In food processor, combine water, chick-peas, garlic, lemon juice, oil and tahini; process until creamy and smooth.

2. Transfer to serving dish; sprinkle with parsley.

PER 1/6TH SERVING

Calories	134
Protein	4 g
Fat	9 g
Carbohydrates	10 g
Sodium	80 mg
Cholesterol	0 mg
Fibre	2 g

ARTICHOKE AND BLUE ····· CHEESE DIP

Serves 4 to 6
or makes 1 1/4 cups
(300 mL).

TIP

If a more subtle flavor is
desired, cut back on the
blue cheese, using only
1 1/2 oz (40 g).

●

Other strong cheeses, such
as grated Parmesan or
Swiss, can replace the blue
cheese.

MAKE AHEAD

Make and refrigerate up to
a day before. Stir just
before serving.

3/4 cup	drained canned artichokes	175 mL
1/4 cup	chopped green onions	50 mL
1/2 tsp	crushed garlic	2 mL
2 oz	blue cheese	50 g
1 tbsp	chopped fresh parsley	15 mL
1/4 cup	2% yogurt	50 mL
	Salt and pepper	

1. In food processor, combine artichokes, onions, garlic, cheese, parsley, yogurt, and salt and pepper to taste; process until smooth. Transfer to serving bowl.

PER 1/6TH SERVING

Calories	53
Protein	3 g
Fat	3 g
Carbohydrates	4 g
Sodium	160 mg
Cholesterol	7 mg
Fibre	1 g

• SPICY MEXICAN DIP • • • • • •

Serves 6 to 8
or makes 2 cups
(500 mL).

TIP

This dip can also be placed in a flour tortilla and slightly warmed.

•

Serve with crackers, vegetables or pita bread.

MAKE AHEAD

Make and refrigerate up to a day before. Stir before garnishing.

1 cup	canned refried beans	250 mL
1/3 cup	minced red onion	75 mL
1/3 cup	finely diced sweet red pepper	75 mL
3/4 tsp	crushed garlic	4 mL
2 tsp	chili powder	10 mL
2 tbsp	chopped fresh parsley	25 mL
2 tbsp	2% yogurt	25 mL
2 tsp	lemon juice	10 mL
3 tbsp	crushed bran cereal*	45 mL
	Parsley sprigs	

* *Use a wheat bran breakfast cereal*

1. In bowl, combine beans, onion, red pepper, garlic, chili powder, parsley, yogurt, lemon juice and cereal; stir until blended. Place in serving bowl and garnish with parsley sprigs.

PER 1/8TH SERVING

Calories	11
Protein	0.6 g
Fat	0 g
Carbohydrates	2 g
Sodium	37 mg
Cholesterol	0 mg
Fibre	0.5 g

•••••••••••••••••••• SPINACH AND RICOTTA DIP ••

PER 1/6TH SERVING

Calories	20
Protein	1 g
Fat	1 g
Carbohydrates	1 g
Sodium	23 mg
Cholesterol	4 mg
Fibre	0 g

Half	pkg (10 oz [284 g]) fresh spinach	Half
1/2 cup	2% yogurt	125 mL
3/4 cup	ricotta cheese	175 mL
1/2 tsp	crushed garlic	2 mL
2 tbsp	chopped fresh parsley	25 mL
2 tbsp	grated Parmesan cheese	25 mL
	Salt and pepper	

1. Rinse spinach and shake off excess water. With just the water clinging to leaves, cook until wilted; drain and squeeze out excess moisture.

2. In food processor, combine spinach, yogurt, ricotta, garlic, parsley, Parmesan cheese, and salt and pepper to taste; process just until still chunky. Do not purée.

SOUPS

1. Always simmer soup, stirring occasionally. Do not allow milk-based soups to boil or they may curdle. Keep covered until ready.

2. Purée soup in batches to achieve an even, smooth texture.

3. If soup appears too thick, add more stock.

4. For more fibre, leave on vegetable peels.

5. Leftover vegetables are ideal for soups.

6. One tablespoon (15 mL) of yogurt or light sour cream can be added as a garnish to a bowl of soup for extra taste and a special appearance.

7. To make your favorite high-fat soup better for you, substitute milk for cream.

••••••••••••••••••••••CAULIFLOWER POTATO SOUP ••

Serves 4 to 6.

TIP

Buy cauliflower with bright, light-colored heads and tightly packed florets.

For a stronger taste, use aged Cheddar or Swiss cheese.

MAKE AHEAD

Prepare and refrigerate up to a day before and reheat before serving, adding more stock if too thick.

1 tbsp	vegetable oil	15 mL
1 tsp	crushed garlic	5 mL
1 cup	chopped onions	250 mL
1	medium cauliflower, separated into florets	1
4 cups	chicken stock	1 L
2	small potatoes, peeled and chopped	2
1/4 cup	shredded Cheddar cheese	50 mL
2 tbsp	chopped fresh chives	25 mL

1. In large nonstick saucepan, heat oil; sauté garlic and onions until softened, approximately 5 minutes.

2. Add cauliflower, stock and potatoes; bring to boil. Cover, reduce heat and simmer for 25 minutes or until tender. Transfer to food processor and purée until creamy and smooth. Return to saucepan and thin with more stock if desired.

3. Ladle into bowls; sprinkle with cheese and chives.

PER 1/6TH SERVING

Calories	99
Protein	6 g
Fat	5 g
Carbohydrates	8 g
Sodium	560 mg
Cholesterol	5 mg
Fibre	2 g

DILL CARROT SOUP

TIP

This soup can be served hot or cold.

•

A dollop of yogurt on each bowlful enhances both the appearance and flavor.

MAKE AHEAD

Make and refrigerate up to a day before. If serving warm, reheat gently.

1 lb	carrots, sliced (6 to 8 medium)	500 g
2 tsp	vegetable oil	10 mL
2 tsp	crushed garlic	10 mL
1 cup	chopped onion	250 mL
3 1/2 cups	chicken stock	875 mL
3/4 cup	2% milk	175 mL
2 tbsp	chopped fresh dill (or 1 tsp [5 mL] dried dillweed)	25 mL
2 tbsp	chopped fresh chives or green onions	25 mL

1. In large saucepan of boiling water, cook carrots just until tender. Drain and return to saucepan; set aside.

2. In nonstick skillet, heat oil; sauté garlic and onion until softened, approximately 5 minutes. Add to carrots along with stock; cover and simmer for 25 minutes.

3. Purée in food processor until smooth, in batches if necessary. Return to saucepan; stir in milk, dill and chives.

PER 1/6TH SERVING

Calories	96
Protein	5 g
Fat	3 g
Carbohydrates	12 g
Sodium	494 mg
Cholesterol	2 mg
Fibre	3 g

• POTATO CORN CHOWDER • • •

Serves 4 or 5.

TIP

Frozen corn niblets would be fine to use. If time is available, make your own stock for a really delicious chowder. (See page 49.)

MAKE AHEAD

Make and refrigerate early in day and reheat gently, adding more stock or milk if too thick.

2 cups	corn niblets (canned or fresh)	500 mL
1 1/2 tsp	margarine	7 mL
1 cup	chopped onions	250 mL
1/2 cup	chopped sweet red pepper	125 mL
1 tsp	crushed garlic	5 mL
1 cup	diced peeled potato	250 mL
1 1/3 cups	chicken stock	325 mL
2 tbsp	all-purpose flour	25 mL
1 1/2 cups	2% milk	375 mL
1/4 tsp	Worcestershire sauce	1 mL
	Pepper	

1. In food processor, process 1 cup (250 mL) of the corn until puréed; add to remaining corn and set aside.

2. In large nonstick saucepan, melt margarine; sauté onions, red pepper and garlic for 5 minutes. Add potato and stock; simmer, covered, until potato is tender, approximately 15 minutes.

3. Add corn mixture to soup; cook for 5 minutes. Stir in flour and cook for 1 minute. Add milk, Worcestershire sauce, and pepper to taste; cook on medium heat for approximately 5 minutes or just until thickened.

PER 1/5TH SERVING

Calories	164
Protein	7 g
Fat	3 g
Carbohydrates	28 g
Sodium	467 mg
Cholesterol	5 mg
Fibre	3 g

•••••••••••••••••••••••••••••• CHILI BEAN STEW •••••••

TIP

Ground chicken or veal can substitute for beef, and other cooked beans can be used instead of kidney beans.

MAKE AHEAD

Make and refrigerate up to a day before. Reheat gently, adding more stock if too thick.

1 1/2 tsp	vegetable oil	7 mL
1 tsp	crushed garlic	5 mL
1 cup	chopped onion	250 mL
8 oz	lean ground beef	250 g
1	can (19 oz [540 mL]) tomatoes, crushed	1
2 cups	beef stock	500 mL
1 1/2 cups	diced peeled potatoes	375 mL
3/4 cup	drained canned red kidney beans	175 mL
3/4 cup	corn niblets	175 mL
2 tbsp	tomato paste	25 mL
1 1/2 tsp	chili powder	7 mL
1 1/2 tsp	each dried oregano and basil	7 mL
1/3 cup	small shell pasta	75 mL

1. In large nonstick saucepan, heat oil; sauté garlic and onion until softened, approximately 5 minutes.

2. Add beef and cook, stirring to break up chunks, until no longer pink; pour off any fat.

3. Add tomatoes, stock, potatoes, kidney beans, corn, tomato paste, chili powder, oregano and basil. Cover and reduce heat; simmer for 40 minutes, stirring occasionally.

4. Add pasta; cook until firm to the bite, approximately 10 minutes.

PER 1/6TH SERVING

Calories	232
Protein	15 g
Fat	6 g
Carbohydrates	30 g
Sodium	580 mg
Cholesterol	22 mg
Fibre	5 g

•••••••••••••••••••GAZPACHO WITH BABY SHRIMP ••

Serves 4 to 6.

TIP

Shrimp can be replaced with crabmeat or imitation seafood.

•

Serve with a spoonful of yogurt on each serving.

MAKE AHEAD

Prepare and refrigerate up to a day before to allow flavors to blend and develop.

2 1/2 cups	tomato juice	625 mL
4 tsp	red wine vinegar	20 mL
1 tsp	crushed garlic	5 mL
1 cup	diced sweet green pepper	250 mL
1 cup	diced sweet red or yellow pepper	250 mL
1 1/4 cups	diced tomatoes	300 mL
1 cup	diced cucumber	250 mL
1 cup	chopped green onions	250 mL
1 cup	diced celery	250 mL
1/4 cup	chopped fresh parsley (or 1 tbsp [15 mL] dried)	50 mL
2 tbsp	chopped fresh basil (or 2 tsp [10 mL] dried)	25 mL
1 tbsp	lemon juice	15 mL
2 oz	cooked baby shrimp	50 g
Dash	Tabasco	Dash
	Pepper	
	Chopped fresh chives	

PER 1/6TH SERVING

Calories	58
Protein	4 g
Fat	0.5 g
Carbohydrates	11 g
Sodium	413 mg
Cholesterol	18 mg
Fibre	3 g

1. In large bowl, combine tomato juice, vinegar and garlic.

2. Mix together green and red peppers, tomatoes, cucumber, green onions and celery; add half to bowl. Place remaining half in food processor; purée until smooth. Add to bowl.

3. Add parsley, basil, lemon juice, shrimp, Tabasco, and pepper to taste; stir gently to combine well. Refrigerate until chilled. To serve, garnish each bowl with sprinkle of chives.

CREAMY BEAN AND CLAM ··· CHOWDER

Serves 4 to 6.

TIP

Try other canned white beans such as navy beans or white pea beans.

MAKE AHEAD

Prepare and refrigerate early in day and reheat gently before serving, adding more stock if too thick.

1 tbsp	vegetable oil	15 mL
1 1/2 cups	chopped onion	375 mL
2 tsp	crushed garlic	10 mL
1	can (5 oz [142 g]) clams	1
2 cups	chicken stock	500 mL
1	medium potato, peeled and diced	1
1 1/2 cups	drained canned white kidney beans	375 mL
2 tbsp	chopped fresh dill (or 1 tsp [5 mL] dried dillweed)	25 mL
2 tbsp	chopped fresh chives or green onions	25 mL
1 tbsp	chopped fresh parsley (or 2 tsp [10 mL] dried)	15 mL

1. In nonstick saucepan, heat oil; sauté onion and garlic until softened, approximately 5 minutes.

2. Drain clams, reserving juice; set clams aside. To saucepan, add clam juice, stock and potato; cover and simmer for 20 minutes or until potato is tender.

3. Add beans; cover and cook for 10 minutes. Purée in food processor until smooth. Return to saucepan; stir in reserved clams, dill, chives and parsley.

PER 1/6TH SERVING

Calories	159
Protein	12 g
Fat	3 g
Carbohydrates	19 g
Sodium	288 mg
Cholesterol	15 mg
Fibre	5 g

CHINESE SCALLOP AND SHRIMP • BROTH WITH SNOW PEAS

Serves 4 to 6.

TIP

Chopped broccoli or asparagus is a good substitute for snow peas.

•

Diced chicken can replace the seafood.

•

Ginger purées or chunks are now available in jars for easier use. One tsp (5 mL) from the jar equals 1 tsp (5 mL) chopped fresh gingerroot.

4 cups	chicken stock	1 L
1 1/2 tsp	minced fresh gingerroot	7 mL
2 cups	chopped snow peas	500 mL
2 oz	scallops, diced	50 g
2 oz	shrimp, diced	50 g
1 tbsp	soya sauce	15 mL
1	green onion, chopped	1

1. In medium saucepan, bring chicken stock and ginger to boil. Add snow peas, scallops, shrimp and soya sauce.

2. Reduce heat and simmer for 2 to 3 minutes or just until scallops are opaque and shrimp are pink. Serve sprinkled with green onion.

PER 1/6TH SERVING

Calories	68
Protein	9 g
Fat	1 g
Carbohydrates	4 g
Sodium	735 mg
Cholesterol	21 mg
Fibre	1 g

· · · · · · · · · · · · · · · · · · · MUSHROOM SPLIT PEA SOUP · ·

Serves 4 or 5.

TIP

Light sour cream can replace the yogurt for a thicker texture.

MAKE AHEAD

Prepare and refrigerate up to a day before and reheat gently before serving, adding more stock if too thick.

1 tbsp	vegetable oil	15 mL
1	medium onion, chopped	1
1 tsp	crushed garlic	5 mL
1	celery stalk, chopped	1
1	medium carrot, chopped	1
1 cup	sliced mushrooms	250 mL
3 1/2 cups	beef or chicken stock	875 mL
3/4 cup	split peas	175 mL
4 tsp	2% yogurt (optional)	20 mL

1. In large nonstick saucepan, heat oil; sauté onion, garlic, celery, carrot and mushrooms until softened, approximately 5 minutes.

2. Add stock and split peas; reduce heat, cover and simmer for 40 minutes or until split peas are tender, stirring occasionally. Purée in food processor until creamy and smooth.

3. Pour into soup bowls and garnish each with yogurt (if using).

PER 1/5TH SERVING

Calories	169
Protein	12 g
Fat	3 g
Carbohydrates	24 g
Sodium	499 mg
Cholesterol	0 mg
Fibre	4 g

••••••••••••••••••• ASPARAGUS AND LEEK SOUP ••

Serves 4 to 6.

TIP

Choose the greenest asparagus with straight, firm stalks. The tips should be tightly closed and firm.

This soup can be served warm or cold.

MAKE AHEAD

Make and refrigerate up to a day before and reheat gently before serving, adding more stock if too thick.

3/4 lb	asparagus	375 g
1 1/2 tsp	vegetable oil	7 mL
1 tsp	crushed garlic	5 mL
1 cup	chopped onion	250 mL
2	leeks, sliced	2
3 1/2 cups	chicken stock	875 mL
1 cup	diced peeled potato	250 mL
	Salt and pepper	
2 tbsp	grated Parmesan cheese	25 mL

1. Trim asparagus; cut stalks into pieces and set tips aside.

2. In large nonstick saucepan, heat oil; sauté garlic, onion, leeks and asparagus stalks just until softened, approximately 10 minutes.

3. Add stock and potato; reduce heat, cover and simmer for 20 to 25 minutes or until vegetables are tender. Purée in food processor until smooth. Taste and adjust seasoning with salt and pepper. Return to saucepan.

4. Steam or microwave reserved asparagus tips just until tender; add to soup. Serve sprinkled with Parmesan cheese.

PER 1/6TH SERVING

Calories	98
Protein	6 g
Fat	3 g
Carbohydrates	13 g
Sodium	491 mg
Cholesterol	1 mg
Fibre	3 g

• • • • • • • • • • • • • • • • • • • BROCCOLI AND LENTIL SOUP ••

Serves 4 to 6.

TIP

A dollop of light sour cream on top of each bowlful gives a great taste and sophisticated look.

MAKE AHEAD

Prepare and refrigerate up to a day before and reheat gently, adding more stock if too thick.

1 1/2 tsp	vegetable oil	7 mL
2 tsp	crushed garlic	10 mL
1	medium onion, chopped	1
1	celery stalk, chopped	1
1	large carrot, chopped	1
4 cups	chicken stock	1 L
2 1/2 cups	chopped broccoli	625 mL
3/4 cup	dried green lentils	175 mL
2 tbsp	grated Parmesan cheese	25 mL

1. In large nonstick saucepan, heat oil; sauté garlic, onion, celery and carrot until softened, approximately 5 minutes.

2. Add stock, broccoli and lentils; cover and simmer for 30 minutes, stirring occasionally, or until lentils are tender.

3. Purée in food processor until creamy and smooth. Serve sprinkled with Parmesan.

PER 1/6TH SERVING

Calories	144
Protein	11 g
Fat	3 g
Carbohydrates	18 g
Sodium	564 mg
Cholesterol	1 mg
Fibre	5 g

Madeira Mushroom and ··· Leek Soup

Serves 4.

Madeira wine gives this soup a subtle sweetness. If unavailable, use a sweet red wine.

MAKE AHEAD

Prepare and refrigerate early in the day and reheat before serving, adding more stock if too thick.

1 1/2 tsp	vegetable oil	7 mL
2 tsp	crushed garlic	10 mL
1 cup	chopped onion	250 mL
1	leek, thinly sliced	1
2 1/2 cups	beef stock	625 mL
1 cup	diced peeled potatoes	250 mL
1 1/2 tsp	margarine	7 mL
12 oz	mushrooms, sliced	375 g
1/3 cup	Madeira wine	75 mL
1/2 cup	2% milk	125 mL

1. In nonstick medium saucepan, heat oil; sauté garlic, onion and leek until softened, approximately 10 minutes.

2. Add stock and potatoes; cover and simmer for 20 to 25 minutes or until softened. Purée in food processor until smooth. Return to saucepan and set aside.

3. In nonstick skillet, melt margarine; sauté mushrooms until softened, approximately 5 minutes. Add Madeira and cook for 2 minutes. Add to soup and stir until combined. Stir in milk.

PER SERVING

Calories	150
Protein	6 g
Fat	4 g
Carbohydrates	18 g
Sodium	444 mg
Cholesterol	2 mg
Fibre	2 g

• BROCCOLI, BARLEY AND • • • •
LEEK SOUP

Serves 4.

TIP

The tops of leeks should be bright green and fresh looking. Only the light green and white of the leek should be used.

•

Cheddar cheese or mozzarella can replace the Swiss cheese.

MAKE AHEAD

Prepare and refrigerate up to a day before and reheat gently, adding more stock if too thick.

1 tbsp	vegetable oil	15 mL
2	large leeks, sliced into thin rounds	2
1 1/2 tsp	crushed garlic	7 mL
2	carrots, diced	2
3 1/2 cups	chicken stock	875 mL
1/3 cup	barley	75 mL
2 cups	chopped broccoli	500 mL
1/2 cup	2% milk	125 mL
3 tbsp	chopped fresh dill (or 1 tsp [5 mL] dried dillweed)	45 mL
2 tbsp	shredded Swiss cheese	25 mL

1. In large nonstick saucepan, heat oil; sauté leeks, garlic and carrots until softened, 10 to 12 minutes, stirring often.

2. Add stock, barley and broccoli; cover and simmer for 30 to 40 minutes or until barley is tender. Purée in food processor until smooth and creamy.

3. Return to pan; stir in milk and dill, blending well. Serve sprinkled with cheese.

PER SERVING

:◼◼◼◼◼◼◼◼◼◼◼◼◼:

Calories	195
Protein	10 g
Fat	6 g
Carbohydrates	25 g
Sodium	734 mg
Cholesterol	5 mg
Fibre	5 g

:◼◼◼◼◼◼◼◼◼◼◼◼◼:

VEGETABLE BEEF BARLEY SOUP

Serves 4.

TIP

Use either pot or pearl barley.

•

Common mushrooms should be firm and dry to the touch. They are very perishable and should be cooked within 48 hours.

MAKE AHEAD

Make and refrigerate up to a day before. Reheat gently just before serving, adding more stock if too thick.

1 tbsp	vegetable oil	15 mL
2 tsp	crushed garlic	10 mL
1	medium onion, diced	1
2	celery stalks, diced	2
2	carrots, diced	2
2 cups	sliced mushrooms	500 mL
3 1/2 cups	(approx) beef stock	875 mL
1/3 cup	barley	75 mL
2	small potatoes, peeled and diced	2
4 oz	stewing beef, diced	125 g
2 tbsp	chopped fresh parsley	25 mL

1. In large nonstick saucepan, heat oil; sauté garlic, onion, celery, carrots and mushrooms until tender, approximately 10 minutes.

2. Add stock, barley, potatoes and beef; cover, reduce heat and simmer approximately 50 minutes or until barley and potatoes are tender, stirring occasionally. Add more stock if too thick. Serve sprinkled with parsley.

PER SERVING

Calories	240
Protein	13 g
Fat	6 g
Carbohydrates	32 g
Sodium	610 mg
Cholesterol	14 mg
Fibre	5 g

ONION SOUP WITH MOZZARELLA

Serves 4.

TIP

The sweeter the onion, the better. Vidalia onions are fabulous and are available during May and June.

•

If ovenproof soup bowls are unavailable, melt cheese in bowls in microwave.

MAKE AHEAD

Make and refrigerate the soup up to a day before. Gently reheat and add bread and cheese prior to serving.

Preheat broiler

1 tbsp	vegetable oil	15 mL
1 tsp	crushed garlic	5 mL
5 cups	thinly sliced onions	1.25 L
1 1/2 tsp	granulated sugar	7 mL
1 1/2 tsp	all-purpose flour	7 mL
3 cups	beef stock	750 mL
1/4 cup	sherry (optional)	50 mL
2	thin slices whole wheat bread, crusts removed	2
1/2 cup	shredded mozzarella cheese	125 mL

1. In medium nonstick saucepan, heat oil; sauté garlic and onions until softened, approximately 5 minutes. Stir in sugar and flour; cover and simmer for 20 minutes, stirring occasionally.

2. Add beef stock, and sherry (if using); cover and simmer for 20 minutes. Pour into individual ovenproof soup bowls.

3. On baking sheet, broil bread until toasted on both sides, 2 to 3 minutes. Cut in half and float on each soup.

4. Sprinkle cheese over toast; broil just until melted and golden. Serve immediately.

PER SERVING

Calories	236
Protein	12 g
Fat	6 g
Carbohydrates	30 g
Sodium	638 mg
Cholesterol	8 mg
Fibre	5 g

VEGETABLE AND BEAN MINESTRONE

Serves 6.

TIP

Any vegetables or beans work well in this versatile soup.

•

If a main dish soup is desired, add 1/2 lb (250 g) raw diced chicken or beef before simmering.

MAKE AHEAD

Make and refrigerate up to a day before and reheat gently before serving, adding more stock if too thick.

PER SERVING

Calories	194
Protein	10 g
Fat	3 g
Carbohydrates	32 g
Sodium	754 mg
Cholesterol	1 mg
Fibre	5 g

1 tbsp	vegetable oil	15 mL
1 tsp	crushed garlic	5 mL
1 1/2 cups	finely chopped onion	375 mL
1	medium carrot, finely chopped	1
1	small celery stalk, finely chopped	1
4 1/2 cups	beef or chicken stock	1.125 L
1 1/2 cups	finely chopped peeled potatoes	375 mL
1 1/2 cups	chopped broccoli	375 mL
1	can (19 oz [540 mL]) tomatoes, crushed	1
3/4 cup	cooked chick-peas	175 mL
2	bay leaves	2
1 1/2 tsp	each dried basil and oregano	7 mL
	Pepper	
1/3 cup	broken spaghetti	75 mL
1 tbsp	grated Parmesan cheese	15 mL

1. In large nonstick saucepan, heat oil; sauté garlic, onion, carrot and celery until softened, approximately 5 minutes.

2. Add stock, potatoes, broccoli, tomatoes, chick-peas, bay leaves, basil and oregano; cover and simmer for approximately 40 minutes or until vegetables are tender, stirring occasionally. Remove bay leaves. Season with pepper to taste.

3. Add pasta; cook for 10 minutes, stirring often, or until spaghetti is firm to the bite. Sprinkle with cheese.

• • • • • • • • • • • • • • • • • • • FRESH TOMATO DILL SOUP • •

1 tbsp	olive oil	15 mL
1 tsp	crushed garlic	5 mL
1	medium carrot, chopped	1
1	celery stalk, chopped	1
1 cup	chopped onion	250 mL
2 cups	chicken stock	500 mL
5 cups	chopped ripe tomatoes	1.25 L
3 tbsp	tomato paste	45 mL
2 tsp	granulated sugar	10 mL
3 tbsp	chopped fresh dill	45 mL

1. In large nonstick saucepan, heat oil; sauté garlic, carrot, celery and onion until softened, approximately 5 minutes.

2. Add stock, tomatoes and tomato paste; reduce heat, cover and simmer for 20 minutes, stirring occasionally.

3. Purée in food processor until smooth. Add sugar and dill; mix well.

PER SERVING

Calories	95
Protein	4 g
Fat	3 g
Carbohydrates	14 g
Sodium	347 mg
Cholesterol	0 mg
Fibre	3 g

······················· Sweet Pea Soup ········

Serves 4.

TIP

If you do not enjoy tarragon, omit it; the soup is delicious either way.

●

Used either canned, fresh or frozen corn niblets.

MAKE AHEAD

Prepare and refrigerate early in day and reheat gently before serving.

1 1/2 tsp	vegetable oil	7 mL
3/4 cup	chopped onion	175 mL
1 tsp	crushed garlic	5 mL
1	carrot, chopped	1
1/4 lb	mushrooms, sliced	125 g
3 cups	chicken stock	750 mL
1	medium potato, peeled and chopped	1
1	pkg (350 g) frozen sweet peas	1
1/2 cup	corn niblets	125 mL
2 tsp	dried tarragon (or 3 tbsp [45 mL] chopped fresh), optional	10 mL

1. In large nonstick saucepan, heat oil; sauté onion, garlic, carrot and mushrooms until softened, approximately 5 minutes.

2. Add stock, potato and all but 1/4 cup (50 mL) of the peas; reduce heat, cover and simmer for 20 to 25 minutes or until potato is tender.

3. Purée soup in food processor until creamy and smooth. Return to pan and add reserved peas and corn niblets. Season with tarragon (if using).

PER SERVING
■■■■■■■■■■■■■■

Calories	174
Protein	10 g
Fat	3 g
Carbohydrates	28 g
Sodium	658 mg
Cholesterol	0 mg
Fibre	7 g

■■■■■■■■■■■■■■

·························· CURRIED SQUASH AND ·····
SWEET POTATO SOUP

Serves 4.

TIP

Other spices that pair with curry are cumin, cardamom, coriander and turmeric; experiment with what you have on hand. Adjust the amount of honey to your taste.

MAKE AHEAD

Make and refrigerate up to the day before and reheat gently before serving, adding more stock if too thick.

2 tsp	vegetable oil	10 mL
1 tsp	crushed garlic	5 mL
1	small onion, chopped	1
1 cup	sliced mushrooms	250 mL
1	butternut squash (8 oz [250 g]), peeled, seeded and chopped	1
1 1/2 cups	chopped peeled sweet potato	375 mL
3 1/4 cups	chicken stock	800 mL
1/2 tsp	ground ginger	2 mL
1 tsp	curry powder	5 mL
1 tbsp	honey	15 mL
1/2 cup	2% milk	125 mL

1. In large nonstick saucepan, heat oil; sauté garlic, onion and mushrooms until softened, approximately 5 minutes.

2. Add squash, sweet potato, stock, ginger and curry powder; reduce heat, cover and simmer for 30 minutes or until vegetables are tender.

3. Purée in food processor until creamy and smooth. Return to saucepan; stir in honey and milk, blending well.

PER SERVING

Calories	188
Protein	7 g
Fat	4 g
Carbohydrates	30 g
Sodium	652 mg
Cholesterol	2 mg
Fibre	4 g

•••••••••••••••••••••• CURRIED PUMPKIN AND ••••
SWEET POTATO SOUP

Serves 4.

TIP

To vary the taste, try adding different amounts of cumin, turmeric and cardamom — the spices that make up curry powder.

MAKE AHEAD

Make and refrigerate up to a day before and reheat gently before serving, adding more milk if too thick.

1 1/2 tsp	vegetable oil	7 mL
1 tsp	crushed garlic	5 mL
1 cup	chopped onion	250 mL
2 1/2 cups	chicken stock	625 mL
8 oz	sweet potatoes, peeled and chopped	250 g
1 cup	puréed cooked canned pumpkin	250 mL
1 1/2 tsp	curry powder	7 mL
1/2 tsp	dried coriander	2 mL
1 tbsp	honey	15 mL
1/2 tsp	ground ginger	2 mL
3/4 cup	2% milk	175 mL
	Chopped fresh parsley	

1. In nonstick saucepan, heat oil; sauté garlic and onion until softened, approximately 5 minutes.

2. Add stock, sweet potatoes, pumpkin, curry powder, coriander, honey and ginger; reduce heat, cover and simmer until potatoes are tender, approximately 40 minutes.

3. Purée in food processor until smooth. Return to saucepan; stir in milk until blended. Sprinkle each serving with chopped parsley.

PER SERVING

Calories	177
Protein	7 g
Fat	4 g
Carbohydrates	30 g
Sodium	517 mg
Cholesterol	3 mg
Fibre	3 g

CARROT, SWEET POTATO •••• AND PARSNIP SOUP

Serves 4.

TIP

You can substitute all carrots for the parsnips or vice versa.

MAKE AHEAD

Make and refrigerate up to a day before and reheat before serving, adding more stock if too thick.

2 tsp	vegetable oil	10 mL
1 tsp	crushed garlic	5 mL
1 cup	chopped onion	250 mL
3 1/2 cups	chicken stock	825 mL
1	small potato, peeled and chopped	1
3/4 cup	chopped carrots	175 mL
3/4 cup	chopped peeled sweet potato	175 mL
1/2 cup	chopped peeled parsnip	125 mL
2 tbsp	chopped fresh dill (or 1 tsp [5 mL] dried dillweed)	25 mL

1. In medium nonstick saucepan, heat oil; sauté garlic and onion for approximately 5 minutes or until softened.

2. Add stock, potato, carrots, sweet potato and parsnip; reduce heat, cover and simmer for 30 to 40 minutes or until vegetables are tender.

3. Purée in food processor until creamy and smooth. Stir in dill.

PER SERVING

Calories	149
Protein	6 g
Fat	4 g
Carbohydrates	23 g
Sodium	692 mg
Cholesterol	0 mg
Fibre	4 g

············· Chicken, Beef or ······· Fish Stock

In 12 cups (3 L) of water, boil a variety of chopped vegetables such as carrots, onions, celery and add your favorite herbs. Add 2 lb (1 kg) of chicken, beef or fish bones and simmer for 2 hours; strain. Use immediately or freeze for up to 2 months.

If homemade stock is unavailable, use canned consommé or bouillon cubes for chicken or beef stock, bottled clam juice or clam water from a can of clams for fish stock.

Stock adds flavor but has no nutrient benefit.

VEGETABLE AND BEAN MINESTRONE (PAGE 43) ➤

OVERLEAF: ASPARAGUS AND LEEK SOUP (PAGE 37)

SALADS

•••••••••••••••••••••••••• SALAD TIPS •••••••••

1. Use fresh crisp vegetables for salads.

2. Wash and dry vegetables carefully before adding to salad to avoid excess liquid. If skins are not bruised, leave skins on for extra fibre.

3. Try a variety of greens for salad, such as Boston, Bibb, radicchio, red leaf and endive. Avoid iceberg lettuce, which has few nutrients and little flavor.

4. Prepare a salad up to four hours before serving, then cover and refrigerate. If prepared earlier, the vegetables will give off excess liquid and lose their crispness.

5. Prepare dressings early in the day or up to 2 days before. Keep covered and refrigerated. Do not pour over salad until just ready to serve. Use between 1 and 2 tbsp (15 and 25 mL) per serving of oil-based dressings and 3 tbsp (45 mL) for yogurt-based dressings.

6. Many of the salads can be served as a main course.

7. To change high-fat dressings to low-fat, low-cholesterol and low-calorie ones, use yogurt or light sour cream instead of mayonnaise. Lessen the oil for four people to 2 tbsp (25 mL) and increase lemon juice, water, vinegar or orange juice.

8. Use only enough dressing to coat the salad lightly. Dressing should not be left in a pool at the bottom of the bowl.

9. Unless otherwise mentioned, vegetable oil should be used for dressings. Excellent oils are canola, soya, sunflower and peanut oil. Olive oil is delicious if it is the main ingredient of the dressing. Sesame oil has an intense flavor and should be used sparingly.

10. Vinegars come in many interesting flavors, such as red or white wine vinegar, herb vinegars, balsamic vinegar, cider vinegar and rice vinegar. Try these instead of white vinegar to enhance flavor.

SEAFOOD SALAD WITH DILL DRESSING

Serves 4.

TIP

Any combination of seafood is good, but these three work very well.

●

Try fresh coriander or Italian parsley instead of the dill.

MAKE AHEAD

Prepare and refrigerate salad and dressing early in day, but do not combine until 2 hours before eating. Stir just before serving.

4 oz	deveined peeled (uncooked) 125 g shrimp, chopped	
4 oz	scallops, chopped	125 g
4 oz	squid, chopped	125 g
1/2 cup	chopped sweet red or yellow pepper	125 mL
1/2 cup	chopped sweet green pepper	125 mL
1/2 cup	chopped celery	125 mL
1/2 cup	chopped red onion	125 mL
1	large green onion, sliced	
	Lettuce leaves	
	Parsley sprigs	

Dressing

1/2 cup	2% yogurt	125 mL
2 tbsp	light mayonnaise	25 mL
3 tbsp	chopped fresh parsley	45 mL
1/4 cup	chopped fresh dill (or 4 tsp [20 mL] dried dillweed)	50 mL
1 tsp	Dijon mustard	5 mL
1 tsp	crushed garlic	5 mL
	Salt and pepper	

1. In shallow saucepan, bring 2 cups (500 mL) water to boil; reduce heat to simmer. Add shrimp, scallops and squid; cover and poach until shrimp are pink and squid and scallops opaque, approximately 2 minutes. Drain and rinse with cold water; drain well and place in bowl. Add red and green peppers, celery and red and green onions.

2. Dressing: In small bowl, combine yogurt, mayonnaise, parsley, dill, mustard, garlic, and salt and pepper to taste, mixing well. Pour over salad and toss well.

3. Line serving bowl with lettuce; top with salad and garnish with parsley.

PER SERVING

Calories	149
Protein	18 g
Fat	4 g
Carbohydrates	10 g
Sodium	236 mg
Cholesterol	120 mg
Fibre	2 g

···················· SALADE NIÇOISE ········

TIP

Fresh tuna, either grilled or broiled, is fabulous. Or try grilled swordfish or shark.

MAKE AHEAD

Prepare salad and dressing early in day, but toss together just before serving.

4 oz	green beans, trimmed	125 g
4 cups	torn leaf lettuce	1 L
2	small potatoes, peeled, cooked and chopped	2
1 cup	chopped tomatoes	250 mL
3/4 cup	chopped sweet red pepper	175 mL
1/2 cup	sliced red onions	125 mL
2	anchovies, minced	2
1	can (7 oz [213 g]) tuna (packed in water), drained and flaked	1
1/2 cup	black olives, pitted and sliced	125 mL
2 tbsp	chopped fresh parsley	25 mL
1/4 cup	chopped fresh dill (or 1 1/2 tsp [7 mL] dried dillweed)	50 mL

Dressing

2 tbsp	water	25 mL
2 tbsp	red wine vinegar	25 mL
2 tbsp	lemon juice	25 mL
1 tsp	crushed garlic	5 mL
1 tsp	Dijon mustard	5 mL
3 tbsp	vegetable oil	45 mL

PER 1/6TH SERVING

Calories	170
Protein	12 g
Fat	8 g
Carbohydrates	12 g
Sodium	187 mg
Cholesterol	7 mg
Fibre	3 g

1. In saucepan of boiling water, blanch green beans just until bright green. Drain and rinse with cold water. Drain and set aside.

2. Place lettuce in large salad bowl. Add green beans, potatoes, tomatoes, red pepper, onion, anchovies, tuna, olives, parsley and dill.

3. Dressing: In small bowl, combine water, vinegar, lemon juice, garlic and mustard; gradually whisk in oil until combined. Pour over salad and toss gently.

WARM MUSHROOM AND SNOW PEA SALAD

Serves 4 to 6.

TIP

Green beans are an excellent substitute for snow peas.

●

This dish can be enhanced by using fresh wild mushrooms.

2 tsp	olive oil	10 mL
1 1/2 tsp	crushed garlic	7 mL
1	medium onion, sliced	1
1 lb	mushrooms, sliced	500 g
8 oz	snow peas	250 g
4 tsp	balsamic or rice vinegar	20 mL
1/2 cup	water chestnuts, drained and chopped	125 mL
	Lettuce leaves	
4 tsp	grated Parmesan cheese	20 mL

1. In nonstick skillet, heat oil; sauté garlic and onion until softened, approximately 5 minutes.

2. Add mushrooms and sauté just until liquid is released; pour off liquid. Add snow peas; cook until tender-crisp, approximately 2 minutes.

3. Stir in vinegar and water chestnuts; cook for 1 minute.

4. Line serving platter with lettuce leaves; pour salad over top. Sprinkle with cheese.

PER 1/6TH SERVING

Calories	68
Protein	4 g
Fat	2 g
Carbohydrates	10 g
Sodium	28 mg
Cholesterol	1 mg
Fibre	2 g

BROCCOLI, SNOW PEA AND BABY CORN SALAD WITH ORANGE DRESSING

Serves 4 to 6.

TIP

Substitute other vegetables for those listed. Try asparagus instead of snow peas, yellow or green pepper instead of red pepper, or choose other lettuces.

MAKE AHEAD

Prepare dressing up to a day before. Toss with salad just before serving.

2 cups	chopped broccoli florets	500 mL
1 cup	snow peas, cut into pieces	250 mL
1/2 cup	sliced red onion	125 mL
Half	medium sweet red pepper, sliced	Half
3 cups	torn romaine lettuce	750 mL
3/4 cup	drained mandarin orange sections	175 mL
1/2 cup	sliced water chestnuts	125 mL
8	drained canned baby corn cobs	8
1 tbsp	raisins	15 mL
1 tbsp	chopped walnuts	15 mL

Dressing

3 tbsp	olive oil	45 mL
3 tbsp	frozen orange juice concentrate, thawed	45 mL
1 1/2 tsp	red wine vinegar	7 mL
1/2 tsp	crushed garlic	2 mL
4 tsp	lemon juice	20 mL
1 tsp	granulated sugar	5 mL

PER 1/6TH SERVING

Calories	150
Protein	3 g
Fat	8 g
Carbohydrates	19 g
Sodium	16 mg
Cholesterol	0 mg
Fibre	3 g

1. Steam or microwave broccoli and snow peas just until tender-crisp. Drain and rinse with cold water; drain again and pat dry. Place in serving bowl.

2. Add onion, red pepper, lettuce, oranges, water chestnuts, corn, raisins and walnuts.

3. Dressing: In small bowl, mix oil, orange juice concentrate, vinegar, garlic, lemon juice and sugar; pour over salad and toss well.

SMOKED SALMON PASTA SALAD

Serves 6 to 8.

TIP

Other smoked fish such as trout, sablefish or sturgeon are also delicious in this recipe.

MAKE AHEAD

Prepare and refrigerate dressing and salad early in day but do not mix. Combine just prior to serving.

8 oz	macaroni or small shell pasta	250 g
4 oz	smoked salmon, chopped	125 g
1	large green onion, chopped	1
1/2 cup	chopped sweet red or green pepper	125 mL
1/4 cup	chopped fresh dill (or 1 1/2 tsp [7 mL] dried dillweed)	50 mL
2 tbsp	chopped fresh parsley	25 mL
	Lettuce leaves	

Dressing

6 tbsp	2% yogurt	90 mL
1/4 cup	light mayonnaise	50 mL
3 tbsp	lemon juice	45 mL
	Salt and pepper	

1. In saucepan of boiling water, cook macaroni according to package directions or until firm to the bite. Drain and rinse with cold water; drain again and place in serving bowl.

2. Add salmon, green onion, red pepper, dill and parsley; mix well.

3. Dressing: In small bowl, blend together yogurt, mayonnaise, lemon juice, and salt and pepper to taste; toss with pasta mixture. Serve on lettuce-lined plates.

PER 1/8TH SERVING

Calories	161
Protein	7 g
Fat	3 g
Carbohydrates	24 g
Sodium	276 mg
Cholesterol	5 mg
Fibre	1 g

SPINACH SALAD WITH ORIENTAL SESAME DRESSING

Serves 4.

MAKE AHEAD

Prepare dressing early in day. Just before serving, prepare salad ingredients and toss with dressing.

5 cups	packed fresh spinach	1.25 mL
3/4 cup	chopped tomatoes	175 mL
1/2 cup	diced red onion	125 mL
1/2 cup	drained mandarin orange segments	125 mL
1/3 cup	sliced water chestnuts	75 mL
1/3 cup	shredded mozzarella cheese	75 mL

Dressing

4 tsp	rice wine vinegar or white wine vinegar	20 mL
1 tbsp	soya sauce	15 mL
1 tbsp	lemon juice	15 mL
1 tsp	sesame seeds	5 mL
1/2 tsp	Dijon mustard	2 mL
4 tsp	vegetable oil	20 mL
1 1/2 tsp	sesame oil	7 mL

1. Remove stems from spinach; tear leaves into bite-sized pieces and place in salad bowl. Add tomatoes, onion, oranges, water chestnuts and cheese.

2. Dressing: In small bowl, combine vinegar, soya sauce, lemon juice, sesame seeds and mustard; whisk in vegetable and sesame oils until well combined. Pour over salad and mix well. Serve immediately.

PER SERVING

Calories	142
Protein	6 g
Fat	8 g
Carbohydrates	12 g
Sodium	385 mg
Cholesterol	5 mg
Fibre	3 g

POTATO SALAD WITH CRISPY ·· FRESH VEGETABLES

Serves 4 to 6.

TIP

Vary the vegetables accompanying the potatoes in this unusual salad.

•

All the vegetables must be fresh, colorful and crisp looking.

MAKE AHEAD

Toss salad with dressing early in day and refrigerate. Stir just before serving.

1/2 cup	chopped broccoli florets	125 mL
1/2 cup	snow peas, sliced	125 mL
4	medium potatoes, peeled, cooked and cubed	4
2	green onions, sliced	2
1/2 cup	chopped sweet red, yellow or green pepper	125 mL
1	celery stalk, diced	1
1/2 cup	finely chopped onions	125 mL
1	medium carrot, sliced	1
3 tbsp	finely chopped fresh dill (or 1 tsp [5 mL] dried dillweed)	45 mL
1/4 tsp	paprika	1 mL
2 tbsp	chopped fresh parsley	25 mL

Dressing

4 tsp	red wine vinegar	20 mL
2 tbsp	2% yogurt	25 mL
3 tbsp	light mayonnaise	45 mL
3 tbsp	lemon juice	45 mL
1 1/2 tsp	Dijon mustard	7 mL
1 tsp	crushed garlic	5 mL
1 tbsp	vegetable oil	15 mL

1. In saucepan, blanch broccoli and snow peas in boiling water for 1 minute or just until color brightens. Drain and rinse with cold water; drain well and place in large salad bowl.
2. Add potatoes, green onions, red pepper, celery, chopped onions, carrot and dill.
3. Dressing: In small bowl, mix together vinegar, yogurt, mayonnaise, lemon juice, mustard, garlic and oil; pour over salad and mix gently. Garnish with paprika and parsley.

PER I/6TH SERVING

:✗✗✗✗✗✗✗✗✗✗✗✗✗:

Calories	128
Protein	3 g
Fat	5 g
Carbohydrates	19 g
Sodium	85 mg
Cholesterol	2 mg
Fibre	2 g

:✗✗✗✗✗✗✗✗✗✗✗✗✗:

GREEK SALAD

Serves 6.

TIP

Use fresh oregano if available.

•

Two ounces (50 g) of cooked baby shrimp is a sophisticated addition if served as a light entrée.

MAKE AHEAD

Prepare dressing up to a day before. Pour over salad just prior to eating.

2	large tomatoes	2
1	medium cucumber	1
1	medium red onion	1
1	sweet red or green pepper	1
3 oz	feta cheese, crumbled	75 g
1/4 cup	black olives, sliced	50 mL

Dressing

3 tbsp	lemon juice	45 mL
4 tsp	red wine vinegar	20 mL
1 tsp	crushed garlic	5 mL
2 tsp	dried oregano (or 2 tbsp [25 mL] chopped fresh)	10 mL
3 tbsp	vegetable oil	45 mL
	Salt and pepper	

1. Cut tomatoes, cucumber, onion and red pepper into large chunks. Place in large salad bowl. Add cheese and olives.

2. Dressing: In small bowl, combine lemon juice, vinegar, garlic and oregano; whisk in oil. Season with salt and pepper to taste. Pour over salad and gently mix well.

PER SERVING

Calories	136
Protein	3 g
Fat	10 g
Carbohydrates	8 g
Sodium	216 mg
Cholesterol	12 mg
Fibre	1 g

CREAMY COLESLAW WITH APPLES AND RAISINS

Serves 4.

TIP

A combination of red and white cabbage is attractive.

●

For curry lovers, 1 tsp (5 mL) curry powder can be added to the dressing.

MAKE AHEAD

Prepare and refrigerate early in day and stir well before serving.

1	medium carrot, diced	1
1/3 cup	finely chopped red onion	75 mL
1/2 cup	finely chopped sweet red or green pepper	125 mL
2	green onions, diced	2
3 cups	thinly sliced white or red cabbage	750 mL
1/3 cup	diced (unpeeled) apple	75 mL
1/3 cup	raisins	75 mL

<u>Dressing</u>

1/4 cup	light mayonnaise	50 mL
2 tbsp	2% yogurt	25 mL
2 tbsp	lemon juice	25 mL
1 1/2 tsp	honey	7 mL
	Salt and pepper	

1. In serving bowl, combine carrot, red onion, red pepper, green onions, cabbage, apple and raisins.

2. Dressing: In small bowl, stir together mayonnaise, yogurt, lemon juice, honey, and salt and pepper to taste, mixing well. Pour over salad and toss gently to combine.

PER SERVING

Calories	137
Protein	2 g
Fat	5 g
Carbohydrates	24 g
Sodium	119 mg
Cholesterol	4 mg
Fibre	3 g

CAESAR SALAD WITH BABY SHRIMP

Serves 4 to 6.

TIP

To make your own croutons, mix 1 tsp (5 mL) each crushed garlic and melted margarine; brush on both sides of 1 slice whole wheat bread. Broil for 3 minutes until browned, then cut into cubes.

MAKE AHEAD

Dressing can be prepared and refrigerated early in the day; toss with salad just before serving.

2 oz	cooked baby shrimp	50 g
1	medium head romaine lettuce, torn into bite-sized pieces	1
1 tbsp	grated Parmesan cheese	15 mL
1 cup	croutons, preferably homemade	250 mL

Dressing

1	egg	1
1 tsp	crushed garlic	5 mL
1	anchovy, minced	1
4 tsp	lemon juice	20 mL
1 tbsp	red wine vinegar	15 mL
1 tsp	Dijon mustard	5 mL
1 tbsp	grated Parmesan cheese	15 mL
2 tbsp	olive oil	25 mL

1. In large bowl, place shrimp, lettuce, cheese and croutons.

2. Dressing: In small bowl, combine egg, garlic, anchovy, lemon juice, vinegar, mustard and cheese; gradually whisk in oil until combined. Pour over salad and toss to coat.

PER 1/6TH SERVING

Calories	113
Protein	6 g
Fat	7 g
Carbohydrates	6 g
Sodium	180 mg
Cholesterol	55 mg
Fibre	1 g

CHICKEN SALAD WITH TARRAGON AND PECANS

Serves 4.

TIP

If tarragon is unavailable, substitute 1/4 cup (50 mL) chopped fresh dill.

●

Fresh tuna or swordfish are delicious substitutes for chicken.

●

Toast pecans in small skillet on medium heat until browned, 2 to 3 minutes.

MAKE AHEAD

Prepare and refrigerate salad and dressing separately early in day, but do not mix until ready to serve.

PER SERVING

Calories	187
Protein	20 g
Fat	6 g
Carbohydrates	13 g
Sodium	151 mg
Cholesterol	42 mg
Fibre	3 g

10 oz	boneless skinless chicken breast, cubed	300 g
3/4 cup	chopped sweet red or green pepper	175 mL
3/4 cup	chopped carrot	175 mL
3/4 cup	chopped broccoli florets	175 mL
3/4 cup	chopped snow peas	175 mL
3/4 cup	chopped red onion	175 mL
1 tbsp	chopped pecans, toasted	15 mL

Dressing

1/2 cup	2% yogurt	125 mL
2 tbsp	lemon juice	25 mL
2 tbsp	light mayonnaise	25 mL
1 tsp	crushed garlic	5 mL
1 tsp	Dijon mustard	5 mL
1/4 cup	chopped fresh parsley	50 mL
2 tsp	dried tarragon (or 3 tbsp [45 mL] chopped fresh)	10 mL
	Salt and pepper	

1. In small saucepan, bring 2 cups (500 mL) water to boil; reduce heat to simmer. Add chicken; cover and cook just until no longer pink inside, 2 to 4 minutes. Drain and place in serving bowl.

2. Add red pepper, carrot, broccoli, snow peas and onion; toss well.

3. Dressing: In small bowl, combine yogurt, lemon juice, mayonnaise, garlic, mustard, parsley, tarragon, and salt and pepper to taste; pour over chicken and mix well. Taste and adjust seasoning. Sprinkle with pecans.

·············· FRESH SALMON AND LEAFY ···
LETTUCE SALAD WITH
CREAMY DILL DRESSING

Serves 4.

TIP

Serve salmon warm
or cold.

●

For a nice change, use
fresh tuna or swordfish.

MAKE AHEAD

Prepare and refrigerate
dressing up to a day
before. Prepare and
refrigerate salmon early in
day if serving cold.

Preheat oven to 400°F (200°C)
Baking sheet sprayed with nonstick vegetable spray

8 oz	salmon fillet	250 g
1 tsp	vegetable oil	5 mL
1 tsp	crushed garlic	5 mL
3 cups	mixed torn lettuce (leaf, Boston, radicchio)	750 mL

Dressing

2 tbsp	buttermilk	25 mL
1/2 tsp	crushed garlic	2 mL
4 tsp	light mayonnaise	20 mL
2 1/2 tsp	lemon juice	12 mL
1 1/2 tsp	water	7 mL
4 tsp	finely chopped fresh dill	20 mL
2 tsp	finely chopped fresh parsley	10 mL
4 tsp	vegetable oil	20 mL

1. Brush salmon with oil and garlic. Place on baking sheet and bake for 10 minutes per inch (2.5 cm) of thickness or until fish flakes easily when tested with fork. Cut into 2-inch (5 cm) pieces.

2. Arrange lettuce on 4 salad plates. Evenly top with salmon.

3. Dressing: In small bowl, combine buttermilk, garlic, mayonnaise, lemon juice, water, dill and parsley; gradually whisk in oil until well blended. Drizzle evenly over salmon.

PER SERVING

Calories	145
Protein	13 g
Fat	9 g
Carbohydrates	2 g
Sodium	59 mg
Cholesterol	23 mg
Fibre	0.5 g

TOMATO, AVOCADO AND SNOW PEA SALAD WITH BLUE CHEESE DRESSING

Serves 4.

4 oz	snow peas, cut in half	125 g
	Lettuce leaves	
Half	medium red or sweet onion, sliced	Half
Half	avocado, sliced thinly	Half
1	large tomato, sliced	1

Dressing

1/4 cup	crumbled blue cheese	50 mL
1/3 cup	2% yogurt	75 mL
1/4 tsp	crushed garlic	1 mL
	Salt and pepper	

1. Steam or microwave snow peas just until tender-crisp. Drain and rinse with cold water; drain well and pat dry.

2. Line serving platter with lettuce leaves. Decoratively arrange onion, avocado, tomato and snow peas over lettuce.

3. Dressing: In food processor, combine blue cheese, yogurt and garlic; process until just combined. Season with salt and pepper to taste. Drizzle over salad.

PER SERVING

Calories	105
Protein	5 g
Fat	6 g
Carbohydrates	8 g
Sodium	140 mg
Cholesterol	7 mg
Fibre	2 g

SWEET PEPPER SALAD WITH •• RED PEPPER DRESSING

Serves 4.

TIP

Double the recipe for red pepper dressing and save half to serve as a wonderful side sauce for fish or chicken.

MAKE AHEAD

Prepare dressing up to a day before. Stir well and pour over salad just prior to serving.

2 cups	chopped sweet red, green or yellow pepper	500 mL
1 cup	chopped cucumber	250 mL
1 cup	cherry tomatoes, cut into quarters	250 mL
1/2 cup	chopped red onion	125 mL
1/2 cup	chopped celery	125 mL

Dressing

2 tbsp	diced red onion	25 mL
1/4 cup	diced sweet red pepper	50 mL
1 tbsp	lemon juice	15 mL
2 tsp	red wine vinegar	10 mL
1 tbsp	water	15 mL
2 tbsp	olive oil	25 mL
1/2 tsp	crushed garlic	2 mL
1/2 tsp	Dijon mustard	2 mL
2 tbsp	chopped fresh parsley	25 mL
	Salt and pepper	

1. In salad bowl, combine red pepper, cucumber, tomatoes, onion and celery.

2. Dressing: In food processor, combine onion, red pepper, lemon juice, vinegar, water, oil, garlic, mustard, parsley, and salt and pepper to taste; process until combined. Pour over salad and toss to combine.

PER SERVING

Calories	102
Protein	1 g
Fat	7 g
Carbohydrates	10 g
Sodium	37 mg
Cholesterol	0 mg
Fibre	2 g

··················· TABBOULEH GREEK STYLE ···

Serves 4 to 6.

TIP

After salad is mixed, it may be chopped in food processor using off/on motion until desired consistency is reached.

●

Fresh herbs can be preserved by standing them in a glass with water covering the stems. Place plastic wrap over the glass and refrigerate.

MAKE AHEAD

Prepare early in day and stir just before serving.

3/4 cup	bulgur	175 mL
1/2 cup	finely chopped red onion	125 mL
1 cup	diced cucumber	250 mL
1 1/2 cups	diced tomatoes	375 mL
2	green onions, sliced thinly	2
1/4 cup	sliced pitted black olives	50 mL
2 oz	feta cheese, crumbled	50 g

Dressing

1/3 cup	chopped fresh parsley	75 mL
1/3 cup	chopped fresh mint	75 mL
2 tbsp	lemon juice	25 mL
2 tbsp	vegetable oil	25 mL
1 tsp	crushed garlic	5 mL
3/4 tsp	dried basil (or 2 tbsp [25 mL] chopped fresh)	4 mL
1/2 tsp	dried oregano (or 1 tbsp [15 mL] chopped fresh)	2 mL

1. Cover bulgur with 2 cups (500 mL) boiling water; soak for 20 minutes. Drain well and place in large serving bowl.

2. Add onion, cucumber, tomatoes, green onions, olives and feta; mix well.

3. Dressing: In small bowl, combine parsley, mint, lemon juice, oil, garlic, basil and oregano; pour over tabbouleh. Mix well. Refrigerate until chilled.

PER 1/6TH SERVING

Calories	152
Protein	4 g
Fat	7 g
Carbohydrates	18 g
Sodium	164 mg
Cholesterol	8 mg
Fibre	4 g

GOAT CHEESE AND SUN-DRIED TOMATO SALAD

Serves 4.

TIP

If goat cheese is unavailable, substitute feta cheese.

•

Toast nuts in skillet on top of stove for 2 minutes until lightly browned.

•

Soften sun-dried tomatoes by placing in boiling water for 10 minutes; then cut.

MAKE AHEAD

Combine dressing ingredients up to a day before. Pour over salad just before serving.

1/2 tsp	crushed garlic	2 mL
1 tsp	Dijon mustard	5 mL
1 tbsp	red wine vinegar	15 mL
2 tbsp	olive oil	25 mL
1 tbsp	lemon juice	15 mL
2 tbsp	water	25 mL
4 cups	torn lettuce (Boston, radicchio or romaine)	1 L
1 tbsp	pine nuts, toasted	15 mL
2 oz	goat cheese, crumbled	50 g
1/4 cup	sun-dried tomatoes, cut into pieces	50 mL

1. In small bowl, combine garlic, mustard, vinegar, oil, lemon juice and water until well mixed.

2. Place lettuce in serving bowl; sprinkle with nuts, goat cheese and tomatoes. Pour dressing over top and toss gently.

PER SERVING

Calories	149
Protein	4 g
Fat	11 g
Carbohydrates	9 g
Sodium	193 mg
Cholesterol	12 mg
Fibre	2 g

• GRILLED VEGETABLE SALAD • • •

Serves 4.

1	medium zucchini	1
1	medium sweet red pepper	1
Half	large red onion	Half
12	small mushrooms	12
3 cups	mixed lettuce leaves (Boston, romaine, radicchio)	750 mL

Dressing

2 tbsp	lemon juice	25 mL
2 tbsp	water	25 mL
1 tbsp	brown sugar	15 mL
4 tsp	balsamic vinegar	20 mL
1 tsp	crushed garlic	5 mL
2 tbsp	olive oil	25 mL
	Salt and pepper	

1. Cut zucchini, red pepper and onion into 2-inch (5 cm) chunks. Alternately thread along with mushrooms onto barbecue skewers.

2. Dressing: In small bowl, combine lemon juice, water, sugar, vinegar and garlic; gradually whisk in oil. Season with salt and pepper to taste. Pour into dish large enough to hold skewers.

3. Add skewers to dressing; marinate for 20 minutes, turning often.

4. Grill vegetables until tender, basting with dressing and rotating often, approximately 15 minutes.

5. Remove vegetables from skewers and place on lettuce-lined serving platter. Pour any remaining dressing over vegetables.

PER SERVING

Calories	107
Protein	2 g
Fat	7 g
Carbohydrates	10 g
Sodium	8 mg
Cholesterol	0 mg
Fibre	2 g

BEAN SALAD WITH FRESH ••• VEGETABLES AND FETA CHEESE

Serves 4.

TIP

Other crisp vegetables such as broccoli, corn or cucumbers can be substituted, as can other cooked beans.

MAKE AHEAD

Combine with dressing a few hours before eating and let marinate. Stir before arranging in lettuce-lined bowl.

3/4 cup	drained cooked white or red kidney beans	175 mL
3/4 cup	drained cooked chick-peas	175 mL
1 cup	chopped tomato	250 mL
1/2 cup	chopped onion	125 mL
1/2 cup	chopped celery	125 mL
1/2 cup	chopped sweet green or red pepper	125 mL
1 oz	feta cheese, crumbled	25 g
	Lettuce leaves	

Dressing

3 tbsp	lemon juice	45 mL
1 tsp	crushed garlic	5 mL
1 tsp	dried basil (or 2 tbsp [25 mL] chopped fresh)	5 mL
1/2 tsp	dried oregano (or 1 tbsp [15 mL] chopped fresh)	2 mL
2 tbsp	vegetable oil	25 mL

1. In bowl, combine beans, chick-peas, tomato, onion, celery, green pepper and feta cheese.

2. Dressing: In small bowl, combine lemon juice, garlic, basil and oregano; whisk in oil. Pour over salad and stir gently to mix well.

3. Line serving bowl with lettuce leaves; top with salad.

PER SERVING

Calories	201
Protein	8 g
Fat	9 g
Carbohydrates	23 g
Sodium	103 mg
Cholesterol	6 mg
Fibre	6 g

JAPANESE SALAD WITH PEANUT DRESSING

4 oz	spaghettini	125 g
1 cup	chopped broccoli florets	250 mL
1 cup	chopped snow peas	250 mL
1 cup	diced sweet red pepper	250 mL
1	green onion, sliced	1
2	small carrots, diced	2
1 tsp	vegetable oil	5 mL
4 oz	lean steak, sliced thinly into strips	125 g
1 tsp	crushed garlic	5 mL

Dressing

3 tbsp	unsalted peanuts	45 mL
1 tsp	minced gingerroot (or 1/4 tsp [1 mL] ground ginger)	5 mL
2 tbsp	lemon juice	25 mL
1 tbsp	soya sauce	15 mL
1 tbsp	honey	15 mL
4 tsp	vegetable oil	20 mL
1 1/2 tsp	sesame oil	7 mL
1 tsp	crushed garlic	5 mL
2 tbsp	water	25 mL

1. In saucepan of boiling water, cook spaghettini according to package directions or just until firm to the bite. Drain and rinse under cold water; drain well and place in serving bowl.

2. In saucepan of boiling water, blanch broccoli and snow peas just until bright green. Drain and rinse under cold water; drain and add to noodles. Add red pepper, onion and carrots.

3. Dressing: In food processor, combine peanuts, gingerroot, lemon juice, soya sauce, honey, vegetable and sesame oils, garlic and water; purée until smooth. Pour over vegetable mixture.

4. In nonstick skillet, heat oil; sauté beef and garlic just until medium or desired doneness. Add to vegetable mixture and combine well. Refrigerate until chilled.

FISH AND SEAFOOD

•••••••••••••••••••• FISH AND SEAFOOD TIPS ••••

1. Fish must be fresh. It should have a bright color, a firm texture and a sweet smell. Whole fish should look plump and have shiny, clear, protruding eyes.

2. Store fish in the coldest part of the refrigerator. Ideally, place whole fish in a dish surrounded with ice. Replace ice when necessary. Do not allow fish to sit in water. Wash fillets, pat dry, then wrap in plastic wrap and keep very cold. Fish will last up to 3 days like this.

3. Wrap frozen fish very tightly so no air can penetrate. Avoid fish with ice crystals or discoloration. These are signs of freezer burn and result in dry fish. Darker, oily fish can be frozen up to 10 weeks, and lean whiter fish up to four months.

4. Defrost fish in refrigerator on a plate, pouring off excess liquid as necessary, or in microwave following manufacturer's instructions.

5. The Canadian Department of Fisheries has developed a guide for fish cookery. Measure fish at the thickest point and bake 10 minutes per inch (2.5 cm) at 425°F to 450°F (220°C to 230°C). If the fish is frozen, double the time. This guideline can be applied to any cooking method. If fish is stuffed or wrapped in foil, cook another 5 to 10 minutes.

6. Overcooked fish will be dry. Properly cooked fish will be moist, tender and flaky. Fish can be baked, broiled, microwaved, grilled or fried. Fish tend to fall into two categories: the darker, oilier firm fish and the whiter, more delicate and leaner fish. Darker fish include such varieties as swordfish, tuna, shark and salmon. These are fattier fish and are best broiled, baked or grilled. The white fish include such varieties as sole, halibut, cod, haddock, orange roughy, snapper, trout, perch, whitefish, grouper and pickerel.

BAKING OR ROASTING

Place fish in baking dish lined with foil. Bake in a 425°F (220°C) oven. Add some moisture such as stock or margarine so fish stays moist.

BROILING

Fattier fish, such as salmon or swordfish, are best broiled. No extra fat is needed during cooking. Add lemon juice, stock or wine to maintain moisture. Broil 4 to 6 inches (10 to 15 cm) from heat for large fish and 4 inches (10 cm) for small fish and fillets, until the flesh is just opaque. Thin fillets do not need to be turned.

POACHING

Poaching is excellent for fish to be served cold and for lean fish, whose meat may dry out in a high heat. Fish can be poached in water, fish stock or court bouillon, which is a combination of water, wine, herbs and vegetables. Wrap the fish tightly in foil or cheesecloth; place in boiling liquid, then reduce to simmer. Cover and cook until done.

STEAMING

Pour 2 to 3 inches (5 to 8 cm) of water into a large pot or a steamer fitted with a rack. Bring water to a boil. Wrap fish tightly in cheesecloth and place fish on rack. Cover and cook. For oven steaming, season fish with herbs and a little lemon juice or wine, then wrap tightly in foil. Place in baking dish and bake at 425°F (220°C).

MICROWAVE

Place fish in microwaveable dish, with herbs and a little lemon juice or wine. Cover with plastic wrap leaving one corner open to let steam out. Microwave on High power 3 to 4 minutes per pound (500 g).

GRILLING

The best fish to grill are salmon, swordfish and tuna steaks about 1-1/2 inches (4 cm) thick. Leave skin on fish if possible, grill on a high heat, basting often, but turning fish only once. If grilling fish kabobs, marinate fish first to keep it moist.

PAN FRYING

Use a nonstick skillet and add 1 tbsp (15 mL) of margarine or oil for 1 lb (500 g) of fish. Dip fish in milk, or egg white, then coat with bread crumbs or flour. Sauté until brown and crisp on both sides and just cooked inside.

• SWORDFISH KABOBS WITH • • • LIME AND GARLIC MARINADE

Serves 4.

1 lb	swordfish, cut into 16 cubes	500 g
16	pieces (2-inch [5 cm]) sweet red pepper	16
16	pieces (2-inch [5 cm]) sweet green pepper	16
16	medium mushroom caps	16
16	pieces (2-inch [5 cm]) onion	16

Marinade

3 tbsp	lime or lemon juice	45 mL
2 tbsp	vegetable oil	25 mL
3 tbsp	chopped fresh coriander or parsley	45 mL
2 tbsp	water	25 mL
1 tsp	crushed garlic	5 mL
1 tsp	Dijon mustard	5 mL

1. Alternately thread 2 pieces each of swordfish, red pepper, green pepper, mushrooms and onion onto 8 barbecue skewers.

2. Marinade: Combine lime juice, oil, coriander, water, garlic and mustard; pour into shallow dish large enough to hold kabobs. Add kabobs; marinate for 30 minutes, turning occasionally.

3. Barbecue kabobs, brushing with marinade and turning carefully, for 10 to 15 minutes or until fish flakes easily when tested with fork.

PER SERVING

Calories	250
Protein	22 g
Fat	12 g
Carbohydrates	12 g
Sodium	80 mg
Cholesterol	60 mg
Fibre	3 g

SWORDFISH PARMIGIANA

Serves 4.

TIP

Any other meaty fish can be substituted for the swordfish. Tuna, marlin or shark are good substitutes.

Preheat oven to 425°F (220°C)

1 1/2 tsp	margarine	7 mL
1 cup	sliced mushrooms	250 mL
1/2 cup	sliced sweet green pepper	125 mL
1/2 cup	sliced onions	125 mL
1 tsp	crushed garlic	5 mL
1/2 tsp	dried basil	2 mL
1/2 tsp	dried oregano	2 mL
1 cup	tomato sauce	250 mL
1 lb	swordfish, cut into 4 serving-sized pieces	500 g
1/2 cup	shredded mozzarella cheese	125 mL

1. In nonstick skillet, melt margarine; sauté mushrooms, green pepper, onions and garlic for 5 minutes or until softened. Add basil, oregano and tomato sauce; simmer for 5 minutes. Pour half of mixture into baking dish. Place fish over top. Pour remaining sauce over top. Sprinkle with cheese.

2. Bake for 10 to 15 minutes or until fish flakes easily when tested with fork.

PER SERVING

Calories	217
Protein	24 g
Fat	9 g
Carbohydrates	8 g
Sodium	520 mg
Cholesterol	67 mg
Fibre	2 g

SOLE WITH SPINACH •••••• AND CREAM SAUCE

Serves 4.

TIP

The fish in this classic entrée can be substituted with trout, flounder, halibut or turbot.

•

You can cook half a package (150g) frozen spinach instead of the fresh, then continue with the recipe.

2 tsp	vegetable oil	10 mL
3/4 cup	chopped onions	175 mL
1 tsp	crushed garlic	5 mL
Half	pkg (10 oz [300 g]) fresh spinach, cooked and drained	Half
	Salt and pepper	
1/3 cup	white wine	75 mL
1 tbsp	lemon juice	15 mL
1 lb	sole fillets	500 g
1 1/2 tsp	margarine	7 mL
1 tbsp	all-purpose flour	15 mL
1/3 cup	2% milk	75 mL
2 tbsp	grated Parmesan cheese	25 mL

1. In small skillet, heat oil; sauté onions and garlic for 3 minutes. Add spinach and cook for 2 minutes. Season with salt and pepper to taste. Spread over flat serving dish. Set aside.

2. In large skillet, bring wine, lemon juice and fish fillets to boil. Reduce heat, cover and simmer just until fish is barely opaque, approximately 3 minutes. With slotted spoon, carefully place fish over spinach mixture, reserving poaching liquid.

3. In small pan, melt margarine; stir in flour and cook for 1 minute. Add milk and reserved poaching liquid; simmer, stirring, until thickened. Stir in 1 tbsp (15 mL) cheese; pour over fish. Sprinkle with remaining cheese.

PER SERVING

Calories	188
Protein	22 g
Fat	6 g
Carbohydrates	7 g
Sodium	182 mg
Cholesterol	56 mg
Fibre	1 g

SOLE WITH ORIENTAL PEANUT SAUCE

Serves 4.

TIP

This intense sauce goes well with lighter flavored fish. Try it over boneless chicken breasts as well.

●

Substitute the peanuts for cashews or almonds for a change.

Preheat oven to 425°F (220°C)
Baking dish sprayed with nonstick vegetable spray

1 lb	sole fillets	500 g
	Salt and pepper	
1/3 cup	Oriental Peanut Sauce (recipe, page 232)	75 mL
1 tbsp	chopped peanuts	15 mL

1. Season fillets with salt and pepper to taste; place in single layer in baking dish.

2. Pour Oriental Peanut Sauce over fish. Cover and bake for 10 to 15 minutes or just until fish flakes easily when tested with fork. Sprinkle nuts over top.

PER SERVING

Calories	149
Protein	20 g
Fat	7 g
Carbohydrates	1 g
Sodium	251 mg
Cholesterol	53 mg
Fibre	0 g

SOLE FILLETS WITH ······ MUSHROOM STUFFING

Serves 4.

TIP

When working with sole, be gentle. It breaks quite easily.

•

A firmer yet still light white fish, such as white fish or orange roughy, can be substituted.

MAKE AHEAD

Prepare stuffing early in the day, but roll up in fillets just before baking.

Preheat oven to 425°F (220°C)
Baking dish sprayed with nonstick vegetable spray

1 lb	fish fillets, cut into 4 serving-sized pieces	500 g
1/3 cup	shredded mozzarella cheese	75 mL
1 tbsp	margarine, melted	15 mL
1 tbsp	lemon juice	15 mL
2 tbsp	chicken stock or white wine	25 mL
2 tbsp	chopped fresh parsley	25 mL

<u>Stuffing</u>

1 tsp	margarine	5 mL
1/2 cup	chopped mushrooms	125 mL
1/3 cup	chopped onions	75 mL
1 tsp	crushed garlic	5 mL
2 tbsp	dry bread crumbs	25 mL
2 tbsp	chopped fresh dill (or 1/2 tsp [2 mL] dried dillweed)	25 mL
1 tbsp	water	15 mL

1. Stuffing: In small nonstick skillet, melt margarine; sauté mushrooms, onions and garlic for 5 minutes. Add crumbs, dill and water; mix well.

2. Divide stuffing among fillets; sprinkle with cheese. Roll up fillets and fasten with toothpicks. Place in single layer in baking dish.

3. Combine margarine, lemon juice and stock; pour over fish. Bake for approximately 10 minutes or until fish flakes easily when tested with fork. Garnish with parsley.

PER SERVING

Calories	175
Protein	22 g
Fat	7 g
Carbohydrates	5 g
Sodium	233 mg
Cholesterol	58 mg
Fibre	1 g

SALMON FILLET WITH SESAME •• SEEDS AND TERIYAKI SAUCE

Serves 4.

TIP

This marinade is ideal for other fish, as well as for chicken or beef.

•

Refrigerate or store ginger in a cool place. Ginger purées are now available in jars for easier use. One tsp (5 mL) from the jar equals 1 tsp (5 mL) chopped fresh gingerroot.

MAKE AHEAD

Prepare the marinade early in the day.

Preheat oven to 425°F (220°C)
Baking dish sprayed with nonstick vegetable spray

1 lb	salmon fillet	500 g
2 tsp	sesame seeds	10 mL

Marinade

3 tbsp	sherry	45 mL
3 tbsp	brown sugar	45 mL
2 tbsp	water	25 mL
2 tbsp	soya sauce	25 mL
2 tbsp	vegetable oil	25 mL
1 1/2 tsp	minced gingerroot	7 mL
2 tsp	crushed garlic	10 mL

1. Marinade: In bowl large enough to hold salmon, combine sherry, sugar, water, soya sauce, oil, ginger, and garlic. Divide fish into serving-sized pieces; place in marinade and let stand for 20 minutes.

2. Remove salmon to baking dish; pour marinade into saucepan. Boil marinade for 3 to 5 minutes or until thick and syrupy; pour over fish. Sprinkle with sesame seeds.

3. Bake fish for 10 to 15 minutes (or 10 minutes per inch [2.5 cm] of thickness) or until fish flakes easily when tested with fork.

PER SERVING

Calories	295
Protein	25 g
Fat	14 g
Carbohydrates	13 g
Sodium	572 mg
Cholesterol	43 mg
Fibre	0 g

• SALMON IN PHYLLO WITH • • • • HERB DRESSING

Serves 4.

TIP

Work quickly with phyllo sheets to prevent them from drying out. Keep unused sheets covered with a damp towel.

MAKE AHEAD

Prepare sauce up to a day before and refrigerate.

•

Prepare phyllo packets just prior to baking, or phyllo will get soggy.

Preheat oven to 425°F (220°C)
Baking sheet sprayed with nonstick vegetable spray

2 tbsp	margarine, melted	25 mL
1 tsp	crushed garlic	5 mL
4	sheets phyllo pastry	4
1 lb	salmon fillet, skinned and divided into 4	500 g

Sauce

1/4 cup	light sour cream	50 mL
1 1/2 tsp	lemon juice	7 mL
1 1/2 tsp	vegetable oil	7 mL
2 tsp	chopped fresh dill (or 1/2 tsp [2 mL] dried dillweed)	10 mL
1 1/2 tsp	chopped fresh basil (or 1/4 tsp [1 mL] dried)	7 mL

1. Sauce: In small bowl, combine sour cream, lemon juice, oil, dill and basil; set aside.

2. Combine margarine and garlic. Cut each sheet of phyllo into 4 to make 16 equal pieces. Lay 1 sheet on work surface; top with second sheet and brush with some margarine mixture. Top with 2 more sheets phyllo; brush again with margarine.

3. Place 1 portion of salmon in centre of phyllo; enclose in phyllo, folding in ends. Brush top with margarine and place on baking sheet. Repeat with remaining phyllo and salmon.

4. Bake for 10 to 15 minutes or just until fish flakes easily when tested with fork and phyllo is golden. Serve with sauce.

PER SERVING

Calories	315
Protein	27 g
Fat	15 g
Carbohydrates	16 g
Sodium	217 mg
Cholesterol	48 mg
Fibre	1 g

BROCCOLI, SNOW PEA AND BABY CORN SALAD
WITH ORANGE DRESSING (PAGE 56) ➤

• SALMON WITH PESTO • • • • • •

Serves 4.

TIP

When making the pesto, use only parsley or only coriander leaves for an unusual taste.

Preheat oven to 425°F (220°C)
Baking sheet sprayed with nonstick vegetable spray

1 lb	salmon steaks or fillet, cut into 4 serving-sized portions	500 g
1 tsp	vegetable oil	5 mL
1 tsp	lemon juice	5 mL
1 tsp	crushed garlic	5 mL
1/4 cup	Pesto Sauce (recipe, page 229)	50 mL

1. Place salmon on baking sheet; brush with oil, lemon juice and garlic. Bake approximately 10 minutes or just until fish flakes easily when tested with fork.

2. Top each serving with 1 tbsp (15 mL) Pesto Sauce.

PER SERVING

Calories	209
Protein	25 g
Fat	11 g
Carbohydrates	1 g
Sodium	70 mg
Cholesterol	44 mg
Fibre	0.5 g

◄ SALMON FILLET WITH SESAME SEEDS AND TERIYAKI SAUCE (PAGE 81)

ORANGE ROUGHY WITH MANDARINS

Serves 4.

TIP

Substitute sole or halibut for the orange roughy.

Preheat oven to 400°F (200°C)
Baking dish sprayed with nonstick vegetable spray

1 lb	orange roughy	500 g
1 cup	orange juice	250 mL
1 tsp	grated orange rind	5 mL
2 tsp	cornstarch	10 mL
1 cup	drained canned mandarin orange segments	250 mL

1. Divide fish into 4 serving-sized pieces. Place in single layer in baking dish; pour in 1/4 cup (50 mL) of the orange juice. Cover and bake for approximately 10 minutes or until fish flakes easily when tested with fork. Gently remove fish to serving platter.

2. Meanwhile, in small saucepan, combine orange rind, cornstarch and remaining 3/4 cup (175 mL) orange juice; cook just until thickened, stirring constantly. Add mandarins and heat through; pour over fish.

PER SERVING

Calories	212
Protein	22 g
Fat	6 g
Carbohydrates	16 g
Sodium	60 mg
Cholesterol	77 mg
Fibre	1 g

LAKE TROUT WITH RED PEPPER SAUCE

Serves 4.

TIP

This fish can also be broiled and the sauce served alongside.

MAKE AHEAD

Prepare and refrigerate sauce up to a day before.

Preheat oven to 425°F (220°C)
Baking dish sprayed with nonstick vegetable spray

1 lb	lake or salmon trout fillets	500 g
1 tsp	vegetable oil	5 mL
	Salt and pepper	

Sauce

1 1/2 tsp	margarine	7 mL
1 tsp	crushed garlic	5 mL
1/4 cup	chopped onion	50 mL
1	medium sweet red pepper, diced	1
1/2 cup	chicken stock	125 mL
1 1/2 tsp	vegetable oil	7 mL

1. Brush fish with oil; season with salt and pepper to taste and place in single layer in baking dish.

2. Sauce: In nonstick skillet, heat margarine; sauté garlic and onion for 2 minutes. Add red pepper and stock; simmer for 5 minutes.

3. Pour sauce into food processor; add oil and purée until smooth. Pour over fish. Bake for 12 to 15 minutes or just until fish flakes easily when tested with fork.

PER SERVING

Calories	204
Protein	25 g
Fat	10 g
Carbohydrates	2 g
Sodium	168 mg
Cholesterol	42 mg
Fibre	0.5 g

HALIBUT WITH LEMON AND PECANS

Serves 4.

TIP

Other white fish, such as sole, flounder or turbot, can be substituted.

•

If using a thin piece of fish, you can probably skip the baking time. The fish will cook through in the skillet.

•

Toast pecans either in 400°F (200°C) oven or in skillet on top of stove for 2 minutes or until brown.

Preheat oven to 400°F (200°C)
Baking dish sprayed with nonstick vegetable spray

1/2 cup	bread crumbs	125 mL
1 tsp	dried parsley	5 mL
1/2 tsp	dried basil	2 mL
1/2 tsp	crushed garlic	2 mL
1 1/2 tsp	grated Parmesan cheese	7 mL
1 lb	halibut, cut into 4 serving-sized pieces	500 g
1	egg white	1
2 tbsp	margarine	25 mL
2 tbsp	white wine	25 mL
4 tsp	lemon juice	20 mL
1 tbsp	chopped fresh parsley	15 mL
1	green onion, chopped	1
1 tbsp	chopped pecans, toasted	15 mL

1. In shallow dish, combine bread crumbs, dried parsley, basil, garlic and cheese. Dip fish pieces into egg white, then into bread crumb mixture.

2. In large nonstick skillet, melt 1 tbsp (15 mL) of the margarine; add fish and cook just until browned on both sides. Transfer fish to baking dish and bake for 5 to 10 minutes or until fish flakes easily when tested with fork. Remove to serving platter and keep warm.

3. To skillet, add remaining margarine, wine, lemon juice, parsley, onions and pecans; cook for 1 minute. Pour over fish.

PER SERVING

Calories	231
Protein	24 g
Fat	9 g
Carbohydrates	10 g
Sodium	302 mg
Cholesterol	61 mg
Fibre	1 g

Halibut with Chunky Tomato Sauce and Black Olives

Serves 4.

TIP

Halibut can be replaced with sole, flounder or turbot.

•

For those with a taste for spicy food, add a sprinkle of chili flakes or powder along with seasonings.

Preheat oven to 425°F (220°C)
Baking dish sprayed with nonstick vegetable spray

1 tbsp	margarine	15 mL
1 tsp	crushed garlic	5 mL
1 cup	sliced mushrooms	250 mL
2/3 cup	chopped onions	150 mL
2	large tomatoes, diced	2
1 tsp	each dried basil and oregano (or 2 tbsp [25 mL] each chopped fresh)	5 mL
1/3 cup	sliced black olives	75 mL
1 lb	halibut, cut into 4 serving-sized pieces	500 g
1 tbsp	grated Parmesan cheese	15 mL

1. In large nonstick skillet, melt margarine; sauté garlic, mushrooms and onions until softened, approximately 3 minutes.

2. Add tomatoes, basil, oregano and olives; simmer for 3 minutes.

3. Place fish in baking dish large enough to arrange in single layer; pour sauce over top. Bake for 10 to 15 minutes or until fish flakes easily when tested with fork. Serve sprinkled with Parmesan cheese.

PER SERVING

Calories	184
Protein	23 g
Fat	6 g
Carbohydrates	8 g
Sodium	262 mg
Cholesterol	61 mg
Fibre	2 g

RED SNAPPER WITH DILL TOMATO SAUCE

Serves 4.

TIP

You can substitute perch, grouper or tilefish for red snapper.

Preheat oven to 425°F (220°C)
Baking dish sprayed with nonstick vegetable spray

1 tbsp	vegetable oil	15 mL
1 tsp	crushed garlic	5 mL
1/2 cup	sliced sweet red pepper	125 mL
1/2 cup	sliced sweet green pepper	125 mL
1/2 cup	sliced onions	125 mL
1/2 cup	sliced mushrooms	125 mL
1 cup	puréed drained canned tomatoes	250 mL
1/2 tsp	dried oregano	2 mL
3 tbsp	chopped fresh dill (or 1 tsp [5 mL] dried dillweed)	45 mL
1 lb	red snapper, divided into 4 portions	500 g
1 tbsp	grated Parmesan cheese	15 mL

1. In large nonstick skillet, heat oil; sauté garlic, red and green peppers, onions and mushrooms until softened, approximately 5 minutes.

2. Add tomatoes and oregano; simmer for 5 minutes. Add dill; cook for 1 more minute.

3. Place red snapper in single layer in baking dish; pour sauce over top. Bake for 18 to 25 minutes or until fish flakes easily when tested with fork. Sprinkle Parmesan over top.

PER SERVING

Calories	170
Protein	23 g
Fat	5 g
Carbohydrates	7 g
Sodium	216 mg
Cholesterol	61 mg
Fibre	2 g

• • • • • • • • • • • • • • • • • • • RED SNAPPER WITH BROCCOLI • AND DILL CHEESE SAUCE

Serves 4.

TIP

Select broccoli with tight green heads on numerous firm stalks, rather than one or two stalks.

•

Fresh cauliflower can replace the broccoli.

Preheat oven to 425°F (220°C)

2 cups	chopped broccoli florets	500 mL
1 lb	red snapper (or any firm fish fillets)	500 g
1 tbsp	margarine	15 mL
1 tbsp	all-purpose flour	15 mL
1 cup	2% milk	250 mL
1/3 cup	shredded Cheddar cheese	75 mL
2 tbsp	chopped fresh dill (or 1/2 tsp [2 mL] dried dillweed)	25 mL
	Salt and pepper	

1. In boiling water, blanch broccoli until still crisp and color brightens; drain and place in baking dish. Place fish in single layer over top.

2. In small saucepan, melt margarine; add flour and cook, stirring, for 1 minute. Add milk and cook, stirring constantly, until thickened, approximately 3 minutes. Stir in cheese, dill, and salt and pepper to taste until cheese has melted; pour over fish.

3. Bake, uncovered, for 15 to 20 minutes or until fish flakes easily when tested with fork.

PER SERVING

Calories	217
Protein	27 g
Fat	8 g
Carbohydrates	7 g
Sodium	232 mg
Cholesterol	74 mg
Fibre	1 g

COD WITH ALMONDS AND LEMON SAUCE

Serves 4.

TIP

Any firm white fish can be substituted, such as haddock or halibut.

●

Pecans also suit this dish.

●

Toast nuts in skillet on top of stove on high, or in 450°F (230°C) oven for 2 minutes or until golden.

Preheat oven to 425°F (220°C)
Baking dish sprayed with nonstick vegetable spray

1 lb	cod, cut into 4 serving-sized pieces	500 g
2 tbsp	chopped fresh dill (or 1 tsp [5 mL] dried dillweed)	25 mL
4 tsp	margarine, melted	20 mL
4 tsp	lemon juice	20 mL
1 tsp	crushed garlic	5 mL
2 tbsp	sliced almonds, toasted	25 mL

1. Place fish in baking dish large enough to arrange in single layer. Combine dill, margarine, lemon juice and garlic; pour over fish.

2. Bake until fish flakes easily when tested with fork, approximately 10 minutes. Sprinkle with almonds.

PER SERVING

Calories	152
Protein	22 g
Fat	6 g
Carbohydrates	1 g
Sodium	146 mg
Cholesterol	60 mg
Fibre	0 g

BAKED WHOLE FISH STUFFED WITH VEGETABLES AND DILLED RICE

Serves 4.

TIP

This stuffing can also be used as a filling between fish fillets. Use whatever vegetables are on hand.

MAKE AHEAD

Make filling early in the day, but do not stuff fish until just before baking.

Preheat oven to 400°F (200°C)

1 tbsp	vegetable oil	15 mL
1 1/2 tsp	crushed garlic	7 mL
1/2 cup	chopped onion	125 mL
1/2 cup	chopped sweet green or red pepper	125 mL
1/3 cup	chopped celery	75 mL
1/2 cup	sliced mushrooms	125 mL
1 1/4 cups	cooked rice	300 mL
1/2 cup	chicken stock	125 mL
2 tbsp	chopped fresh dill (or 1 tsp [5 mL] dried dillweed)	25 mL
2 tbsp	chopped fresh parsley	25 mL
1 tbsp	grated Parmesan cheese	15 mL
	Salt and pepper	
1	whole trout, pickerel or salmon (2 to 3 lb [1 to 1.5 kg]), cleaned, boned if possible	1
4	slices lemon	4

PER SERVING

Calories	412
Protein	59 g
Fat	8 g
Carbohydrates	22 g
Sodium	618 mg
Cholesterol	157 mg
Fibre	2 g

1. In large nonstick skillet, heat oil; sauté garlic, onion, green pepper and celery until softened, approximately 5 minutes. Add mushrooms and cook for 3 minutes.

2. Add rice, stock, dill, parsley, cheese, and salt and pepper to taste; cook for 1 minute, mixing to combine, or until stock is evaporated.

3. Place fish on large sheet of lightly oiled foil. Stuff with rice mixture; place lemon slices over top. Fold foil to enclose fish completely; place on baking sheet and bake for approximately 30 minutes, or 10 minutes per inch (2.5 cm) of thickness, or until fish flakes easily when tested with fork.

FISH FILLETS WITH DATES, APRICOTS AND ORANGE SAUCE

Serves 4.

TIP

Homemade whole-wheat bread crumbs are delicious and add extra fibre to your diet, along with the bran cereal. (See Italian Seasoned Bread Crumbs, page 239.)

•

If sauce appears too thick to pour, add a little more orange juice.

Preheat oven to 425°F (220°C)
Baking dish sprayed with nonstick vegetable spray

1/2 cup	bran cereal*	125 mL
1/4 cup	dry bread crumbs	50 mL
1 lb	firm fish fillets (cod, haddock, orange roughy)	500 g
1	egg white	1
2 tbsp	margarine	25 mL
1 tbsp	all-purpose flour	15 mL
1 cup	orange juice	250 mL
1/2 cup	chopped dates	125 mL
1/4 cup	chopped dried apricots	50 mL

* Use a wheat bran breakfast cereal.

1. In food processor, process bran cereal and bread crumbs until in crumbs; place in shallow dish. Dip fillets into egg white, then into crumb mixture to coat all over; refrigerate.

2. In nonstick saucepan, melt 1 tbsp (15 mL) of the margarine; add flour and cook, stirring, for 1 minute. Add orange juice and cook, stirring continuously, for 2 to 3 minutes or until thickened. Add dates and apricots; set aside.

3. In large nonstick skillet sprayed with nonstick vegetable spray, melt remaining margarine; cook fish just until browned on both sides. Place in single layer in baking dish; pour sauce over top. Bake for 10 to 15 minutes or until fish flakes easily when tested with fork.

PER SERVING

Calories	314
Protein	25 g
Fat	7 g
Carbohydrates	38 g
Sodium	276 mg
Cholesterol	60 mg
Fibre	3 g

FISH FILLETS WITH APPLES, RAISINS AND PECANS

Serves 4.

TIP

Any white fish is suitable. Try grouper, cod, halibut or haddock.

Preheat oven to 425°F (220°C)
Baking dish sprayed with nonstick vegetable spray

1 lb	firm white fish fillets	500 g
1 tbsp	margarine	15 mL
1 cup	chopped peeled apples	250 mL
1/3 cup	raisins	75 mL
1/4 cup	chopped pecans or walnuts	50 mL
4 tsp	brown sugar	20 mL
1/2 tsp	cinnamon	2 mL
1 tbsp	all-purpose flour	15 mL
1 cup	apple juice	250 mL

1. Place fish in single layer in baking dish.

2. In nonstick skillet, melt margarine; sauté apples, raisins, pecans, sugar and cinnamon for 3 minutes or until apples are tender.

3. Mix flour with apple juice until dissolved; add to pan and cook until thickened, stirring constantly, 2 to 3 minutes.

4. Pour sauce over fish; cover and bake for approximately 15 minutes or until fish flakes easily when tested with fork.

PER SERVING

Calories	288
Protein	22 g
Fat	9 g
Carbohydrates	28 g
Sodium	194 mg
Cholesterol	60 mg
Fibre	2 g

MONKFISH AND ASPARAGUS •• IN HOISIN SAUCE

Serves 4.

TIP

Monkfish has the texture of lobster. You can substitute lobster, shrimp or crayfish.

●

Use broccoli or snow peas if asparagus is unavailable.

MAKE AHEAD

Prepare sauce up to a day before.

1/2 lb	asparagus, trimmed and cut into 1-inch (2.5 cm) pieces	250 g
1-1/2 tsp	vegetable oil	7 mL
1 tsp	crushed garlic	5 mL
1/2 cup	chopped sweet red pepper	125 mL
1 lb	monkfish, cut into 1-inch (2.5 cm) chunks	500 g
2	green onions, chopped	2

Sauce

2 tbsp	soya sauce	25 mL
2 tbsp	water	25 mL
1 tbsp	brown sugar	15 mL
1 tbsp	dry sherry or rice wine vinegar	15 mL
4 tsp	hoisin sauce	20 mL
2 tsp	sesame oil	10 mL
1 tsp	cornstarch	5 mL
1 1/2 tsp	minced gingerroot (or 3/4 tsp [4 mL] ground ginger)	7 mL

1. Sauce: In small bowl, combine soya sauce, water, brown sugar, sherry, hoisin sauce, oil, cornstarch and ginger; mix well. Set aside.

2. Blanch asparagus in boiling water for 2 minutes; drain and set aside.

3. In large nonstick skillet, heat oil; sauté garlic and red pepper for 3 minutes. Add monkfish and asparagus; cook for 3 minutes.

4. Stir sauce and add to pan; cook just until thickened and fish flakes easily when tested with fork, 1 to 2 minutes. Pour onto serving plate and sprinkle green onions over top.

PER SERVING

Calories	184
Protein	25 g
Fat	5 g
Carbohydrates	8 g
Sodium	841 mg
Cholesterol	62 mg
Fibre	2 g

•••••••••••••••••• BAKED SQUID STUFFED WITH ••
RED PEPPER AND ONION

Serves 4.

TIP

This is a most unusual, exciting and delicious way to eat squid. Serve with a simple pasta or vegetable. The colors are sensational.

MAKE AHEAD

Squid can be stuffed early in the day and refrigerated. Bake just prior to serving.

Preheat oven to 400°F (200°C)

1 tbsp	vegetable oil	15 mL
1 tsp	crushed garlic	5 mL
3/4 cup	chopped onion	175 mL
3/4 cup	chopped sweet red pepper	175 mL
1/3 cup	dry bread crumbs	75 mL
2 tsp	lemon juice	10 mL
2 tsp	water	10 mL
1 lb	whole large squid, cleaned and tentacles removed (4 large squid)	500 g
3/4 cup	tomato sauce	175 mL

1. In medium nonstick skillet, heat oil; sauté garlic, onion and red pepper just until softened approximately 5 minutes. Transfer to food processor; process using on/off motion just until combined. Do not purée. Stir in bread crumbs, lemon juice and water until combined.

2. With small spoon, carefully fill squid with stuffing. Pour tomato sauce into baking dish; place squid over top. Cover and bake for 25 to 30 minutes or until squid is tender.

PER SERVING
■■■■■■■■■■■■■

Calories	203
Protein	20 g
Fat	5 g
Carbohydrates	17 g
Sodium	393 mg
Cholesterol	271 mg
Fibre	2 g

■■■■■■■■■■■■■

MUSSELS WITH TOMATOES, ••• BASIL AND GARLIC

Serves 4.

TIP

The shells of mussels should be tightly closed when buying.

•

Fresh juicy tomatoes are excellent when in season.

•

Substitute clams for the mussels.

2 lb	mussels	1 kg
1 1/2 tsp	vegetable oil	7 mL
1/2 cup	finely diced onions	125 mL
2 tsp	crushed garlic	10 mL
1	can (14 oz [398 mL]) tomatoes, drained and chopped	1
1/3 cup	dry white wine	75 mL
1 tbsp	chopped fresh basil (or 1/2 tsp [2 mL] dried)	15 mL
1 1/2 tsp	chopped fresh oregano (or 1/4 tsp [1 mL] dried)	7 mL

1. Scrub mussels under cold water; pull off hairy beards. Discard any that do not close when tapped. Set aside.

2. In large nonstick saucepan, heat oil; sauté onions and garlic for 2 minutes. Add tomatoes, wine, basil and oregano; cook for 3 minutes, stirring constantly.

3. Add mussels; cover and cook until mussels fully open, 4 to 5 minutes. Discard any that do not open. Arrange mussels in bowls; pour sauce over top.

PER SERVING

Calories	108
Protein	10 g
Fat	2 g
Carbohydrates	8 g
Sodium	351 mg
Cholesterol	22 mg
Fibre	2 g

SCALLOPS WITH BASIL TOMATO SAUCE

Serves 4.

TIP

Shrimp or squid can be used in place of the scallops, or try a combination of the two.

1 tbsp	margarine	15 mL
3/4 cup	chopped onions	175 mL
1 tsp	crushed garlic	5 mL
3/4 cup	diced sweet green pepper	175 mL
3/4 cup	sliced mushrooms	175 mL
2 tsp	all-purpose flour	10 mL
1 cup	2% milk	250 mL
2 tbsp	tomato paste	25 mL
1 1/4 tsp	dried basil (or 2 tbsp [25 mL] chopped fresh)	6 mL
1 lb	scallops, sliced in half if large	500 g
1 tbsp	grated Parmesan cheese	15 mL

1. In large nonstick skillet, melt margarine; sauté onions, garlic, green pepper and mushrooms until softened, approximately 5 minutes. Stir in flour and cook for 1 minute, stirring.

2. Add milk, tomato paste and basil; cook, stirring continuously, until thickened, 2 to 3 minutes.

3. Add scallops; cook just until opaque, 2 to 3 minutes. Place on serving dish; sprinkle with Parmesan cheese.

PER SERVING

Calories	226
Protein	29 g
Fat	6 g
Carbohydrates	14 g
Sodium	459 mg
Cholesterol	41 mg
Fibre	2 g

SHRIMP AND SCALLOPS WITH CHEESY CREAM SAUCE

Serves 4.

TIP

Other firm white fish such as grouper, cod or halibut can be cut into chunks, to substitute for the seafood.

•

Freeze shrimp with their shells to preserve the best taste.

1 tbsp	margarine	15 mL
1 tsp	crushed garlic	5 mL
1/3 cup	chopped green onions	75 mL
1 lb	seafood (shrimp, scallops or combination)	500 g
1/4 cup	chopped fresh parsley	50 mL
2 oz	goat or feta cheese, crumbled	50 g

Sauce

1 tbsp	margarine	15 mL
2 1/2 tsp	all-purpose flour	12 mL
1/3 cup	dry white wine	75 mL
1/2 cup	2% milk	125 mL

1. Sauce: In small saucepan, melt margarine; stir in flour and cook, stirring, for 1 minute. Add wine and milk; cook, stirring, until thickened and smooth, approximately 2 minutes. Set aside and keep warm.

2. In nonstick skillet, melt margarine; sauté garlic, green onions and seafood just until seafood is opaque. Remove from stove; add sauce and mix well.

3. Pour into serving dish; sprinkle parsley and cheese over top.

PER SERVING

Calories	234
Protein	25 g
Fat	10 g
Carbohydrates	6 g
Sodium	498 mg
Cholesterol	113 mg
Fibre	0.5 g

CHINESE SHRIMP SAUTÉ WITH ·· GREEN ONIONS AND PECANS

Serves 4.

TIP

The shrimp can be replaced with scallops or a combination of both.

1 1/2 cups	chopped broccoli florets	375 mL
1 1/2 cups	snow peas, trimmed	375 mL
2/3 cup	chicken stock	150 mL
2 tbsp	hoisin sauce	25 mL
1 tbsp	cornstarch	15 mL
1 tsp	minced gingerroot (or 1/2 tsp [2 mL] ground)	5 mL
1 tbsp	olive oil	15 mL
1 1/2 tsp	crushed garlic	7 mL
3/4 cup	chopped sweet red pepper	175 mL
1 lb	medium shrimp, peeled and deveined	500 g
1 tbsp	chopped pecans	15 mL
1	green onion, finely chopped	1

1. Blanch broccoli and snow peas in boiling water just until color brightens; drain and set aside.

2. Combine chicken stock, hoisin sauce, cornstarch and ginger until mixed. Set aside.

3. In large skillet, heat oil; sauté garlic and red pepper for 2 minutes. Add shrimp and hoisin mixture; sauté just until shrimp turns pink and sauce thickens. Add broccoli, snow peas and pecans; toss well. Sprinkle with green onions.

PER SERVING

Calories	244
Protein	29 g
Fat	6 g
Carbohydrates	17 g
Sodium	779 mg
Cholesterol	221 mg
Fibre	4 g

SEAFOOD KABOBS WITH SNOW PEAS AND RED PEPPER

Serves 4.

TIP

Try this recipe with a combination of firm fish such as tuna, monkfish or swordfish.

1 lb	seafood (shrimp, scallops, squid or combination)	500 g
1	large sweet red pepper	1
Half	medium onion	Half
16	snow peas, trimmed	16

Marinade

3 tbsp	sherry or rice wine vinegar	45 mL
3 tbsp	vegetable oil	45 mL
2 tbsp	soya sauce	25 mL
2 tbsp	water	25 mL
4 tsp	brown sugar	20 mL
1 1/2 tsp	minced gingerroot	7 mL
1 tsp	crushed garlic	5 mL

1. If necessary, cut seafood into equal-sized pieces. Cut red pepper and onion into 2-inch (5 cm) pieces. Alternately thread seafood, peppers, snow peas and onions onto 8 barbecue skewers.

2. Marinade: Combine sherry, oil, soya sauce, water, sugar, ginger and garlic; pour into dish large enough to hold kabobs. Add kabobs; marinate for 15 minutes, turning occasionally.

3. Barbecue kabobs, brushing with marinade and turning once, for 5 minutes or until seafood is opaque.

PER SERVING

Calories	246
Protein	19 g
Fat	11 g
Carbohydrates	13 g
Sodium	680 mg
Cholesterol	140 mg
Fibre	1 g

SEAFOOD TOMATO STEW

Serves 6.

TIP

Known as a cioppino, this seafood dish can be made with any combination of seafood. Other chopped vegetables can also be added.

●

Serve with French or Italian bread.

MAKE AHEAD

Follow steps 1 to 3 early in day. Later, reheat the sauce, then add seafood and cook as directed.

1 tbsp	vegetable oil	15 mL
Half	medium onion, chopped	Half
Half	celery stalk, chopped	Half
1 tsp	crushed garlic	5 mL
1/4 lb	mushrooms, sliced	125 g
2	cans (each 19 oz [540 mL]) tomatoes, crushed	2
2 tbsp	tomato paste	25 mL
1/3 cup	white wine or fish stock	75 mL
1 1/2 tsp	dried oregano	7 mL
1 1/2 tsp	dried basil	7 mL
2	bay leaves	2
24	mussels	24
1/2 lb	shrimp, peeled and deveined	250 g
1/2 lb	scallops	250 g
1/2 lb	firm white fish (cod, halibut, haddock), cut into bite-sized pieces	250 g
	Chopped fresh parsley	

1. In large nonstick saucepan, heat oil; sauté onion, celery, garlic and mushrooms until softened, approximately 5 minutes.
2. Add tomatoes, tomato paste, wine, oregano, basil and bay leaves; cover and simmer for 25 minutes, stirring occasionally.
3. Scrub mussels under cold water; remove any beards. Discard any that do not close when tapped.
4. Add mussels, shrimp, scallops and fish to pot; cover and cook for 5 to 8 minutes or until mussels open, shrimp are pink and scallops and fish are opaque. Discard any mussels that do not open. Discard bay leaves. Serve immediately.

PER SERVING

Calories	238
Protein	33 g
Fat	6 g
Carbohydrates	14 g
Sodium	749 mg
Cholesterol	106 mg
Fibre	3 g

SEAFOOD WITH RICE, MUSHROOMS AND TOMATOES

Serves 4 to 6.

TIP

Try brown rice instead of plain rice to increase the fibre. Cook 10 minutes longer.

MAKE AHEAD

Prepare a couple of hours before serving and serve at room temperature.

1 lb	cooked seafood (any combination of shrimp, scallops, squid or firm white fish)	500 g
1 tbsp	vegetable oil	15 mL
1 1/2 tsp	crushed garlic	7 mL
1 cup	chopped onions	250 mL
3/4 cup	chopped sweet green or red pepper	175 mL
1 cup	sliced mushrooms	250 mL
1 cup	rice	250 mL
2 1/2 cups	chicken stock	625 mL
1 cup	frozen peas	250 mL
1 cup	chopped tomatoes	250 mL
1 1/2 tsp	each dried oregano and basil (or 2 tbsp [25 mL] each chopped fresh)	7 mL
1 tbsp	grated Parmesan cheese	15 mL
	Chopped fresh parsley	

1. Cut seafood into bite-sized pieces and set aside.

2. In large nonstick saucepan, heat oil; sauté garlic, onions, green peppers and mushrooms until softened. Add rice and sauté, stirring, just until rice begins to turn brown, 3 to 5 minutes. Add stock; cover and simmer for 20 to 30 minutes or until rice is tender and most liquid is absorbed.

3. Add peas, tomatoes, oregano and basil; cook on medium heat for 3 minutes or until peas are cooked. Add seafood and cook until heated through. Place in serving dish. Sprinkle Parmesan and parsley over top.

PER 1/6TH SERVING

Calories	281
Protein	21 g
Fat	5 g
Carbohydrates	37 g
Sodium	823 mg
Cholesterol	88 mg
Fibre	3 g

CHICKEN

•••••••••••••••••••••••••••• CHICKEN TIPS ••••••••••

1. Boneless chicken breasts that are to be stuffed should be pounded flat between two sheets of waxed paper with a mallet or rolling pin. The thinner the chicken breast is the easier it is to stuff and roll.

2. A serving-sized piece of chicken is a quarter chicken, or two drumsticks, two thighs, or a half breast. A 2 to 3 lb (1 to 1.5 kg) chicken will serve four people. One pound (500 g) of boneless chicken meat serves four people.

3. The nutritional analysis for some chicken recipes includes cooking with the skin on, but removing the skin before eating. In this way, the chicken retains the flavor through the cooking, but the fat consumption is greatly reduced.

4. Buy chicken with moist skin, tender flesh and a fresh smell.

5. At home, remove the wrapping and wash the chicken with cold water. Wrap chicken loosely in foil and place in the coldest part of the refrigerator for up to 48 hours. If freezing, wrap chicken in a plastic freezer bag and freeze up to four months. A whole chicken can be frozen up to eight months.

6. Thaw poultry in the refrigerator (5 hours per pound [10 hours per kilogram]), in a bowl of cold water (1 hour per pound [2 hours per kilogram]), or in the microwave. Do not defrost at room temperature; harmful bacteria may develop. Never refreeze raw chicken after thawing. Cooked chicken may be frozen.

7. Stuff a bird just before roasting; harmful bacteria could infect the stuffing if done earlier.

8. Always cook chicken until it is no longer pink and juices run clear. It must never be served rare, since harmful bacteria may remain. Overcooked chicken becomes dry.

9. Chicken can be prepared in a variety of ways — grilled, baked, roasted, poached, steamed or braised — and can be served as an appetizer, entrée, side dish or in soups or salads.

10. If chicken is grilled, baked or roasted, baste often to maintain moisture. Dark meat takes longer to cook than white meat.

11. Whenever possible, purchase free-range chickens. They are tastier and have been raised in a more humane environment.

•••••••••••••••••••••LEMON CHICKEN WITH •••••
NUTTY COATING

4	boneless skinless chicken breasts	4
	Salt and pepper	
1/2 cup	dry bread crumbs	125 mL
1/4 cup	bran cereal*	50 mL
2 tbsp	sliced almonds or hazelnuts	25 mL
1	egg white	1
1 tbsp	vegetable oil	15 mL
1 1/2 tsp	margarine	7 mL
1/4 cup	chopped green onions	50 mL
1/2 cup	chopped mushrooms	125 mL
1/2 cup	chicken stock	125 mL
2 tbsp	lemon juice	25 mL

Use a wheat bran breakfast cereal.

1. Pound chicken between 2 sheets of waxed paper until flattened. Sprinkle with salt and pepper to taste. Set aside.

2. In food processor, process bread crumbs, cereal and nuts until finely ground. Transfer to shallow dish. Dip chicken into egg white, then into bread crumb mixture to coat well.

3. In nonstick skillet sprayed with nonstick vegetable spray, heat oil; sauté chicken until browned on both sides and no longer pink inside. Place on serving dish; cover and keep warm.

4. In same skillet, melt margarine; sauté onions and mushrooms until softened. Add stock and lemon juice; reduce heat and simmer for 2 minutes. Pour over chicken.

PER SERVING

:✖✖✖✖✖✖✖✖✖✖✖✖✖:

Calories:	292
Protein:	30 g
Fat:	12 g
Carbohydrates:	15 g
Sodium:	353 mg
Cholesterol:	66 mg
Fibre:	3 g

:✖✖✖✖✖✖✖✖✖✖✖✖✖:

CHICKEN BREASTS STUFFED WITH GOAT CHEESE AND PECANS IN LEEK SAUCE

Serves 4.

TIP

To wash leeks properly, separate leaves and rinse under running water to remove all dirt trapped between leaves.

MAKE AHEAD

Assemble and refrigerate breasts early in day; brown and bake just before serving. Prepare and refrigerate sauce, adding more stock if too thick when reheating.

Preheat oven to 400°F (200°C)
Baking dish sprayed with nonstick vegetable spray

4	boneless skinless chicken breasts	4
2 oz	goat cheese	50 g
1 tbsp	chopped pecans	15 mL
1	egg white	1
1/3 cup	dry bread crumbs	75 mL
1 tbsp	vegetable oil	15 mL
1 1/2 tsp	margarine	7 mL
1	medium leek, thinly sliced	1
1/2 tsp	crushed garlic	2 mL
1 tbsp	all-purpose flour	15 mL
3/4 cup	chicken stock	175 mL
1/3 cup	2% milk	75 mL

1. Place chicken between 2 sheets of waxed paper; pound until flattened and thin.

2. Combine cheese and pecans until mixed; divide among breasts and roll up to enclose. Fasten with toothpicks. Dip into egg white, then into bread crumbs until well coated.

3. In nonstick skillet, heat oil; brown breasts all over, approximately 5 minutes. Place in baking dish; cover and bake for approximately 10 minutes or until chicken is no longer pink inside. Place on serving plate.

4. Meanwhile, add margarine to skillet; sauté leeks and garlic until softened, approximately 10 minutes. Add flour and cook, stirring, for 1 minute. Gradually stir in stock and milk; cook, stirring, until thickened, approximately 3 minutes. Pour over chicken.

PER SERVING

Calories:	304
Protein:	32 g
Fat:	13 g
Carbohydrates:	11 g
Sodium:	472 mg
Cholesterol:	81 mg
Fibre:	1 g

•CHICKEN BREASTS STUFFED • • • WITH RED PEPPER PURÉE IN CREAMY SAUCE

Serves 4.

TIP

Try yellow pepper instead of the red.

•

Fresh herbs will last longer if placed in a glass with some water covering the stems and plastic wrap to cover the glass. Store in the refrigerator.

MAKE AHEAD

Assemble stuffed breasts early in day and refrigerate. Bake just before serving. Prepare sauce early in day and reheat gently, adding a little more milk if too thick.

PER SERVING

Calories:	251
Protein:	30 g
Fat:	11 g
Carbohydrates:	7 g
Sodium:	211 mg
Cholesterol:	71 mg
Fibre:	1 g

Preheat oven to 375°F (190°C)
Baking dish sprayed with nonstick vegetable spray

4	boneless skinless chicken breasts	4
1 tbsp	vegetable oil	15 mL
1/2 tsp	crushed garlic	2 mL
3/4 cup	diced sweet red pepper	175 mL
1 tbsp	water	15 mL
2 tbsp	chopped fresh dill (or 1/2 tsp [2 mL] dried dillweed)	25 mL
2 tbsp	dry bread crumbs	25 mL
1 1/2 tsp	grated Parmesan cheese	7 mL
1 tbsp	toasted pine nuts	15 mL
	Salt and pepper	
1/4 cup	chicken stock or water	50 mL

Sauce

1 1/2 tsp	margarine	7 mL
1 1/2 tsp	all-purpose flour	7 mL
3/4 cup	2% milk	175 mL
1 tbsp	grated Parmesan cheese	15 mL
1 tbsp	chopped fresh dill (or 1/4 tsp [1 mL] dried dillweed)	15 mL
Pinch	paprika	Pinch

1. Place chicken between 2 sheets of waxed paper; pound until flattened. Set aside.

2. In nonstick skillet, heat oil; sauté garlic and red pepper for 3 minutes; stir in water. Transfer to food processor and purée; pour into bowl. Stir in dill, bread crumbs, cheese, pine nuts, and salt and pepper to taste, mixing well and adding a little water if too dry.

3. Divide purée among chicken breasts; roll up and fasten with toothpicks. Place in baking dish; pour in stock. Cover and bake for about 15 minutes or until chicken is no longer pink inside. Transfer to serving dish.

4. Sauce: Meanwhile, in saucepan, melt margarine; add flour and cook, stirring, for 1 minute. Gradually add milk and cook, stirring, until thickened, approximately 3 minutes. Stir in cheese, dill and paprika. Pour over chicken.

CHICKEN BREASTS STUFFED WITH SPINACH AND CHEESE WITH TOMATO GARLIC SAUCE

Serves 4.

TIP

Be sure not to overcook the chicken or it will become dry.

●

If using fresh spinach, use 1 1/2 cups (375 mL). Cook, drain well and chop.

MAKE AHEAD

Assemble and refrigerate stuffed breasts early in day, but bake just before eating.

Preheat oven to 400°F (200°C)
Baking dish sprayed with nonstick vegetable spray

4	boneless skinless chicken breasts	4
1 1/2 tsp	vegetable oil	7 mL
1/2 tsp	crushed garlic	2 mL
1	medium green onion, finely chopped	1
1/4 cup	drained cooked chopped spinach	50 mL
1/4 cup	diced mushrooms	50 mL
1/4 cup	shredded mozzarella cheese	50 mL
1/4 cup	chicken stock	50 mL

Sauce

1 1/2 tsp	margarine	7 mL
1 tsp	crushed garlic	5 mL
1 1/2 cups	diced tomatoes	375 mL
1/3 cup	chicken stock	75 mL
1 tbsp	chopped fresh parsley	15 mL

1. Place chicken between 2 sheets of waxed paper; pound until flattened. Set aside.

2. In nonstick skillet, heat oil; sauté garlic, onion, spinach and mushrooms until softened. Spoon evenly over breasts; sprinkle with cheese. Roll up and fasten with toothpicks.

3. Place chicken in baking dish; pour in stock. Cover and bake for 10 minutes or until chicken is no longer pink. Remove chicken to serving dish and keep warm.

4. Sauce: Meanwhile, in small saucepan, melt margarine; sauté garlic for 1 minute. Stir in tomatoes and chicken stock; cook for 3 minutes or until heated through. Add parsley and serve over chicken.

PER SERVING

Calories:	216
Protein:	30 g
Fat:	8 g
Carbohydrates:	4 g
Sodium:	247 mg
Cholesterol:	70 mg
Fibre:	1 g

•••••••••••••••••••CHICKEN BREASTS STUFFED •••
WITH APPLE AND ALMONDS

Serves 4.

TIP

Apple cider gives the
sauce a more intense
flavor than apple juice
does.

MAKE AHEAD

Assemble and refrigerate
chicken rolls early in day.
Brown and bake just
before serving. Prepare
and refrigerate sauce,
adding more stock if too
thick when reheating.

Preheat oven to 400°F (200°C)
Baking dish sprayed with nonstick vegetable spray

1 1/2 tsp	margarine	7 mL
1/2 cup	chopped peeled apple	125 mL
1 tbsp	almond slices	15 mL
1/4 tsp	cinnamon	1 mL
4	boneless skinless chicken breasts	4
1	egg white	1
1/2 cup	dry bread crumbs	125 mL
1 1/2 tsp	vegetable oil	7 mL

Sauce

1 tbsp	margarine	15 mL
1 tbsp	all-purpose flour	15 mL
3/4 cup	apple juice or cider	175 mL
1/4 cup	chicken stock	50 mL
1/4 tsp	cinnamon	1 mL
1 1/2 tsp	brown sugar	7 mL

PER SERVING

Calories:	318
Protein:	29 g
Fat:	12 g
Carbohydrates:	20 g
Sodium:	274 mg
Cholesterol:	66 mg
Fibre:	1 g

1. In small nonstick skillet, melt margarine; sauté apple, almonds and cinnamon just until apple is tender, approximately 5 minutes.

2. Place chicken between 2 sheets of waxed paper; pound until flattened. Top each evenly with apple mixture; carefully roll up and secure with toothpicks. Dip into egg white, then into bread crumbs.

3. In large nonstick skillet, heat oil; sauté breasts just until browned on all sides. Place in baking dish.

4. Sauce: In small saucepan, melt margarine; add flour and cook, stirring, for 1 minute. Add apple juice, stock, cinnamon and sugar; cook, stirring, until thickened, approximately 3 minutes. Pour over chicken; cover and bake for 10 to 15 minutes or just until chicken is no longer pink inside.

CHICKEN BREASTS WRAPPED IN PHYLLO WITH BASIL AND TOMATOES

Serves 4.

TIP

When testing doneness, carefully place tip of knife into chicken, trying not to break phyllo package.

MAKE AHEAD

Prepare filling ahead of time; assemble and bake right before eating or phyllo will get soggy.

Preheat oven to 400°F (200°C)
Baking sheet sprayed with nonstick vegetable spray

4	boneless skinless chicken breasts	4
1 1/2 tsp	margarine	7 mL
1/2 tsp	crushed garlic	2 mL
1/2 cup	chopped onion	125 mL
1/2 cup	chopped mushrooms	125 mL
1/4 cup	chopped tomatoes	50 mL
1/4 tsp	dried basil (or 2 tbsp [25 mL] chopped fresh)	1 mL
4	sheets phyllo	4
4 tsp	margarine, melted	20 mL
1/2 cup	tomato sauce, warmed	125 mL

1. Place chicken between 2 sheets of waxed paper; pound until thin and flattened. Set aside.

2. In small nonstick skillet, melt margarine; sauté garlic, onion and mushrooms until softened, approximately 3 minutes. Add tomatoes and basil; cook for 1 minute. Spoon evenly over breasts. Roll up carefully and fasten with toothpicks.

3. Layer phyllo sheets; cut into 4 to make 16 squares. Place 2 squares on flat surface; brush with some margarine. Place 2 more squares over top. Place rolled breast over top and enclose with phyllo. Brush with margarine; place on baking sheet. Repeat with 3 other breasts.

4. Bake for 15 to 20 minutes or just until phyllo is golden and chicken is no longer pink. Serve with warmed tomato sauce.

PER SERVING

Calories:	274
Protein:	28 g
Fat:	8 g
Carbohydrates:	18 g
Sodium:	391 mg
Cholesterol:	66 mg
Fibre:	2 g

•••••••••••••••••••••••••CHICKEN WITH TERIYAKI ••••
VEGETABLES

Serves 4.

TIP

Chicken quarters or
breasts with the bone in
can also be used. Bake for
20 to 30 minutes or until
no longer pink inside.

Preheat oven to 425°F (220°C)
Baking dish sprayed with nonstick vegetable spray

4	boneless skinless chicken breasts	4
1 tsp	vegetable oil	5 mL
1 tsp	crushed garlic	5 mL
1	large sweet red pepper, sliced thinly	1
1 cup	snow peas, trimmed	250 mL

Marinade

3 tbsp	sherry	45 mL
3 tbsp	brown sugar	45 mL
2 tbsp	water	25 mL
2 tbsp	soya sauce	25 mL
2 tbsp	vegetable oil	25 mL
1 1/2 tsp	minced gingerroot	7 mL

1. Marinade: In medium bowl, combine sherry, sugar, water, soya sauce, oil and ginger. Set aside.

2. Place chicken between 2 sheets of waxed paper; pound until thin and flattened. Add to bowl and marinate for 30 minutes.

3. Remove chicken and place in baking dish. Pour marinade into saucepan; cook for 3 to 4 minutes or until thickened and syrupy. Set 2 tbsp (25 mL) aside; brush remainder over chicken. Cover and bake for 10 to 15 minutes or until no longer pink inside.

4. Meanwhile, in large nonstick skillet, heat oil; sauté garlic, red pepper and snow peas for 2 minutes. Add reserved marinade; cook for 2 minutes, stirring constantly. Serve over chicken.

PER SERVING

Calories:	221
Protein:	26 g
Fat:	7 g
Carbohydrates:	9 g
Sodium:	318 mg
Cholesterol:	62 mg
Fibre:	1 g

CHICKEN WITH RED PEPPER •• AND ONIONS

Serves 4.

TIP

This red pepper sauce can also be puréed.

Preheat oven to 400°F (200°C)
Baking dish sprayed with nonstick vegetable spray

| 4 | chicken breasts or legs | 4 |
| | All-purpose flour for dusting | |

Sauce

1 tbsp	margarine	15 mL
1 1/2 tsp	crushed garlic	7 mL
3/4 cup	diced onion	175 mL
1 1/2 cups	diced sweet red pepper	375 mL
1 tbsp	all-purpose flour	15 mL
1 1/3 cups	chicken stock	325 mL
	Parsley sprigs	

1. Dust chicken with flour. In large nonstick skillet sprayed with nonstick vegetable spray, brown chicken on both sides, approximately 10 minutes. Place in baking dish; cover and bake for 20 to 30 minutes or until no longer pink inside and juices run clear when chicken is pierced.

2. Sauce: Meanwhile, in small saucepan, melt margarine; sauté garlic, onion and red pepper for 5 minutes or until softened. Add flour and cook, stirring, for 1 minute. Add stock and cook, stirring, just until thickened, approximately 3 minutes.

3. Place chicken on serving dish; pour sauce over top. Garnish with parsley. Remove skin before eating.

PER SERVING

Calories:	250
Protein:	35 g
Fat:	8 g
Carbohydrates:	13 g
Sodium:	383 mg
Cholesterol:	84 mg
Fibre:	0 g

SEAFOOD TOMATO STEW (PAGE 101) ➤

·········· BAKED CHICKEN WITH ····· TOMATOES, RAISINS AND ALMONDS

Serves 4.

TIP

Adjust the amount of curry powder to your taste.

•

Toast nuts either in 400°F (200°C) oven or in a skillet on top of stove for 3 to 5 minutes.

Preheat oven to 400°F (200°C)

1 tbsp	vegetable oil	15 mL
4	chicken breasts or legs	4
2 tsp	crushed garlic	10 mL
3/4 cup	chopped red onion	175 mL
3/4 cup	chopped sweet green pepper	175 mL
1/3 cup	chopped carrots	75 mL
2 tsp	curry powder	10 mL
1	can (19 oz [540 mL]) tomatoes, crushed or puréed	1
1/3 cup	sliced pitted black olives	75 mL
1/3 cup	raisins	75 mL
2 tbsp	sliced almonds, toasted	25 mL

1. In large nonstick skillet, heat half the oil; brown chicken on both sides, approximately 10 minutes. Remove chicken to baking dish. Pour off extra fat.

2. To skillet, add remaining oil, garlic, onion, green pepper and carrots; sauté until softened, approximately 5 minutes.

3. Stir in curry powder, tomatoes, olives and raisins; reduce heat, cover and simmer for 15 minutes, stirring occasionally.

4. Pour sauce over chicken; cover and bake for 30 minutes or until chicken is no longer pink inside and juices run clear when chicken is pierced. Sprinkle with almonds. Remove skin before eating.

PER SERVING

Calories:	260
Protein:	30 g
Fat:	5 g
Carbohydrates:	29 g
Sodium:	410 mg
Cholesterol:	66 mg
Fibre:	4 g

◀ CHICKEN KABOBS WITH GINGER LEMON MARINADE (PAGE 124)

◀ SAUTÉED RICE WITH ALMONDS, CURRY AND GINGER (PAGE 195)

CHICKEN WITH PAPRIKA •••• IN VEGETABLE CREAM SAUCE

Serves 4.

TIP

For an extravagant change, try fresh wild mushrooms, such as oyster mushrooms.

4	chicken breasts or legs	4
	All-purpose flour for dusting	
1 tbsp	vegetable oil	15 mL
2 tsp	crushed garlic	10 mL
3/4 cup	chopped onion	175 mL
3/4 cup	chopped sweet red or green pepper	175 mL
3/4 cup	sliced mushrooms	175 mL
1 cup	chicken stock	250 mL
2 tsp	paprika	10 mL
2 tsp	all-purpose flour	10 mL
1/4 cup	light sour cream	50 mL

1. Dust chicken with flour. In large nonstick skillet sprayed with nonstick vegetable spray, sauté chicken until browned on both sides, approximately 10 minutes. Remove and set aside.

2. In same skillet, heat oil; sauté garlic, onion, red pepper and mushrooms until softened, approximately 5 minutes. Add chicken stock.

3. Return chicken to pan; sprinkle chicken with paprika. Cover and simmer for 20 to 30 minutes or until chicken is no longer pink inside and juices run clear when chicken is pierced. Remove chicken to serving platter.

4. Mix flour with sour cream until well combined; add to skillet and cook on low heat, stirring, until thickened, 3 to 4 minutes. Pour over chicken. Remove skin before eating.

PER SERVING

Calories:	215
Protein:	31 g
Fat:	5 g
Carbohydrates:	15 g
Sodium:	279 mg
Cholesterol:	72 mg
Fibre:	2 g

•CHICKEN WITH RED WINE • • •
SAUCE AND CHOPPED DATES

Serves 4.

TIP

Instead of dates, try
chopped prunes for a
change.

•

Store dry herbs in tightly
closed containers away
from heat, light and
moisture.

Preheat oven to 400°F (200°C)

4	chicken breasts or legs	4
	All-purpose flour for dusting	
1 tbsp	vegetable oil	15 mL
1	medium onion, chopped	1
2 tsp	crushed garlic	10 mL
2	large carrots, sliced	2
1/2 lb	mushrooms, sliced	250 g
1 1/4 cups	chicken stock	300 mL
2/3 cup	dry red wine	150 mL
2 tbsp	tomato paste	25 mL
1 tsp	dried oregano	5 mL
1 tsp	dried basil	5 mL
1/2 tsp	dried rosemary	2 mL
1/2 cup	chopped dates	125 mL
	Parsley sprigs	

1. Dust chicken with flour. In large nonstick skillet sprayed with nonstick vegetable spray, sauté chicken until browned on both sides, approximately 10 minutes. Place in baking dish.

2. In same skillet, heat oil; sauté onion, garlic, carrots and mushrooms until softened, 5 to 8 minutes. Add stock, wine, tomato paste, oregano, basil and rosemary; cover and simmer for 10 minutes, stirring occasionally. Stir in dates.

3. Pour sauce over chicken. Bake for 30 minutes, basting occasionally, or until chicken is no longer pink inside and juices run clear when chicken is pierced. Garnish with parsley. Remove skin before eating.

PER SERVING
✖✖✖✖✖✖✖✖✖✖✖✖✖✖

Calories:	310
Protein:	31 g
Fat:	5 g
Carbohydrates:	36 g
Sodium:	393 mg
Cholesterol:	66 mg
Fibre:	5 g

✖✖✖✖✖✖✖✖✖✖✖✖✖✖

CHICKEN WITH LEEKS, SWEET POTATOES AND DATES

Serves 4.

TIP

If leeks are unavailable, use the same measurement of sliced onions.

•

Dried apricots or raisins can replace the dates, or use a combination.

•

If using a food processor to chop the dates, oil the blade first to avoid sticking.

Preheat oven to 400°F (200°C)

4	chicken breasts or legs	4
	All-purpose flour for dusting	
1 tbsp	margarine	15 mL
2 tsp	crushed garlic	10 mL
2 cups	chopped leeks	500 mL
2 cups	chopped peeled sweet potatoes	500 mL
1 1/2 cups	chicken stock	375 mL
1/3 cup	white wine	75 mL
1/2 tsp	cinnamon	2 mL
1/2 tsp	ground ginger	2 mL
1/2 cup	chopped dates	125 mL

1. Dust chicken with flour. In nonstick skillet sprayed with nonstick vegetable spray, brown chicken on both sides, approximately 10 minutes. Place in baking dish.

2. In same skillet, melt margarine; sauté garlic, leeks and potatoes until softened, approximately 10 minutes, stirring constantly. Add chicken stock, wine, cinnamon and ginger; cover and simmer for 10 minutes. Stir in dates.

3. Pour sauce over chicken; bake for 20 to 30 minutes, basting occasionally, or until chicken is no longer pink inside and juices run clear when chicken is pierced. Remove skin before eating.

PER SERVING

Calories:	400
Protein:	34 g
Fat:	8 g
Carbohydrates:	48 g
Sodium:	427 mg
Cholesterol:	84 mg
Fibre:	5 g

ROASTED CHICKEN WITH PINEAPPLE, CARROTS AND GINGER

Serves 4.

TIP

Try red pepper in place of the green pepper for a more dramatic appearance.

●

Also try a sprinkle of cinnamon and nutmeg.

●

If using canned pineapple, use juice from can.

MAKE AHEAD

Sauté chicken early in day and keep refrigerated. Make sauce early in day and pour over chicken before baking.

Preheat oven to 400°F (200°C)

4	chicken breasts or legs	4
1 tbsp	margarine	15 mL
1 cup	chopped sweet green pepper	250 mL
1/2 cup	chopped onion	125 mL
1 cup	chopped carrot	250 mL
1 1/2 tsp	crushed garlic	7 mL
2 tsp	minced gingerroot	10 mL
1/2 cup	pineapple juice	125 mL
1 tbsp	cornstarch	15 mL
4 tsp	soya sauce	20 mL
2 tbsp	brown sugar	25 mL
1/2 cup	chicken stock	125 mL
1 cup	pineapple chunks	250 mL

1. In large nonstick skillet sprayed with nonstick vegetable spray, sauté chicken until browned on both sides, approximately 10 minutes. Place chicken in baking dish.

2. Pour off fat in skillet; add margarine. Add green pepper, onion, carrot, garlic and ginger; cook until vegetables are softened, approximately 5 minutes.

3. Meanwhile, combine pineapple juice, cornstarch, soya sauce, brown sugar and stock until well mixed. Pour into skillet along with pineapple chunks; cook for 3 to 4 minutes or until thickened.

4. Pour sauce over chicken; bake for 30 to 40 minutes or until juices run clear when chicken is pierced. Remove skin before eating.

PER SERVING

Calories:	325
Protein:	31 g
Fat:	9 g
Carbohydrates:	26 g
Sodium:	576 mg
Cholesterol:	90 mg
Fibre:	3 g

•••••••••••••••••••• CHICKEN CACCIATORE WITH •• THICK TOMATO SAUCE

Serves 4.

TIP

You can use vegetables such as zucchini or eggplant to replace the peppers and mushrooms.

4	chicken drumsticks, skinned	4
4	chicken thighs, skinned	4
	All-purpose flour for dusting	
1 tbsp	vegetable oil	15 mL
2 tsp	crushed garlic	10 mL
1 cup	chopped onion	250 mL
1/2 cup	chopped sweet green pepper	125 mL
1 cup	sliced mushrooms	250 mL
1	can (19 oz [540 mL]) tomatoes, crushed	1
2 tbsp	tomato paste	25 mL
1 tsp	dried basil	5 mL
1 tsp	dried oregano	5 mL
1/4 cup	red wine	50 mL
1 tbsp	grated Parmesan cheese	15 mL
1/4 cup	chopped fresh parsley	50 mL

1. Dust chicken with flour. In large nonstick skillet, heat oil; sauté chicken just until browned on all sides. Remove and set aside.

2. To skillet, add garlic, onion, green pepper and mushrooms; sauté for 5 minutes or until softened. Add tomatoes, tomato paste, basil, oregano and wine; stir to mix well.

3. Return chicken to skillet; cover and simmer for 20 to 30 minutes or until juices run clear when chicken is pierced, stirring occasionally and turning pieces over. Serve sprinkled with cheese and parsley.

PER SERVING

Calories:	192
Protein:	17 g
Fat:	7 g
Carbohydrates:	13 g
Sodium:	341 mg
Cholesterol:	4 mg
Fibre:	3 g

••••••••••••••••••••• ROASTED CHICKEN WITH ••• ASIAN GLAZE AND FRUIT SAUCE

Serves 4.

TIP

This glaze can also be used over Cornish hens or game birds.

•

Substitute dried prunes or raisins for the dates or apricots for a change.

Preheat oven to 400°F (200°C)

1	whole chicken (2 1/2 to 3 lb [1.25 to 1.5 kg])	1
Glaze		
1 tsp	crushed garlic	5 mL
1 tsp	minced gingerroot (or 1/4 tsp [1 mL] ground ginger)	5 mL
1/4 cup	honey	50 mL
1/4 cup	sweet dessert wine (plum wine)	50 mL
Pinch	chili flakes	Pinch
1 tbsp	margarine, melted	15 mL
Pinch	dried coriander and/or cumin	Pinch
	Salt and pepper	
1/2 cup	chicken stock	125 mL
Sauce		
1 tbsp	cornstarch	15 mL
1/2 cup	chicken stock	125 mL
1/4 cup	chopped dates	50 mL
1/4 cup	chopped dried apricots	50 mL

1. Place chicken in roasting pan.

2. Glaze: In small bowl, mix together garlic, ginger, honey, wine, chili flakes, margarine, coriander, salt and pepper to taste and stock; set half aside for sauce. Brush some of the remaining mixture over chicken. Bake for 50 to 60 minutes or until meat thermometer registers 185°F (85°C), basting with more honey mixture every 15 minutes.

3. Cut chicken into 4 quarters; place on serving dish and keep warm.

4. Sauce: Pour reserved honey mixture into small saucepan; stir in cornstarch, mixing well. Add chicken stock along with dates and apricots; cook over medium heat, stirring, for 2 minutes or until thickened. Pour over chicken. Remove skin before eating.

PER SERVING

Calories:	367
Protein:	36 g
Fat:	9 g
Carbohydrates:	35 g
Sodium:	378 mg
Cholesterol:	100 mg
Fibre:	1 g

·················· ROASTED CHICKEN STUFFED ·· WITH APPLES AND RAISINS

Serves 4.

TIP

Stuff birds just prior to cooking to avoid contaminating with harmful bacteria.

•

Dry dates or apricots can replace the raisins.

MAKE AHEAD

Stuffing can be made and refrigerated up to the day before.

Preheat oven to 375°F (190°C)

1	whole chicken (2 1/2 to 3 lb [1.25 to 1.5 kg])	1

Stuffing

1 1/2 tsp	margarine	7 mL
1/2 cup	diced onions	125 mL
1/3 cup	diced carrots	75 mL
1 cup	diced peeled apple	250 mL
1/4 cup	raisins	50 mL
4 tsp	brown sugar	20 mL
1/2 tsp	cinnamon	2 mL
1 cup	cooked rice (preferably brown)	250 mL

Basting Sauce

2 tbsp	brown sugar	25 mL
1/2 cup	orange juice	125 mL
2 tsp	grated orange rind	10 mL
1/2 tsp	ground ginger	2 mL

PER SERVING

Calories:	355
Protein:	35 g
Fat:	8 g
Carbohydrates:	40 g
Sodium:	261 mg
Cholesterol:	104 mg
Fibre:	2 g

1. Stuffing: In nonstick skillet, melt margarine; sauté onions and carrots until onions are softened. Add apple, raisins, sugar and cinnamon; cook, stirring, for 3 minutes. Stir in rice.

2. Basting Sauce: Meanwhile, in small saucepan, combine sugar, orange juice, orange rind and ginger; heat thoroughly.

3. Spoon stuffing into chicken and truss chicken. Place in roasting pan and pour sauce over chicken. Roast for about 1 1/4 hours or until meat thermometer registers 185°F (85°C), basting often with sauce. Tent chicken with foil if browning too fast. Serve with pan juices. Remove skin before eating.

CHICKEN, RED PEPPER AND SNOW PEA STIR-FRY

Serves 4.

TIP

You can substitute other vegetables, such as asparagus, broccoli or bean sprouts, for the snow peas.

•

Tender beef or veal can replace the chicken.

8 oz	boneless skinless chicken breasts, cubed	250 g
	All-purpose flour for dusting	
1 tbsp	vegetable oil	15 mL
1 tsp	sesame oil	5 mL
1 tsp	crushed garlic	5 mL
1 cup	thinly sliced sweet red pepper	250 mL
1 cup	sliced water chestnuts	250 mL
1 cup	snow peas, cut in half	250 mL
1/4 cup	cashews, coarsely chopped	50 mL
1	large green onion, chopped	1

Sauce

1/2 cup	chicken stock	125 mL
1 tbsp	soya sauce	15 mL
1 tbsp	hoisin sauce	15 mL
2 tsp	cornstarch	10 mL
1 tsp	minced gingerroot	5 mL

1. Sauce: In small bowl, mix together stock, soya sauce, hoisin sauce, cornstarch and ginger; set aside.

2. Dust chicken cubes with flour. In nonstick skillet, heat vegetable and sesame oils; sauté garlic, chicken, red pepper, water chestnuts and snow peas over high heat just until vegetables are tender-crisp, approximately 2 minutes.

3. Add sauce to skillet; cook for 2 minutes or just until chicken is no longer pink inside and sauce has thickened. Garnish with cashews and green onions.

PER SERVING

Calories:	248
Protein:	17 g
Fat:	10 g
Carbohydrates:	21 g
Sodium:	614 mg
Cholesterol:	31 mg
Fibre:	3 g

•••••••••••••••••••••••••• CHICKEN KABOBS WITH ••••
GINGER LEMON MARINADE

Serves 4.

TIP

This tart yet sweet
marinade complements
veal and firm white fish,
too.

•

For a change, try a
combination of red or
yellow pepper instead of
the green pepper.

8 oz	boneless skinless chicken breasts, cut into 2-inch (5 cm) cubes	250 g
16	squares sweet green pepper	16
16	pineapple chunks (fresh or canned)	16
16	cherry tomatoes	16

Ginger Lemon Marinade

3 tbsp	lemon juice	45 mL
2 tbsp	water	25 mL
1 tbsp	vegetable oil	15 mL
2 tsp	sesame oil	10 mL
1 1/2 tsp	red wine vinegar	7 mL
4 tsp	brown sugar	20 mL
1 tsp	minced gingerroot (or 1/4 tsp [1 mL] ground)	5 mL
1/2 tsp	ground coriander	2 mL
1/2 tsp	ground fennel seeds (optional)	2 mL

1. Ginger Lemon Marinade: In small bowl, combine lemon juice, water, vegetable oil, sesame oil, vinegar, brown sugar, ginger, coriander, and fennel seeds (if using); mix well. Add chicken and mix well; marinate for 20 minutes.

2. Alternately thread chicken cubes, green pepper, pineapple and tomatoes onto 4 long or 8 short barbecue skewers. Barbecue for 15 to 20 minutes or just until chicken is no longer pink inside, brushing often with marinade and rotating every 5 minutes.

PER SERVING

✖✖✖✖✖✖✖✖✖✖✖✖✖✖

Calories:	110
Protein:	13 g
Fat:	2 g
Carbohydrates:	10 g
Sodium:	35 mg
Cholesterol:	31 mg
Fibre:	2 g

✖✖✖✖✖✖✖✖✖✖✖✖✖✖

·················· CHICKEN TETRAZZINI ·····

Serves 4 to 6.

TIP

Try this dish with macaroni or penne instead of spaghetti.

•

Substitute fresh tuna or swordfish for the chicken.

•

Mozzarella cheese can replace the Cheddar.

•

Substitute the chicken with 4 oz (125 g) of cooked seafood for a change.

PER 1/6TH SERVING

Calories:	318
Protein:	17 g
Fat:	9 g
Carbohydrates:	40 g
Sodium:	505 mg
Cholesterol:	29 mg
Fibre:	2 g

Preheat broiler

8 oz	spaghetti	250 g
4 tsp	margarine	20 mL
1 1/2 tsp	crushed garlic	7 mL
1 cup	chopped onion	250 mL
1 cup	chopped sweet red pepper	250 mL
1 cup	sliced mushrooms	250 mL
3 tbsp	all-purpose flour	45 mL
1 1/2 cups	chicken stock	375 mL
1 cup	2% milk	250 mL
3 tbsp	white wine	45 mL
1 1/2 tsp	Dijon mustard	7 mL
4 oz	cooked boneless skinless chicken pieces	125 g
1/2 cup	shredded Cheddar cheese	125 mL
1 tbsp	grated Parmesan cheese	15 mL
	Chopped fresh parsley	

1. In saucepan of boiling water, cook spaghetti according to package directions or until firm to the bite; drain.

2. Meanwhile, in nonstick saucepan, melt margarine; sauté garlic, onion, red pepper and mushrooms until softened, approximately 5 minutes. Add flour and cook, stirring, for 1 minute.

3. Add stock, milk, wine and mustard; cook, stirring, for 3 minutes or until thickened. Add chicken.

4. Add sauce to spaghetti and toss to mix well; place in baking dish. Sprinkle Cheddar and Parmesan cheeses over top; bake until top is golden, approximately 5 minutes. Garnish with parsley.

WARM CHICKEN SALAD WITH ORANGE DRESSING

Serves 6.

TIP

The orange juice concentrate gives this dressing an intense flavor. If a lighter taste is desired, omit the concentrate.

MAKE AHEAD

Prepare dressing up to a day before. Refrigerate.

1 1/2 cups	snow peas, sliced in half	375 mL
8 oz	boneless skinless chicken breasts, cubed	250 g
1	large head romaine lettuce, torn	1
1 cup	mandarin orange segments	250 mL
1/2 cup	sliced water chestnuts	125 mL
2 tbsp	pecans	25 mL

Dressing

2 tsp	grated orange rind	10 mL
1/4 cup	orange juice	50 mL
1/2 tsp	crushed garlic	2 mL
1 tbsp	frozen orange juice concentrate, thawed	15 mL
2 tbsp	light mayonnaise	25 mL
3 tbsp	vegetable oil	45 mL
1 tbsp	chopped fresh tarragon (or 1 tsp [5 mL] dried)	15 mL

1. Dressing: In small bowl, whisk together orange rind and juice, garlic, orange juice concentrate, mayonnaise, oil and tarragon until well blended. Set aside.

2. Steam or microwave snow peas just until tender-crisp. Drain and place in salad bowl.

3. In saucepan, pour in just enough water to cover chicken; bring to boil. Reduce heat, cover and simmer for 2 to 3 minutes or until no longer pink; drain and add to snow peas.

4. Add lettuce, oranges and chestnuts to salad bowl. Pour dressing over top and toss. Sprinkle with pecans.

PER SERVING

Calories	216
Protein	11 g
Fat	11 g
Carbohydrates	18 g
Sodium	59 mg
Cholesterol	22 mg
Fibre	2 g

CHICKEN AND ASPARAGUS SALAD WITH LEMON DILL VINAIGRETTE

Serves 4 to 6.

TIP

Containing both protein and carbohydrates, this salad is a complete meal.

•

Substitute broccoli or fresh green beans for the asparagus.

12	baby red potatoes (or 4 small white)	12
8 oz	boneless skinless chicken breasts, cubed	250 g
1/4 cup	water	50 mL
1/4 cup	white wine	50 mL
8 oz	asparagus, trimmed and cut into small pieces	250 g
2	small heads Boston lettuce, torn into pieces	2

Lemon Dill Vinaigrette

3 tbsp	balsamic vinegar	45 mL
2 tbsp	lemon juice	25 mL
1 tbsp	water	15 mL
1	large green onion, minced	1
3/4 tsp	garlic	4 mL
2 tbsp	chopped fresh dill (or 1 tsp [5 mL] dried dillweed)	25 mL
3 tbsp	olive oil	45 mL

PER 1/6TH SERVING

Calories	199
Protein	11 g
Fat	8 g
Carbohydrates	19 g
Sodium	33 mg
Cholesterol	20 mg
Fibre	3 g

1. In saucepan of boiling water, cook potatoes until just tender. Peel and cut into cubes. Place in salad bowl and set aside.

2. In saucepan, bring chicken, water and wine to boil; reduce heat, cover and simmer for approximately 2 minutes or until chicken is no longer pink. Drain and add to potatoes in bowl.

3. Steam or microwave asparagus until just tender-crisp; drain and add to bowl. Add lettuce.

4. Lemon Dill Vinaigrette: In bowl, whisk together vinegar, lemon juice, water, onion, garlic and dill; whisk in oil until combined. Pour over chicken mixture; toss to coat well.

CHICKEN AND RICE SALAD ·· WITH CREAMY GARLIC DRESSING

Serves 4.

TIP

This salad has enough nutrients to be served as an entire meal.

•

Bok choy or nappa cabbage can be found in Chinese vegetable markets and many supermarkets. If unavailable, use romaine lettuce.

2 cups	cubed cooked chicken	500 mL
3/4 cup	cooked rice (preferably brown)	175 mL
1/3 cup	bran cereal*	75 mL
1/2 cup	thinly sliced celery	125 mL
1/2 cup	thinly sliced sweet red pepper	125 mL
1/4 cup	sliced green onions	50 mL
3 cups	finely chopped bok choy or nappa cabbage	750 mL
1/2 cup	Creamy Garlic Dressing (recipe, page 214)	125 mL

* *Use a wheat bran breakfast cereal.*

1. In large serving bowl, combine chicken, rice, cereal, celery, red pepper, onions and bok choy. Toss with Creamy Garlic Dressing.

PER SERVING

Calories:	225
Protein:	23 g
Fat:	8 g
Carbohydrates:	16 g
Sodium:	300 mg
Cholesterol:	58 mg
Fibre:	4 g

MEAT

1. Tender cuts of beef from the rib and sirloin areas contain a lot of fat and calories. Choose those from the flank, chuck or round. Buy lean cuts of meat and trim all excess fat.

2. Pork should be thoroughly cooked until no longer pink. Do not overcook or meat becomes dry. Choose lean cuts of loin chops or tenderloin.

3. Lean cuts of meat to be grilled should be left in a marinade at least 20 minutes, preferably more, in order to tenderize and flavor it.

4. When roasting or grilling, baste meat often to retain moisture. To prevent harmful bacteria from contaminating the food, never serve leftover marinade with cooked meat.

5. After sautéeing ground beef for spaghetti sauce, pour off excess fat before continuing with the recipe. If you are using fatter meat in stews, cook it the day before, refrigerate, then skim off the fat layer.

6. Tightly wrapped fresh meat can be kept refrigerated for 2 days in a cold section of the refrigerator. Meat can be frozen for up to 6 months. Do not use meat that has freezer burn or discoloration.

7. Defrost meat in the refrigerator, or wrap in plastic and place in a bowl of cold water to quicken defrosting. An even faster method is to defrost in microwave. Rotate meat every few minutes to ensure even defrosting.

VEAL CHOPS WITH CREAMY MUSHROOM SAUCE

Serves 4.

TIP

Marsala wine gives this dish a subtle sweetness.

•

Avoid overcooking the veal as it toughens.

•

Substitute pork chops or lamb chops for a change.

Preheat oven to 425°F (220°C)

4	veal chops (6 oz [175 g] each)	4
	All-purpose flour for dusting	
2 tbsp	margarine	25 mL
2 tsp	crushed garlic	10 mL
1 1/2 cups	sliced mushrooms	375 mL
2 tbsp	all-purpose flour	25 mL
1/4 cup	Marsala wine or sweet red wine	50 mL
3/4 cup	2% milk	175 mL
1/3 cup	chicken stock	75 mL

1. Dust chops with flour.

2. In large nonstick skillet, melt 1 tbsp (15 mL) of the margarine; sauté garlic for 1 minute. Add veal and sauté until browned on both sides, approximately 5 minutes. Place in baking dish; cover and bake just until tender, approximately 10 minutes.

3. Meanwhile, add remaining margarine and mushrooms to skillet; cook, stirring occasionally, until softened and liquid is absorbed. Add flour and cook for 1 minute. Add wine, milk and stock; simmer until thickened, stirring continuously, approximately 2 minutes. Place veal on serving dish and pour sauce over top.

PER SERVING

Calories	239
Protein	18 g
Fat	10 g
Carbohydrates	14 g
Sodium	202 mg
Cholesterol	65 mg
Fibre	1 g

• • • • • • • • • • • • • • • • • • VEAL STUFFED WITH CHEESE • • IN MUSHROOM SAUCE

Serves 4.

TIP

If the veal seems tough, marinate it in milk 2 hours before using. Be sure not to overcook the veal, which will make it tough.

•

You can substitute boneless chicken breasts for the veal.

MAKE AHEAD

Assemble and refrigerate veal rolls early in the day. Make sauce ahead of time but add sour cream after reheating.

PER SERVING

Calories	222
Protein	24 g
Fat	10 g
Carbohydrates	7 g
Sodium	360 mg
Cholesterol	82 mg
Fibre	1 g

Preheat oven to 400°F (200°C)

1 lb	veal cutlets	500 g
1 tsp	vegetable oil	5 mL
1/2 cup	finely diced mushrooms	125 mL
1/4 cup	finely diced onions	50 mL
1 tsp	crushed garlic	5 mL
1/3 cup	shredded mozzarella cheese	75 mL
1/4 cup	beef stock	50 mL
	Chopped fresh parsley	

Sauce

1 tbsp	margarine	15 mL
1 1/2 cups	sliced mushrooms	375 mL
2 tbsp	all-purpose flour	25 mL
1 cup	beef stock	250 mL
1 tbsp	sherry (optional)	15 mL
2 tbsp	light sour cream	25 mL

1. Pound veal until flat and divide into 4 serving pieces.

2. In small nonstick skillet, heat oil; sauté mushrooms, onions and garlic until softened, approximately 3 minutes. Remove from heat.

3. Divide vegetable mixture among cutlets. Sprinkle cheese over top. Roll up and secure with toothpick. Place in baking dish and add stock. Cover and bake for 8 to 10 minutes or just until veal is tender. Remove rolls to serving platter. Keep warm.

4. Sauce: In small nonstick skillet, melt margarine; sauté mushrooms until softened and liquid is released. Add flour and cook, stirring, for 1 minute. Add stock, and sherry (if using); cook until thickened, approximately 2 minutes, stirring constantly. If too thick, add more stock. Remove from heat and stir in sour cream; pour over veal. Garnish with parsley.

•••••••••••••••••••••••••• BARBECUED VEAL AND •••••
VEGETABLE KABOBS

12 oz	veal, cut into 1-inch (2.5 cm) cubes	375 g
16	pieces (1-inch [2.5 cm]) sweet red pepper	16
16	pieces (1-inch [2.5 cm]) onion	16
16	small mushrooms	16
16	pieces (1-inch [2.5 cm]) green apple	16

<u>Marinade</u>

2 tbsp	frozen apple juice concentrate, thawed	25 mL
2 tbsp	water	25 mL
1 tbsp	lemon juice or cider vinegar	15 mL
1 tbsp	honey, warmed	15 mL
1 tbsp	soya sauce	15 mL
1 tsp	dried rosemary (or 1 tbsp [15 mL] chopped fresh)	5 mL
1 tbsp	vegetable oil	15 mL

1. Marinade: In bowl, combine apple juice concentrate, water, lemon juice, honey, soya sauce, rosemary and oil. Add veal and marinate for 30 minutes, or longer in refrigerator.

2. Remove veal from marinade. Pour marinade into small saucepan; boil until thick and syrupy, 2 to 4 minutes.

3. Thread veal, red peppers, onions, mushrooms and apples alternately onto 8 metal skewers. Place on greased grill and barbecue for 15 to 20 minutes, turning often and brushing with marinade, or just until meat is tender. Serve with any remaining marinade.

SAUTÉED VEAL WITH LEMON GARLIC SAUCE

Serves 4.

TIP

You can prepare your own scaloppine by pounding veal cutlets until flat and thin.

•

If you use an economical cut, marinate it in milk for at least 2 hours before cooking.

•

Pork or chicken cutlets can also be substituted.

2/3 cup	dry bread crumbs	150 mL
1 1/2 tsp	grated Parmesan cheese	7 mL
4 tsp	chopped fresh parsley	20 mL
	Salt and pepper	
1 lb	veal scaloppine, divided into 4 serving pieces	500 g
1	egg white	1
4 tsp	vegetable oil	20 mL
2 tsp	crushed garlic	10 mL
2 tbsp	lemon juice	25 mL
3 tbsp	beef or chicken stock	45 mL
1 tbsp	white wine	15 mL
1 tbsp	margarine	15 mL
	Lemon slices	
	Chopped fresh parsley	

1. In shallow bowl, combine bread crumbs, cheese, parsley, and salt and pepper to taste.

2. Dip cutlets into egg white, then crumb mixture to coat well on both sides.

3. In nonstick skillet sprayed with nonstick vegetable spray, heat oil; sauté half of the garlic for 1 minute. Add veal and cook on both sides until cooked through and browned, approximately 3 minutes. Remove to serving dish.

4. To skillet, add remaining garlic, lemon juice, stock, wine and margarine; cook for 1 minute. Pour over veal. Garnish with lemon slices and parsley.

PER SERVING

Calories	256
Protein	21 g
Fat	12 g
Carbohydrates	13 g
Sodium	279 mg
Cholesterol	75 mg
Fibre	1 g

VEAL SCALOPPINE WITH GOAT • CHEESE AND TOMATO SAUCE

Serves 4.

TIP

Feta cheese or shredded mozzarella can be substituted for the goat cheese in this interesting version of veal parmigiana.

•

Boneless chicken or pork cutlets can replace the veal.

MAKE AHEAD

Assemble and refrigerate up to 1 day ahead. Bring to room temperature, then bake for 5 minutes to heat through.

Preheat oven to 450°F (230°C)

1 lb	veal cutlets, pounded until thin	500 g
1	egg white	1
1/2 cup	dry bread crumbs	125 mL
1 tbsp	vegetable oil	15 mL
2 tsp	crushed garlic	10 mL
1 cup	tomato sauce	250 mL
2 oz	goat cheese, crumbled	50 g
	Chopped fresh parsley	

1. Dip veal in egg white, then in bread crumbs until coated.

2. In large nonstick skillet sprayed with nonstick vegetable spray, heat oil; sauté garlic for 1 minute. Add veal and cook just until tender and browned on both sides. Remove from heat.

3. Place tomato sauce in baking dish. Top with veal and sprinkle with goat cheese. Bake, uncovered, for 5 minutes or until heated through. Garnish with parsley.

PER SERVING

Calories	253
Protein	23 g
Fat	11 g
Carbohydrates	14 g
Sodium	697 mg
Cholesterol	87 mg
Fibre	1 g

VEAL STEW IN CHUNKY TOMATO SAUCE

Serves 4.

TIP

For a different version, try beef or lamb and other vegetables.

•

The longer the veal stews, the more tender the meat.

MAKE AHEAD

Prepare up to a day before and refrigerate, or freeze for longer storage. Reheat gently on a low heat.

1 lb	boneless stewing veal, cut into 1-inch (2.5 cm) cubes	500 g
	All-purpose flour for dusting	
1 tbsp	vegetable oil	15 mL
2 tsp	crushed garlic	10 mL
1 cup	chopped onions	250 mL
1/2 cup	chopped sweet green pepper	125 mL
1 cup	chopped carrots	250 mL
1 1/2 cups	sliced mushrooms	375 mL
1 1/2 cups	beef stock	375 mL
1	bay leaf	1
1 tsp	dried oregano	5 mL
1 1/2 tsp	dried basil (or 2 tbsp [25 mL] chopped fresh)	7 mL
1 cup	chopped peeled potato	250 mL
1 cup	tomato sauce	250 mL
2 tbsp	tomato paste	25 mL
1/4 cup	red wine	50 mL

1. Dust veal cubes in flour.

2. In large nonstick Dutch oven, heat oil; sauté veal for 2 minutes. Remove veal and set aside.

3. To pan, add garlic, onions, green pepper, carrots and mushrooms; sauté until softened, approximately 5 minutes.

4. Add stock, bay leaf, oregano, basil, potato, tomato sauce, tomato paste and wine. Return veal to pan; cover and simmer for 1 hour or until veal is tender, stirring occasionally. Discard bay leaf.

PER SERVING

Calories	289
Protein	24 g
Fat	8 g
Carbohydrates	30 g
Sodium	753 mg
Cholesterol	72 mg
Fibre	5 g

CHILI WITH VEAL AND KIDNEY BEANS

Serves 6.

TIP

Making chili with veal rather than beef gives it a light touch. Add chili powder to your taste.

MAKE AHEAD

Make and refrigerate up to a day before. This dish can also be frozen.

1 1/2 tsp	vegetable oil	7 mL
2 tsp	crushed garlic	10 mL
1 cup	diced onion	250 mL
1 cup	diced sweet green pepper	250 mL
1 cup	diced carrots	250 mL
1 lb	ground veal	500 g
1	can (28 oz [796 mL]) tomatoes, puréed	1
2	cans (each 19 oz [540 mL]) kidney beans (preferably white and red)	2
2 tbsp	tomato paste	25 mL
1 tbsp	chili powder	15 mL
3/4 tsp	dried oregano	4 mL
3/4 tsp	dried basil	4 mL

1. In large nonstick saucepan, heat oil; sauté garlic, onion, green pepper and carrots until softened. Add veal and sauté until no longer pink.

2. Add tomatoes, beans, tomato paste, chili powder, oregano and basil. Cover and simmer for 30 minutes.

PER SERVING

Calories	382
Protein	31 g
Fat	5 g
Carbohydrates	54 g
Sodium	758 mg
Cholesterol	54 mg
Fibre	17 g

•••••••••••••••••• GROUND VEAL WITH SWEET ••
POTATOES AND CHEDDAR
CHEESE

Serves 4.

TIP

Sweet potatoes give a
natural sweetness to this
fabulous variation of
classic shepherd's pie.

•

Children love this dish.
Mozzarella cheese can
replace the Cheddar.

MAKE AHEAD

Prepare and refrigerate up
to a day ahead and bake
just before serving. Great
reheated.

Preheat oven to 375°F (190°C)
8-inch (2 L) square baking dish

1/2 lb	lean ground veal or beef	250 g
1 tsp	vegetable oil	5 mL
1/2 cup	chopped onions	125 mL
2 tsp	crushed garlic	10 mL
1 tbsp	all-purpose flour	15 mL
1/2 cup	beef stock	125 mL
1 tbsp	tomato paste	15 mL
12 oz	sweet potatoes, peeled and diced	375 g
1/4 cup	2% milk	50 mL
	Salt and pepper	
1/2 cup	shredded Cheddar cheese	125 mL

1. In large nonstick skillet, sauté veal in oil until no
   longer pink. Pour off any excess fat. Add onions and
   garlic; sauté until softened, approximately 5 minutes.
   Add flour and cook for 1 minute.

2. Add stock and tomato paste; cook, stirring, until liquid
   is absorbed and mixture thickens, approximately 2
   minutes. Process in food processor using on/off motion
   until still slightly chunky. Place in baking dish.

3. In saucepan of boiling water, cook sweet potatoes until
   tender, approximately 10 minutes. Drain and mash
   with fork or purée slightly. Add milk and combine;
   season with salt and pepper to taste. Spread over meat
   mixture. Sprinkle cheese over top and bake, uncovered, for 20 minutes or until cheese browns.

PER SERVING

Calories	247
Protein	16 g
Fat	8 g
Carbohydrates	26 g
Sodium	251 mg
Cholesterol	56 mg
Fibre	3 g

SPICY VEAL MEATBALLS WITH TOMATO SAUCE

Serves 4 to 6.

TIP

Chicken can be substituted for the veal.

•

Adjust the chili powder to your taste.

•

Serve over plain spaghetti or rice.

MAKE AHEAD

Prepare and refrigerate meatballs up to a day before serving, then reheat on low temperature.

Preheat oven to 450°F (230°C)
Baking sheet sprayed with nonstick vegetable spray

12 oz	ground veal	375 g
1/4 cup	finely chopped onion	50 mL
2 tsp	crushed garlic	10 mL
1/4 cup	finely chopped sweet red pepper	50 mL
1	egg	1
1 1/2 tsp	grated Parmesan cheese	7 mL
1/3 cup	dry bread crumbs	75 mL
2 tbsp	chili sauce or ketchup	25 mL
2 tbsp	chopped fresh basil (or 1 tsp [5 mL] dried)	25 mL
1 tsp	chili powder	5 mL
1 3/4 cups	tomato sauce, heated	425 mL

1. In large bowl, mix together veal, onion, garlic, red pepper, egg, cheese, bread crumbs, chili sauce, basil and chili powder until well combined. Roll into 1-inch (2.5 cm) balls and place on baking sheet.

2. Bake for approximately 10 minutes or until no longer pink inside. Place in serving dish and pour tomato sauce over top.

PER 1/6TH SERVING

Calories	130
Protein	13 g
Fat	3 g
Carbohydrates	12 g
Sodium	585 mg
Cholesterol	76 mg
Fibre	2 g

· HAMBURGERS STUFFED WITH · ·
CHEESE AND ONIONS

Serves 4 or 5.

TIP

Try ground veal or chicken for a change.

●

Substitute other cheeses, such as Swiss or mozzarella.

MAKE AHEAD

Make patties in advance and freeze. Thaw and barbecue just prior to serving.

Barbecue or preheat oven to 450°F (230°C)

1 lb	lean ground beef	500 g
2 tsp	crushed garlic	10 mL
1/4 cup	finely chopped green onion	50 mL
2 tbsp	ketchup	25 mL
	Salt and pepper	
1	egg	1
2 tbsp	dry bread crumbs	25 mL
1/2 cup	finely chopped onions	125 mL
1 tsp	vegetable oil	5 mL
1/4 cup	shredded Cheddar cheese	50 mL

1. In bowl, mix together beef, garlic, green onion, ketchup, salt and pepper to taste, egg and bread crumbs until well combined. Form into 4 or 5 hamburgers.

2. In small nonstick skillet, sauté onions in oil until softened. Make pocket in each hamburger and evenly stuff with onions and cheese. Press meat mixture around opening to seal.

3. Place on greased grill and barbecue, or place on rack on baking sheet and bake for 10 to 15 minutes or until no longer pink inside, turning patties once.

PER 1/5TH SERVING

Calories	240
Protein	21 g
Fat	13 g
Carbohydrates	5 g
Sodium	181 mg
Cholesterol	102 mg
Fibre	1 g

BEEF, MACARONI AND CHEESE CASSEROLE

Serves 4.

TIP

Children love this version of packaged Beefaroni. It is not only more delicious, it is healthier for them.

●

Double this recipe and serve it to a group.

●

Substitute ground chicken or veal for the beef.

MAKE AHEAD

Cook and refrigerate up to a day before, then reheat to serve.

1 1/2 tsp	vegetable oil	7 mL
2 tsp	crushed garlic	10 mL
1/2 cup	chopped onion	125 mL
12 oz	lean ground beef	375 g
1	can (19 oz [540 mL]) tomatoes, crushed	1
1 tsp	dried basil	5 mL
1 tsp	dried oregano	5 mL
1 cup	macaroni	250 mL
2 tbsp	grated Parmesan cheese	25 mL

1. In large nonstick skillet, heat oil; sauté garlic and onion for 3 minutes. Add beef and sauté until no longer pink, stirring constantly to break up beef.

2. Add tomatoes, basil and oregano; cover and cook for 15 minutes, stirring occasionally.

3. Meanwhile, cook macaroni according to package directions or until firm to the bite. Drain and place in serving bowl. Toss with sauce and sprinkle with cheese.

PER SERVING

Calories	350
Protein	24 g
Fat	13 g
Carbohydrates	34 g
Sodium	446 mg
Cholesterol	53 mg
Fibre	3 g

···· MEATLOAF TOPPED WITH ····
SAUTÉED VEGETABLES AND
TOMATO SAUCE

Serves 6.

TIP

Try other vegetables for a change, or substitute veal or chicken for the beef.

MAKE AHEAD

Assemble and refrigerate dish early in the day. Bake as directed. Or bake early in the day and reheat before serving.

Preheat oven to 375°F (190°C)
9- x 5-inch (2 L) loaf pan sprayed with nonstick vegetable spray

1 1/2 tsp	vegetable oil	7 mL
1 tsp	crushed garlic	5 mL
1/2 cup	finely diced onions	125 mL
1/2 cup	finely diced sweet red pepper	125 mL
1/2 cup	thinly sliced mushrooms	125 mL
1/2 cup	tomato sauce, heated	125 mL

Meatloaf

1 lb	lean ground beef	500 g
1	green onion, finely chopped	1
2 tsp	crushed garlic	10 mL
1	egg	1
1/3 cup	dry bread crumbs	75 mL
1 tbsp	grated Parmesan cheese	15 mL
2 tbsp	chili sauce or ketchup	25 mL
1/2 tsp	dried basil	2 mL
1/2 tsp	dried oregano	2 mL
1/2 cup	tomato sauce	125 mL

1. Meatloaf: In bowl, mix together beef, onion, garlic, egg, bread crumbs, cheese, chili sauce, basil, oregano and tomato sauce until well combined. Pat into loaf pan.

2. In small nonstick skillet, heat oil; sauté garlic, onions, red pepper and mushrooms until softened, about 5 minutes. Spoon over meatloaf. Bake, uncovered, for 40 to 50 minutes or until meat thermometer registers 170°F (75°C). Cover and let stand for 20 minutes before serving. Serve with tomato sauce.

PER SERVING

Calories	219
Protein	18 g
Fat	11 g
Carbohydrates	11 g
Sodium	411 mg
Cholesterol	82 mg
Fibre	2 g

CHINESE BEEF WITH CRISP VEGETABLES

Serves 4.

1 tbsp	vegetable oil	15 mL
2 tsp	crushed garlic	10 mL
8 oz	lean beef, thinly sliced	250 g
1 1/2 cups	chopped broccoli	375 mL
1 1/2 cups	thinly sliced sweet red pepper	375 mL
1 1/2 cups	snow peas	375 mL

Sauce

1 tbsp	cornstarch	15 mL
3/4 cup	beef stock	175 mL
2 tbsp	soya sauce	25 mL
1/4 cup	brown sugar	50 mL
2 tbsp	sherry or rice vinegar	25 mL
1 1/2 tsp	minced gingerroot (or 1/4 tsp [1 mL] ground)	7 mL

1. Sauce: In small bowl, combine cornstarch, beef stock, soya sauce, sugar, sherry and ginger; mix well and set aside.

2. In large nonstick skillet, heat oil; sauté garlic and beef just until beef is browned but not cooked through. Remove beef and set aside.

3. To skillet, add broccoli, red pepper and snow peas; sauté for 2 minutes. Return beef to pan. Stir sauce and add to pan; cook just until beef is cooked and sauce has thickened, approximately 2 minutes, stirring constantly.

......STEAK KABOBS WITH ......
HONEY GARLIC MARINADE

Serves 4.

TIP

The longer you marinate the meat, the better the flavor will be.

●

Change the kind of vegetables used for a variation.

●

Pineapple is a delicious substitute for any of the vegetables.

MAKE AHEAD

Prepare steak up to a day before and allow it to sit in marinade, turning occasionally. Assemble kabobs and barbecue just prior to serving.

2 tbsp	soya sauce	25 mL
2 tbsp	sherry or rice vinegar	25 mL
4 tsp	honey	20 mL
2 tsp	crushed garlic	10 mL
1 1/2 tsp	sesame oil	7 mL
4 tsp	vegetable oil	20 mL
1 tbsp	water	15 mL
3/4 lb	lean steak, cut into cubes	375 g
16	pieces (1-inch [2.5cm]) sweet green pepper	16
16	pieces (1-inch [2.5cm]) onion	16
16	small mushrooms	16
16	snow peas	16

1. In bowl, combine soya sauce, sherry, honey, garlic, sesame and vegetable oils and water. Add steak and marinate for 30 minutes, or longer in refrigerator.

2. Remove beef from marinade. Place marinade in small saucepan and cook for 3 to 5 minutes or until thick and syrupy.

3. Thread beef, green pepper, onion, mushrooms and snow peas alternately onto 8 metal skewers. Place on greased grill and barbecue for 10 to 15 minutes, turning often and brushing with marinade, or until cooked as desired. Serve with any remaining marinade.

PER SERVING

Calories	228
Protein	20 g
Fat	9 g
Carbohydrates	16 g
Sodium	553 mg
Cholesterol	47 mg
Fibre	2 g

Tortillas Stuffed with Sautéed Vegetables, Beans and Beef

Serves 4.

TIP

This can also be served as an appetizer or vegetable dish.

MAKE AHEAD

Make early in the day and bake just prior to serving.

Preheat oven to 375°F (190°C)
Baking sheet sprayed with nonstick vegetable spray

1 1/2 tsp	vegetable oil	7 mL
1 tsp	crushed garlic	5 mL
2/3 cup	diced onion	150 mL
2/3 cup	diced mushrooms	150 mL
4 oz	lean ground beef, veal or chicken	125 g
1 1/3 cups	finely diced tomatoes	325 mL
1 cup	drained canned red kidney beans	250 mL
2 tsp	chili powder	10 mL
8	small flour tortillas	8
1/2 cup	shredded Cheddar cheese	125 mL

1. In large nonstick skillet, heat oil; sauté garlic, onion and mushrooms until softened. Add beef and cook, stirring to break up, until no longer pink.

2. Add tomatoes, beans and chili powder; cook, stirring occasionally, for 2 minutes. Divide among tortillas. Sprinkle cheese over top. Roll up and place on baking sheet. Bake for approximately 10 minutes or until hot.

PER SERVING

Calories	348
Protein	17 g
Fat	13 g
Carbohydrates	15 g
Sodium	146 mg
Cholesterol	9 mg
Fibre	1 g

·················ROASTED LEG OF LAMB WITH ··
CRUNCHY GARLIC TOPPING

Serves 6 to 8.

Preheat oven to 375°F (190°C)

TIP

If you suspect the lamb
will be tough, marinate it
in milk, turning occasionally, for at least 3 hours
before baking.

MAKE AHEAD

Prepare topping up to a
day before. Pat on meat
prior to baking.

1 tbsp	margarine	15 mL
2 tsp	crushed garlic	10 mL
1/3 cup	finely chopped onion	75 mL
1/2 cup	dry bread crumbs	125 mL
1/4 cup	crushed bran cereal*	50 mL
1/4 cup	chopped fresh parsley	50 mL
1/3 cup	chicken stock	75 mL
1	leg of lamb (2 1/2 to 3 lb [1.25 to 1.5 kg]), deboned	1
1/3 cup	red wine	75 mL
1/3 cup	beef stock	75 mL

Use a wheat bran breakfast cereal

1. In large nonstick skillet, melt margarine; sauté garlic
and onion until softened. Add bread crumbs, cereal,
parsley and chicken stock; mix until well combined. If
too dry, add more chicken stock.

2. Place lamb in roasting pan and pat bread crumb mixture over top. Pour wine and beef stock into pan. Cover
and bake for 20 minutes. Uncover and bake for 15 to
20 minutes or until meat thermometer registers 140°F
(60°C) for rare or until desired doneness. Serve with
pan juices.

PER 1/8TH SERVING

Calories	227
Protein	25 g
Fat	9 g
Carbohydrates	6 g
Sodium	197 mg
Cholesterol	77 mg
Fibre	1 g

ROASTED CHICKEN WITH ASIAN GLAZE AND FRUIT SAUCE (PAGE 121) ➤

• CURRIED LAMB CASSEROLE • • •
WITH SWEET POTATOES

Serves 4.

TIP

Other vegetables can be used in this recipe.

•

Adjust the curry powder to your taste.

•

Serve over rice, linguine or couscous.

MAKE AHEAD

Make and refrigerate up to a day ahead and reheat on low heat. This dish can also be frozen.

3/4 lb	lamb, cut into 3/4-inch (2 cm) cubes	375 g
	All-purpose flour for dusting	
1 tbsp	vegetable oil	15 mL
2 tsp	crushed garlic	10 mL
1 cup	chopped onion	250 mL
1 cup	finely chopped carrots	250 mL
1/2 cup	finely chopped sweet green pepper	125 mL
1 cup	cubed peeled sweet potatoes	250 mL
1 1/2 cups	sliced mushrooms	375 mL
2 1/2 cups	beef stock	625 mL
1/3 cup	red wine	75 mL
3 tbsp	tomato paste	45 mL
2 tsp	curry powder	10 mL

1. Dust lamb with flour.

2. In large nonstick Dutch oven, heat oil, sauté lamb for 2 minutes or just until seared all over. Remove lamb and set aside.

3. To skillet, add garlic, onion, carrots, green pepper and sweet potatoes; cook, stirring often, for 8 to 10 minutes or until tender. Add mushrooms and cook until softened, approximately 3 minutes.

4. Add stock, wine, tomato paste and curry powder. Return lamb to pan; cover and simmer for 1 1/2 hours, stirring occasionally.

◄ CURRIED LAMB CASSEROLE WITH SWEET POTATOES (PAGE 147)

◄ COUSCOUS WITH RAISINS, DATES AND CURRY (PAGE 202)

PER SERVING

Calories	296
Protein	22 g
Fat	8 g
Carbohydrates	30 g
Sodium	556 mg
Cholesterol	47 mg
Fibre	5 g

················ PORK TENDERLOIN ROAST ···
WITH DRIED FRUIT

Serves 4 or 5.

TIP

A great way to bring out the best flavor of pork. The dried fruits go well with the meat and increase the fibre content.

•

Substitute veal or beef tenderloin.

Preheat oven to 375°F (190°C)

1 1/2 lb	pork tenderloin	750 g
1/4 cup	brown sugar	50 mL
1/4 cup	orange marmalade	50 mL
1/4 cup	beef stock	50 mL
1/4 cup	red wine	50 mL
1/4 cup	chopped dates	50 mL
1/4 cup	chopped dried apricots	50 mL
1/4 cup	raisins	50 mL

1. Place meat in roasting pan. In small saucepan, heat sugar and marmalade; brush over pork.

2. Add stock, wine, dates, apricots and raisins to roasting pan.

3. Bake, covered, for 35 to 45 minutes or until no longer pink and meat thermometer registers 160° to 170°F (70° to 75°C), basting every 10 minutes with pan juices.

4. To serve, slice meat thinly and spoon sauce and fruit over meat.

PER 1/5TH SERVING

Calories	379
Protein	40 g
Fat	6 g
Carbohydrates	38 g
Sodium	138 mg
Cholesterol	126 mg
Fibre	1 g

VEGETABLES

•••••••••••••••••••••••••••••• VEGETABLE TIPS ••••••••

1. Use fresh crisp vegetables that are in season. If out-of-season vegetables are needed, use frozen, never canned. Canned vegetables have a high salt content and lack good color. Keep vegetables in refrigerator in designated section.

2. Stop cooking vegetables when they are tender-crisp and still retain their color. Overcooked vegetables are dull and soft, and most of the nutrients are lost.

3. Leaving the skin on vegetables, if not discolored or bruised, increases the fibre content.

STEAM COOKING

Steam cooking is one of the best ways to cook vegetables because they retain their color, vitamins and flavor.

Place a strainer or rack in a saucepan. Add enough water to just reach bottom of strainer. Place evenly cut vegetables on rack, cover tightly and cook just until tender and color brightens.

MICROWAVE

Place evenly cut vegetables in a microwaveable dish with small amount of water. Cover with plastic wrap, leaving one corner open. Cook on High power just until crisp and color is brightened. Drain and serve immediately or rinse with cold water to stop cooking process.

BOILING

Vegetables can be placed in just enough water to cover and boiled until tender-crisp. Nutrients are often lost through this method. Rinse vegetables immediately when done to stop cooking.

GRILLING

This is a delicious way to cook vegetables. Grill vegetables directly over heat, basting occasionally with marinade. Or place evenly cut vegetables on foil, moisten with margarine, juice or stock and seal tightly; vegetables steam in their own juices. Vegetables such as sweet potatoes, potatoes, fennel and turnips can be precooked in the microwave to lessen grilling time.

• • • • • • • • • • • • • • • • • • POTATO CHEESE CASSEROLE • •

Serves 4 or 5.

TIP

The potatoes can also be diced.

•

Substitute another cheese of your choice, such as Swiss or mozzarella.

MAKE AHEAD

This casserole can be prepared and refrigerated up to 24 hours ahead of time and baked just prior to eating.

Preheat oven to 375°F (190°C)

4	medium potatoes, peeled and thinly sliced	4
1 1/2 tsp	margarine	7 mL
1 cup	chopped onions	250 mL
1 tsp	crushed garlic	5 mL
2 tbsp	all-purpose flour	25 mL
1 3/4 cups	2% warm milk	425 mL
3 tbsp	chopped fresh dill (or 1 tsp [5 mL] dried dillweed)	45 mL
	Salt and pepper	
1/2 cup	shredded Cheddar cheese	125 mL

1. In saucepan of boiling water, cook potatoes just until fork-tender, approximately 10 minutes; drain. Arrange in baking dish just large enough to lay in single layer of overlapping slices.

2. In medium nonstick saucepan, melt margarine; sauté onions and garlic for 5 minutes or until softened. Add flour and cook, stirring, for 1 minute. Slowly stir in milk, simmer until thickened, stirring constantly, 3 to 4 minutes. Add dill; season with salt and pepper to taste.

3. Pour sauce over potatoes; sprinkle with cheese. Cover and bake for approximately 1 hour or until potatoes are tender.

PER 1/5TH SERVING

Calories	207
Protein	8 g
Fat	6 g
Carbohydrates	29 g
Sodium	134 mg
Cholesterol	18 mg
Fibre	2 g

CHEESE AND RED PEPPER STUFFED POTATOES

Serves 4.

TIP

Use ricotta instead of cottage cheese for a creamier consistency. There will, however, be slightly more calories per serving.

MAKE AHEAD

Prepare and refrigerate up to a day before. Bake just before serving.

Preheat oven to 425°F (220°C)

2	large baking potatoes	2
1/3 cup	2% cottage cheese	75 mL
1/4 cup	2% yogurt	50 mL
2 tbsp	2% milk	25 mL
1 tsp	vegetable oil	5 mL
1 1/2 tsp	crushed garlic	7 mL
1/4 cup	finely diced onion	50 mL
1/4 cup	finely diced sweet red pepper	50 mL
2 tbsp	chopped fresh dill (or 1 tsp [5 mL] dried dillweed)	25 mL
	Salt and pepper	
2 tbsp	grated Parmesan cheese	25 mL

1. Pierce potatoes with fork; bake or microwave just until tender. Cool and slice lengthwise in half; carefully scoop out pulp, leaving shell intact. Place pulp in mixing bowl or food processor.

2. Add cottage cheese, yogurt and milk; mix well. (Or process using on/off motion; do not purée.) Set aside.

3. In nonstick skillet, heat oil; sauté garlic, onion and red pepper until tender. Add dill, and salt and pepper to taste; add to potato mixture and mix well. Do not purée.

4. Stuff into potato shells; sprinkle with Parmesan. Place on baking sheet and bake for 10 minutes or until hot.

PER SERVING

Calories	170
Protein	7 g
Fat	3 g
Carbohydrates	30 g
Sodium	147 mg
Cholesterol	5 mg
Fibre	2 g

CHEDDAR CHEESE POTATO SKINS

Serves 4.

TIP

These taste great dipped in yogurt or low-fat sour cream.

●

Sprinkle other herbs or diced vegetables over top.

MAKE AHEAD

Assemble and refrigerate potato shells early in day. Bake just prior to serving.

Preheat oven to 425°F (220°C)

2	medium baking potatoes	2
4 tsp	margarine, melted	20 mL
1 1/2 tsp	crushed garlic	7 mL
1 tbsp	finely chopped fresh parsley	15 mL
	Salt and pepper	
1/4 cup	shredded Cheddar cheese	50 mL

1. Bake potatoes for 1 hour or until tender. (Or pierce skins and microwave at High for 8 to 10 minutes.) Cool and slice lengthwise in half; carefully remove pulp, leaving skin intact. (Reserve pulp for another use.) Place skins on baking sheet.

2. In small bowl, combine margarine, garlic, parsley, and salt and pepper to taste. Spread over potato shells. Top with cheese and bake for 20 minutes or until crisp.

PER SERVING

Calories	114
Protein	3 g
Fat	6 g
Carbohydrates	12 g
Sodium	99 mg
Cholesterol	7 mg
Fibre	1 g

•••••••••••••••••••• BAKED FRENCH WEDGE •••• POTATOES

Serves 6.

TIP

These "french fries" beat those cooked in lots of oil. Children and adults can't stop eating them. Try different spices.

•

Potatoes should be firm, heavy and smooth. Keep in a cool place for 2 to 3 weeks where there is ventilation to keep them dry.

Preheat oven to 375°F (190°C)
Baking sheet sprayed with nonstick vegetable spray

4	medium potatoes, unpeeled	4
2 tbsp	margarine, melted	25 mL
1/2 tsp	chili powder	2 mL
1/2 tsp	dried basil	2 mL
1 tsp	crushed garlic	5 mL
1 1/2 tsp	chopped fresh parsley	7 mL
1 tbsp	grated Parmesan cheese	15 mL

1. Scrub potatoes; cut each into 8 wedges. Place on baking sheet.

2. In small bowl, combine margarine, chili powder, basil, garlic and parsley; brush half over potatoes. Sprinkle with half of the Parmesan; bake for 30 minutes. Turn wedges over; brush with remaining mixture and sprinkle with remaining cheese. Bake for 30 minutes longer.

PER SERVING

Calories	127
Protein	2 g
Fat	4 g
Carbohydrates	21 g
Sodium	73 mg
Cholesterol	1 mg
Fibre	2 g

SWEET POTATO, APPLE AND RAISIN CASSEROLE

Serves 6.

TIP

The darker the skin of the sweet potato, the moister it is.

●

Sweet potatoes are sweet on their own. Lessen the honey or maple syrup if desired.

●

Chopped dates or apricots can replace the raisins.

MAKE AHEAD

Prepare casserole without apples up to the day before. Add apples, toss and bake just prior to serving.

Preheat oven to 350°F (180°C)
Baking dish sprayed with nonstick vegetable spray

1 lb	sweet potatoes, peeled and cubed	500 g
3/4 tsp	ground ginger	4 mL
1/4 cup	honey or maple syrup	50 mL
3/4 tsp	ground cinnamon	4 mL
2 tbsp	margarine, melted	25 mL
1/4 cup	raisins	50 mL
2 tbsp	chopped walnuts	25 mL
3/4 cup	cubed peeled sweet apples	175 mL

1. Steam or microwave sweet potatoes just until slightly underdone. Drain and place in baking dish.

2. In small bowl, combine ginger, honey, cinnamon, margarine, raisins, walnuts and apples; mix well. Pour over sweet potatoes and bake, uncovered, for 20 minutes or until tender.

PER SERVING

Calories	187
Protein	2 g
Fat	5 g
Carbohydrates	34 g
Sodium	62 mg
Cholesterol	0 mg
Fibre	3 g

CAULIFLOWER, BROCCOLI AND GOAT CHEESE BAKE

Serves 4.

TIP

Cut the cauliflower and broccoli into florets and 2-inch (5 cm) stem pieces.

•

The goat cheese can be replaced with mozzarella or Cheddar.

•

If in a hurry, omit the topping.

MAKE AHEAD

Sauce and topping can be prepared early in day. Warm sauce gently before pouring over vegetables. Add a little more milk to thin.

PER SERVING

Calories	148
Protein	7 g
Fat	8 g
Carbohydrates	15 g
Sodium	405 mg
Cholesterol	15 mg
Fibre	5 g

Preheat broiler
Baking dish sprayed with nonstick vegetable spray

2 1/2 cups	chopped cauliflower	625 mL
2 1/2 cups	chopped broccoli	625 mL
1 tbsp	margarine	15 mL
1 tbsp	all-purpose flour	15 mL
1/2 cup	2% milk	125 mL
1/2 cup	chicken stock	125 mL
2 oz	goat cheese	50 g
2 tbsp	diced sweet red pepper	25 mL

Topping

1/3 cup	bran cereal*	75 mL
1 tsp	margarine, melted	5 mL
1/2 tsp	crushed garlic	2 mL

* Use a wheat bran breakfast cereal

1. Steam or microwave cauliflower and broccoli until just tender. Drain and place in baking dish.

2. In small saucepan, melt margarine; add flour and cook, stirring, for 1 minute. Add milk and stock; cook, stirring continuously, until thickened, approximately 5 minutes. Remove from stove. Stir in goat cheese until melted; pour over vegetables. Sprinkle red pepper over top.

3. Topping: In food processor, combine cereal, margarine and garlic; process using on/off motion until crumbly. Sprinkle over vegetables. Broil until browned, approximately 2 minutes.

BROCCOLI WITH FETA CHEESE AND RED PEPPER

Serves 4.

TIP

For a change, substitute asparagus for the broccoli, and goat cheese for the feta.

4 cups	chopped broccoli florets and 2-inch (5 cm) stalk pieces	1 L
2 tsp	vegetable oil	10 mL
2 tsp	crushed garlic	10 mL
3/4 cup	diced onion	175 mL
1/2 cup	diced red pepper	125 mL
1/3 cup	sliced black olives	75 mL
1 cup	diced tomatoes	250 mL
2 tbsp	chicken stock	25 mL
1 tsp	dried oregano (or 2 tbsp [25 mL] chopped fresh)	5 mL
1 1/2 oz	feta cheese, crumbled	40 g

1. Steam or microwave broccoli just until barely tender. Drain and set aside.

2. In nonstick skillet, heat oil; sauté garlic and onion just until softened, approximately 3 minutes. Add broccoli, red pepper, olives, tomatoes, chicken stock and oregano; cook for 3 minutes. Place in serving dish. Sprinkle with feta cheese.

PER SERVING

Calories	111
Protein	5 g
Fat	6 g
Carbohydrates	11 g
Sodium	270 mg
Cholesterol	9 mg
Fibre	4 g

FETA AND SPINACH PHYLLO WHEELS

TIP

You can cook three-quarters of a package (225g) frozen spinach instead of the fresh, then continue recipe.

•

When working with phyllo pastry, keep reserved sheets covered with damp tea towel to prevent them from drying out. Leftover phyllo can be rewrapped and returned to the freezer.

•

Try Cheddar or Swiss cheese instead of feta.

MAKE AHEAD

Make filling up to a day before, but fill phyllo just prior to baking to prevent it from becoming soggy.

PER SERVING

Calories	143
Protein	4 g
Fat	7 g
Carbohydrates	15 g
Sodium	273 mg
Cholesterol	14 mg
Fibre	1 g

Preheat oven to 375°F (190°C)
Baking sheet sprayed with nonstick vegetable spray

5 cups	fresh spinach	1.25 L
2 tsp	vegetable oil	10 mL
2 tsp	crushed garlic	10 mL
2	green onions, chopped	2
1 cup	chopped onions	250 mL
1 cup	diced mushrooms	250 mL
3 1/2 oz	feta cheese, crumbled	90 g
5	sheets phyllo pastry	5
1 tbsp	margarine, melted	15 mL

1. Rinse spinach and shake off excess water. With just the water clinging to leaves, cook until wilted. Drain and squeeze out excess moisture. Finely chop and set aside.

2. In nonstick skillet, heat oil; sauté garlic, green onions and onions for 2 minutes. Add mushrooms and spinach; sauté for 3 minutes or until mushrooms are softened. Add cheese; cook for 1 minute. Remove from heat.

3. Lay out 2 sheets of phyllo and brush with some of the margarine. Repeat with two more sheets. Place last sheet over top. Spread spinach filling over top and roll up like jelly roll. Brush with margarine. Place on baking sheet and bake for 20 to 25 minutes or until crisp and golden. Cut into slices to serve.

• FENNEL PARMIGIANA • • • • • •

Serves 4.

TIP

The stalks and bulbs of fennel should be firm.

•

If fennel is unavailable, replace with 1 large sliced zucchini or half a small sliced eggplant.

MAKE AHEAD

Prepare and refrigerate early in day. Bake just before eating. This tastes great reheated.

Preheat oven to 350°F (180°C)
8-inch (2 L) square baking dish

1	medium fennel bulb, trimmed and sliced thinly	1
1 1/2 tsp	vegetable oil	7 mL
2 tsp	crushed garlic	10 mL
1/2 cup	chopped onion	125 mL
2 cups	tomato sauce	500 mL
2 tbsp	chopped fresh dill (or 1 tsp [5 mL] dried dillweed)	25 mL
1/2 cup	shredded mozzarella cheese	125 mL

1. In saucepan of boiling water, cook fennel just until tender, 5 to 8 minutes. Drain and set aside.

2. In nonstick skillet, heat oil; sauté garlic and onion until softened. Add tomato sauce and dill.

3. Add half of the tomato sauce mixture to baking dish. Add fennel; pour remaining sauce over top. Top with cheese. Bake for 20 minutes or until hot and cheese melts.

PER SERVING

Calories	122
Protein	7 g
Fat	4 g
Carbohydrates	16 g
Sodium	928 mg
Cholesterol	7 mg
Fibre	4 g

•••••••••••••••••••••••TOMATOES STUFFED WITH ••••
SPINACH AND RICOTTA CHEESE

Serves 4.

TIP

For a different texture, try crushed bran cereal for the topping instead of bread crumbs.

•

Use cottage cheese instead of ricotta to reduce the calories.

•

If frozen spinach is used, use 2/3 cup (150 mL) cooked and well drained.

MAKE AHEAD

Make early in day and refrigerate. Bake just prior to serving.

Preheat oven to 350°F (180°C)
Baking dish sprayed with nonstick vegetable spray

4 cups	fresh spinach	1 L
4	medium tomatoes	4
2 1/2 tsp	vegetable oil	12 mL
2 tsp	crushed garlic	10 mL
2/3 cup	chopped onion	150 mL
2/3 cup	ricotta cheese	150 mL
	Salt and pepper	

<u>Topping</u>

1 tbsp	dry bread crumbs	15 mL
1 tbsp	chopped fresh parsley	15 mL
1 tsp	margarine	5 mL
1 tsp	grated Parmesan cheese	5 mL

1. Rinse spinach and shake off excess water. With just the water clinging to leaves, cook until wilted. Squeeze out excess moisture; chop and set aside.

2. Slice off tops of tomatoes. Scoop out pulp, leaving shell of tomato intact. (Reserve pulp for another use.)

3. In nonstick skillet, heat oil; sauté garlic and onion until softened. Remove from heat. Add spinach, cheese, and salt and pepper to taste; mix well. Fill tomatoes with cheese mixture and place in baking dish.

4. Topping: Combine bread crumbs, parsley, margarine and cheese; sprinkle over tomatoes. Bake for 15 minutes or until heated through and topping is golden brown.

PER SERVING

Calories	132
Protein	7 g
Fat	6 g
Carbohydrates	13 g
Sodium	108 mg
Cholesterol	12 mg
Fibre	3 g

·················· ASPARAGUS WITH LEMON ··· AND GARLIC

Serves 4.

TIP

Adjust the lemon to taste.

•

If asparagus is not available, try broccoli or snow peas.

MAKE AHEAD

Make this early in day if it is to be served cold, to allow the asparagus a chance to marinate.

1/2 lb	asparagus, trimmed	250 g
2 tsp	vegetable oil	10 mL
1 tsp	crushed garlic	5 mL
1/4 cup	diced sweet red pepper	50 mL
1	green onion, sliced	1
2 tbsp	white wine	25 mL
4 tsp	lemon juice	20 mL
2 tbsp	chicken stock	25 mL
	Pepper	

1. Steam or boil asparagus just until tender-crisp. Do not overcook. Drain and set aside.

2. In large nonstick skillet, heat oil; sauté garlic and red pepper until softened.

3. Reduce heat and add green onion, wine, lemon juice, chicken stock, pepper to taste and asparagus. Cook for 1 minute. Place asparagus mixture in serving dish.

PER SERVING

Calories	46
Protein	2 g
Fat	2 g
Carbohydrates	4 g
Sodium	29 mg
Cholesterol	0 mg
Fibre	1 g

ASPARAGUS WITH CAESAR DRESSING

Serves 4.

TIP

Broccoli can replace asparagus.

•

Serve warm or cold.

•

Use less mustard if you prefer.

MAKE AHEAD

Make dressing at any time. Just before serving, cook asparagus.

1 lb	asparagus, trimmed	500 g
2 tsp	crushed garlic	10 mL
1 tbsp	Dijon mustard	15 mL
1 tbsp	lemon juice	15 mL
2 tbsp	olive oil	25 mL
1 tbsp	grated Parmesan cheese	15 mL

1. Steam or microwave asparagus until just tender. Drain and place on serving dish.

2. In small bowl, mix garlic, mustard, lemon juice and oil until combined; pour over asparagus. Sprinkle with cheese.

PER SERVING

Calories	101
Protein	4 g
Fat	7 g
Carbohydrates	6 g
Sodium	76 mg
Cholesterol	1 mg
Fibre	2 g

•••••••••••••••••••• BRUSSELS SPROUTS WITH ••••
PECANS AND SWEET POTATOES

Serves 4.

TIP

Brussels sprouts can have a slightly bitter taste, especially if overcooked. The addition of sweet potatoes and pecans balances the flavor.

•

Toast pecans in 400°F (200°C) oven or in skillet on top of stove for 2 minutes or until brown.

1 1/2 cups	cubed peeled sweet potatoes	375 mL
3/4 lb	brussels sprouts, cut in half	375 g
1 tbsp	margarine	15 mL
1/2 cup	chopped onion	125 mL
1 tsp	crushed garlic	5 mL
1/4 cup	chicken stock	50 mL
4 tsp	brown sugar or honey	20 mL
1/4 tsp	cinnamon	1 mL
2 tbsp	pecan pieces, toasted	25 mL

1. In saucepan of boiling water, cook sweet potatoes until just tender; drain and reserve. Repeat with brussels sprouts. Set aside.

2. In nonstick skillet, melt margarine; sauté onion and garlic just until tender. Add sweet potatoes, brussels sprouts, stock, sugar, cinnamon and pecans; cook for 3 minutes or until vegetables are tender.

PER SERVING

Calories	182
Protein	5 g
Fat	6 g
Carbohydrates	30 g
Sodium	142 mg
Cholesterol	0 mg
Fibre	6 g

CARROTS AND SNOW PEAS ···
WITH MAPLE SYRUP AND PECANS

Serves 4.

TIP

Smaller carrots are more tender and sweeter than larger ones.

•

Green beans can be a good substitute for snow peas.

•

Walnuts or pine nuts can replace pecans.

•

Toast pecans in small skillet on stove for 2 minutes or in 400°F (200°C) oven until golden.

1/2 lb	carrots, sliced thinly	250 g
1/2 lb	snow peas	250 g
1 1/2 tsp	margarine	7 mL
3 tbsp	maple syrup	45 mL
2 tbsp	chopped fresh parsley	25 mL
2 tbsp	chopped pecans, toasted	25 mL
1/2 tsp	cinnamon	2 mL

1. Steam or microwave carrots at High just until barely tender, approximately 2 minutes. Drain and set aside.

2. Steam or microwave snow peas just until barely tender, approximately 2 minutes. Drain and set aside.

3. In nonstick skillet, heat margarine and maple syrup. Add carrots, snow peas and parsley; cook for 1 minute. Serve sprinkled with pecans and cinnamon.

PER SERVING

Calories	125
Protein	3 g
Fat	4 g
Carbohydrates	20 g
Sodium	72 mg
Cholesterol	0 mg
Fibre	3 g

SNOW PEAS WITH SESAME SEEDS

Serves 4.

TIP

This dish is also great with asparagus instead of snow peas.

●

Other nuts such as toasted pine nuts can be substituted.

●

Toast sesame seeds in small skillet on high heat for 2 minutes until brown, stirring continuously.

MAKE AHEAD

If serving cold as a salad, prepare early in the day and stir just before serving.

1 tbsp	vegetable oil	15 mL
1 1/2 tsp	crushed garlic	7 mL
1 lb	snow peas, trimmed	500 g
1/2 cup	diced sweet red peppers	125 mL
2 tsp	sesame oil	10 mL
1 1/2 tsp	sesame seeds, toasted	7 mL
4	medium green onions, sliced	4

1. In nonstick skillet, heat vegetable oil; sauté garlic, snow peas and red peppers until tender-crisp.

2. Add sesame oil and seeds and green onions; cook for 1 minute. Serve immediately.

PER SERVING

Calories	112
Protein	4 g
Fat	6 g
Carbohydrates	10 g
Sodium	8 mg
Cholesterol	0 mg
Fibre	3 g

MUSHROOMS STUFFED WITH SPINACH AND RICOTTA CHEESE

Serves 8.

TIP

Instead of fresh spinach, you can use 1/3 cup (75 mL) frozen spinach, cooked and well drained.

•

Cherry tomatoes can replace the mushrooms.

•

Serve as an appetizer or side dish.

MAKE AHEAD

Prepare early in day and refrigerate. Bake just before serving.

PER SERVING

Calories	51
Protein	2 g
Fat	3 g
Carbohydrates	3 g
Sodium	33 mg
Cholesterol	5 mg
Fibre	1 g

Preheat oven to 400°F (200°C)

2 cups	fresh spinach	500 mL
16	medium mushrooms	16
1 tbsp	vegetable oil	15 mL
2 tsp	crushed garlic	10 mL
1/4 cup	finely chopped onions	50 mL
1/3 cup	ricotta cheese	75 mL
1 tbsp	grated Parmesan cheese	15 mL
	Salt and pepper	

1. Rinse spinach and shake off excess water. With just the water clinging to leaves, cook until wilted. Drain and squeeze out excess moisture; chop finely and set aside.

2. Remove stems from mushrooms. Place caps on baking sheet. Dice half of the stems and reserve. Use remaining stems for another use.

3. In small nonstick saucepan, heat oil; sauté garlic, onions and diced stems until softened. Add spinach and cook for 1 minute. Remove from heat.

4. Add ricotta, half the Parmesan, and salt and pepper to taste; mix well and carefully fill mushroom caps. Sprinkle with remaining Parmesan. Bake for 8 to 10 minutes or just until mushrooms release their liquid.

GREEN BEANS AND DICED TOMATOES

Serves 4.

TIP

Snow peas or asparagus can replace the green beans.

MAKE AHEAD

If serving cold, prepare early in day and allow flavors to blend.

8 oz	green beans, trimmed	250 g
1 1/2 tsp	vegetable oil	7 mL
1 tsp	crushed garlic	5 mL
3/4 cup	chopped onion	175 mL
1/3 cup	chopped sweet red or yellow pepper	75 mL
1 1/2 cups	diced tomatoes	375 mL
1/2 tsp	dried basil (or 1 tbsp [15 mL] fresh)	2 mL
1/2 tsp	dried oregano	2 mL
2 tbsp	chicken stock	25 mL
2 tsp	lemon juice	10 mL
2 tsp	grated Parmesan cheese (optional)	10 mL

1. Steam or microwave green beans just until tender. Set aside.

2. In nonstick skillet, heat oil; sauté garlic, onion and red pepper just until tender.

3. Add green beans, tomatoes, basil, oregano, stock and lemon juice; cook for 2 minutes, stirring constantly. Serve sprinkled with Parmesan (if using).

PER SERVING

Calories	65
Protein	2 g
Fat	2 g
Carbohydrates	10 g
Sodium	55 mg
Cholesterol	1 mg
Fibre	3 g

• CHEESY RATATOUILLE BEAN • • •
CASSEROLE

Serves 4 or 5.

TIP

Any beans can be used. Try red or white kidney beans, chick-peas or navy beans.

•

Other vegetables such as sweet peppers, parsnips or carrots can be substituted.

•

For extra fibre, leave on the skin of the zucchini and eggplant.

MAKE AHEAD

Prepare and refrigerate up to a day before and bake just before serving. This is delicious reheated.

PER 1/5TH SERVING

Calories	210
Protein	12 g
Fat	7 g
Carbohydrates	26 g
Sodium	395 mg
Cholesterol	12 mg
Fibre	6 g

Preheat oven to 400°F (200°C)

1 tbsp	vegetable oil	15 mL
2 tsp	crushed garlic	10 mL
1	medium onion, diced	1
1 cup	sliced mushrooms	250 mL
1 cup	thickly sliced zucchini	250 mL
2 cups	cubed eggplant	500 mL
1 cup	cubed peeled potatoes	250 mL
1	can (19 oz/540 mL) tomatoes, crushed	1
1 cup	drained cooked beans	250 mL
1 tsp	dried oregano	5 mL
1 tsp	dried basil	5 mL
1 cup	shredded mozzarella cheese	250 mL

1. In large nonstick saucepan, heat oil over medium heat; cook garlic, onion, mushrooms, zucchini and eggplant, stirring constantly, for about 10 minutes or until softened.

2. Add potatoes, tomatoes, beans, oregano and basil; simmer for 30 minutes or until potatoes are tender.

3. Pour into large baking dish and sprinkle with mozzarella. Bake for 10 minutes or until cheese melts.

•••••••••••••••••• ZUCCHINI BOATS STUFFED •••
WITH CHEESE AND VEGETABLES

Serves 6.

TIP

For a main course version, 1/4 lb (125 g) ground beef, veal or chicken can be added when the vegetables are sautéed. Serve 2 boats per person.

MAKE AHEAD

Prepare early in the day and refrigerate. Bake just before serving.

Preheat oven to 375°F (190°C)

3	medium zucchini	3
1 tbsp	vegetable oil	15 mL
2 tsp	crushed garlic	10 mL
1/2 cup	finely diced onions	125 mL
1/2 cup	finely diced mushrooms	125 mL
1/4 cup	finely diced sweet red pepper	50 mL
2 tbsp	chopped fresh dill (or 1 tsp [5 mL] dried dillweed)	25 mL
3 tbsp	dry bread crumbs	45 mL
4 tsp	grated Parmesan cheese	20 mL
	Salt and pepper	
1/4 cup	shredded mozzarella cheese	50 mL

1. Trim off ends of zucchini. Cook zucchini in boiling water for 3 minutes or until tender. Drain and rinse with cold water. Slice each lengthwise in half. With sharp knife, carefully remove pulp, leaving shell intact. Finely dice pulp and squeeze out excess moisture.

2. In nonstick skillet, heat oil; sauté garlic, onions, mushrooms, red pepper and zucchini until softened, approximately 10 minutes. Add dill, bread crumbs, Parmesan, and salt and pepper to taste; mix well.

3. Spoon filling evenly into zucchini shells and place in baking dish. Top each with mozzarella. Bake for 10 minutes or until hot and cheese melts.

PER SERVING

Calories	74
Protein	4 g
Fat	4 g
Carbohydrates	7 g
Sodium	73 mg
Cholesterol	3 mg
Fibre	2 g

• ROASTED GARLIC SWEET • • • • PEPPER STRIPS

Serves 4.

TIP

Add a sprinkle of fresh herbs such as parsley or basil to oil mixture.

MAKE AHEAD

These peppers can be prepared ahead of time and served cold.

Preheat oven to 400°F (200°C)

4	large sweet peppers (combination of green, red and yellow)	4
2 tbsp	olive oil	25 mL
1 1/2 tsp	crushed garlic	7 mL
1 tbsp	grated Parmesan cheese	15 mL

1. On baking sheet, bake whole peppers for 15 to 20 minutes, turning occasionally, or until blistered and blackened. Place in paper bag; seal and let stand for 10 minutes.

2. Peel off charred skin from peppers; cut off tops and bottoms. Remove seeds and ribs; cut into 1 inch (2.5 cm) wide strips and place on serving platter.

3. Mix oil with garlic; brush over peppers. Sprinkle with cheese.

PER SERVING

Calories	95
Protein	1 g
Fat	7 g
Carbohydrates	7 g
Sodium	26 mg
Cholesterol	1 mg
Fibre	2 g

SPAGHETTI SQUASH WITH ··· VEGETABLES AND TOMATO SAUCE

Serves 4 to 6.

TIP

Instead of microwaving it, you can bake the squash in 350°F (180°C) oven for 40 to 50 minutes or until tender.

●

For an attractive dish, serve in the spaghetti squash shells.

MAKE AHEAD

This can be prepared and baked ahead, then reheated in 325°F (160°C) oven until warm. It is best, however, if served immediately after baking.

Preheat broiler

1 to 2 lb	spaghetti squash	500 g to 1 kg
1 tbsp	margarine	15 mL
3/4 cup	chopped onions	175 mL
2 tsp	crushed garlic	10 mL
1 1/2 cups	sliced mushrooms	375 mL
3/4 cup	diced sweet green pepper	175 mL
1 cup	tomato sauce	250 mL
1 tsp	dried oregano	5 mL
1 tsp	dried basil	5 mL
1/4 cup	grated Parmesan cheese	50 mL

1. Pierce squash in several places. In microwave, cook squash at High for 8 to 10 minutes or until soft. Cool and slice lengthwise in half. Discard seeds and with fork, scrape out spaghetti-like strands and set aside.

2. In large nonstick skillet, melt margarine; sauté onions, garlic, mushrooms and green pepper for about 5 minutes or until tender. Add spaghetti squash strands and cook for 2 more minutes.

3. Add tomato sauce, oregano and basil; combine well. Place in baking dish and sprinkle with Parmesan. Broil for 2 minutes or until browned.

PER 1/6TH SERVING

Calories	102
Protein	3 g
Fat	4 g
Carbohydrates	16 g
Sodium	337 mg
Cholesterol	3 mg
Fibre	4 g

• TERIYAKI SESAME VEGETABLES • •

Serves 4.

TIP

Use any other combination of vegetables. Keep colors contrasting.

•

Remember to cook on a high heat and not to overcook.

1 1/2 tsp	vegetable oil	7 mL
1 tsp	crushed garlic	5 mL
Half	large sweet red or yellow pepper, sliced thinly	Half
Half	large sweet green pepper, sliced thinly	Half
1 1/2 cups	snow peas	375 mL
1	large carrot, sliced thinly	1
1/2 tsp	sesame seeds	2 mL

<u>Sauce</u>

1 tsp	crushed garlic	5 mL
1 tbsp	soya sauce	15 mL
1 tbsp	rice wine vinegar or white wine vinegar	15 mL
1/2 tsp	minced gingerroot	2 mL
1/2 tsp	sesame oil	2 mL
1 tbsp	water	15 mL
1 tbsp	brown sugar	15 mL
1 1/2 tsp	vegetable oil	7 mL

1. Sauce: In small saucepan, combine garlic, soya sauce, vinegar, ginger, sesame oil, water, sugar and vegetable oil; cook for 3 to 5 minutes or until thickened and syrupy.

2. In large nonstick skillet, heat oil; sauté garlic, red and green peppers, snow peas and carrot, stirring constantly, for 2 minutes.

3. Add sauce; sauté for 2 minutes or just until vegetables are tender-crisp. Place in serving dish and sprinkle with sesame seeds.

PER SERVING

Calories	96
Protein	2 g
Fat	4 g
Carbohydrates	12 g
Sodium	271 mg
Cholesterol	0 mg
Fibre	2 g

•••••••••••••••••••••• CHEESE AND VEGETABLE •••• STUFFED TORTILLAS

Serves 8.

TIP

These tortillas can be served as an appetizer or side dish.

•

Serve with salsa, yogurt or light sour cream.

•

Vary the vegetables if desired.

Preheat oven to 400°F (200°C)

1 tbsp	margarine	15 mL
1 tsp	crushed garlic	5 mL
1 cup	finely chopped onions	250 mL
1 cup	finely chopped sweet green or red pepper	250 mL
2/3 cup	finely chopped broccoli	150 mL
	Salt and pepper	
1	large green onion, sliced	1
4	tortillas	4
1/2 cup	shredded Cheddar cheese	125 mL

1. In nonstick skillet, melt margarine; sauté garlic, onions, green pepper, broccoli, and salt and pepper to taste until just tender. Add green onion and mix.

2. Divide vegetables among tortillas and spread over top; sprinkle with cheese. Roll up and place on baking sheet. Bake for 3 to 5 minutes or until hot and cheese melts. Cut in half to serve.

PER SERVING

Calories	119
Protein	4 g
Fat	5 g
Carbohydrates	15 g
Sodium	146 mg
Cholesterol	9 mg
Fibre	1 g

PASTA AND GRAINS

• • • • • • • • • • • • • • • • • • • PASTA AND GRAINS TIPS • • •

1. Cook pasta in a large pot of boiling water. Use 12 to 16 cups (3 to 4 L) water for each pound (500 g) of pasta. Add a little oil to prevent pasta from sticking. Stir pasta occasionally while cooking.

2. Cook pasta "al dente," firm to the bite. Never overcook it until it becomes soft and loses all its texture. When cooked, drain in colander, then transfer to a serving dish. If pasta is to be eaten right away, immediately add sauce and toss. If not, add a little sauce or water so pasta does not stick, then cover and set aside. Do not add sauce to pasta until just ready to serve, or pasta will absorb the sauce and there will appear to be not enough sauce.

3. Cook the sauce while the pasta is cooking. Plan ahead so the sauce will be completed at the same time the pasta is cooked.

4. For a main entrée, 8 oz (1/2 lb [250 g]) dry pasta serves four people.

5. If you are entertaining and don't have time to cook pasta before serving, cook it a few hours in advance, drain and place in a bowl of cold water. Before serving drain pasta and plunge in boiling water until warm, approximately two to three minutes.

6. Do not overcook rice or it becomes too soft. Wild rice begins to fall apart if overcooked.

7. Grains are wonderfully versatile. By adding vegetables, cheese, meat, fish or poultry, these foods can become an entire meal. They can be served as salads, appetizers, main entrées or as side dishes, and can be eaten warm or cold.

······················ TORTELLINI WITH CREAMY ··· TOMATO SAUCE

Serves 4 to 6.

TIP

In my book on pasta, I recommend using whipping cream for this recipe. However, I find that using milk or light cream provides just as much taste — with a significant reduction in fat.

MAKE AHEAD

Make sauce and refrigerate a day before, then gently rewarm before pouring over cooked pasta.

1 lb	cheese tortellini	500 g
2 cups	tomato sauce	500 mL
2 tbsp	chopped fresh basil (or 1 tsp [5 mL] dried)	25 mL
2 tbsp	chopped fresh parsley (or 2 tsp [10 mL] dried)	25 mL
	Pepper	
1/2 cup	milk	125 mL
3 tbsp	grated Parmesan cheese	45 mL

1. Cook tortellini according to package directions or until firm to the bite. Drain and place in serving bowl.

2. Meanwhile, in medium saucepan, bring tomato sauce, basil, parsley, and pepper to taste to simmer. Add milk and 2 tbsp (25 mL) of the Parmesan; cook for 1 minute. Pour over pasta and mix well; sprinkle with remaining cheese.

PER 1/6TH SERVING

Calories	218
Protein	14 g
Fat	6 g
Carbohydrates	25 g
Sodium	733 mg
Cholesterol	110 mg
Fibre	2 g

ROTINI WITH TOMATOES, BLACK OLIVES AND GOAT CHEESE

Serves 4 to 6.

TIP

This is delicious served warm or cold.

●

The goat cheese can be substituted with feta cheese.

MAKE AHEAD

If serving cold, prepare and refrigerate early in day and toss again prior to serving.

1 tbsp	vegetable oil	15 mL
1 1/2 tsp	crushed garlic	7 mL
1 cup	chopped onions	250 mL
1	can (19 oz [540 mL]) tomatoes, puréed	1
1/4 cup	sliced pitted black olives	50 mL
1 tsp	dried basil (or 2 tbsp [25 mL] chopped fresh)	5 mL
	Red pepper flakes	
2 oz	goat cheese	50 g
12 oz	rotini	375 g
1 tbsp	grated Parmesan cheese	15 mL
	Chopped fresh parsley	

1. In large nonstick saucepan, heat oil; sauté garlic and onions for 5 minutes. Add tomatoes, olives, basil, and red pepper flakes to taste; cover and simmer for 10 minutes, stirring often. Add goat cheese, stirring until melted.

2. Meanwhile, cook pasta according to package directions or until firm to the bite. Drain and place in serving bowl. Toss with sauce. Sprinkle with Parmesan cheese and garnish with parsley.

PER 1/6TH SERVING

Calories	305
Protein	10 g
Fat	6 g
Carbohydrates	51 g
Sodium	539 mg
Cholesterol	9 mg
Fibre	3 g

SWEET POTATO, APPLE AND RAISIN CASSEROLE (PAGE 155) ➤

CHILLED PENNE SALAD WITH •• FRESH TOMATOES, YELLOW PEPPER AND BASIL

Serves 4 to 6.

TIP

Substitute rotini or medium shell pasta for the noodles.

MAKE AHEAD

Make early in day. Toss well just before serving.

8 oz	penne noodles	250 g
2 1/2 cups	chopped tomatoes	625 mL
1 cup	thinly sliced sweet yellow or green pepper	250 mL
1/2 cup	chopped fresh basil (or 1 1/2 tsp [7 mL] dried)	125 mL
1/3 cup	shredded mozzarella cheese	75 mL
1 tsp	crushed garlic	5 mL
2 tbsp	olive oil	25 mL
1 tbsp	lemon juice	15 mL
2	green onions, sliced	2

1. Cook penne according to package directions or until firm to the bite. Drain and place in serving bowl.

2. Add tomatoes, yellow pepper, basil, cheese, garlic, oil and lemon juice; toss well. Sprinkle with green onions. Chill for at least 2 hours before serving.

PER 1/6TH SERVING

Calories	228
Protein	7 g
Fat	6 g
Carbohydrates	35 g
Sodium	189 mg
Cholesterol	3 mg
Fibre	2 g

◄ BAKED FRENCH WEDGE POTATOES (PAGE 154)

PENNE WITH SPICY MARINARA SAUCE

Serves 4.

TIP

Other pastas such as rotini or even fettuccine will suit this spicy tomato sauce.

•

For a spicier sauce, increase the capers and red pepper flakes.

MAKE AHEAD

Sauce can be prepared and refrigerated 2 days in advance, or frozen up to 1 month.

1 1/2 tsp	vegetable oil	7 mL
1/2 cup	chopped onion	125 mL
1 tsp	crushed garlic	5 mL
1 1/2 tsp	capers	7 mL
1	can (19 oz [540 mL]) tomatoes, puréed	1
1/3 cup	sliced pitted black olives	75 mL
1 tbsp	tomato paste	15 mL
1 1/2 tsp	dried basil (or 3 tbsp [45 mL] chopped fresh)	7 mL
1/2 tsp	dried oregano	2 mL
1	bay leaf	1
	Red pepper flakes	
8 oz	penne noodles	250 g
4 tsp	grated Parmesan cheese	20 mL

1. In large nonstick skillet, heat oil; sauté onion, garlic and capers for 3 minutes.

2. Add tomatoes, olives, tomato paste, basil, oregano, bay leaf, and red pepper flakes to taste; cover and simmer for 10 to 15 minutes or until thickened slightly and flavors are blended. Discard bay leaf.

3. Meanwhile, cook penne according to package directions or until firm to the bite. Drain and place in serving bowl. Toss with sauce. Sprinkle with cheese.

PER SERVING

Calories	296
Protein	10 g
Fat	5 g
Carbohydrates	54 g
Sodium	603 mg
Cholesterol	1 mg
Fibre	4 g

FETTUCCINE ALFREDO WITH RED PEPPER AND SNOW PEAS

Serves 4.

TIP

Try asparagus, broccoli or yellow pepper for a variation of this colorful dish.

MAKE AHEAD

Sauce can be made in advance and refrigerated; reheat gently, adding more milk to thin.

8 oz	fettuccine noodles	250 g
1 1/2 tsp	margarine	7 mL
1/2 cup	sliced sweet red pepper	125 mL
1/2 cup	snow peas	125 mL
2 tbsp	chopped fresh parsley	25 mL

Sauce

1 tbsp	margarine	15 mL
1 tbsp	all-purpose flour	15 mL
1/2 cup	2% milk	125 mL
3/4 cup	chicken stock	175 mL
1/3 cup	grated Parmesan cheese	75 mL
	Pepper	

1. Cook pasta according to package directions or until firm to the bite. Drain and place in serving bowl.

2. Meanwhile, in nonstick skillet, melt margarine; sauté red pepper and snow peas just until tender. Add to pasta.

3. Sauce: In small nonstick saucepan, melt margarine; add flour and cook, stirring, for 1 minute. Add milk and stock; simmer, stirring constantly, just until thickened, 3 to 5 minutes. Stir in cheese until melted. Season with pepper to taste. Pour over pasta mixture and combine well. Garnish with parsley.

PER SERVING

Calories	306
Protein	12 g
Fat	9 g
Carbohydrates	42 g
Sodium	587 mg
Cholesterol	56 mg
Fibre	3 g

• LINGUINE ALFREDO • • • • • • •

Serves 4.

3/4 lb	linguine noodles	375 g
4 tsp	margarine	20 mL
2 tbsp	all-purpose flour	25 mL
2 cups	2% milk	500 mL
1/4 cup	grated Parmesan cheese	50 mL
1/4 tsp	nutmeg	1 mL
	Pepper	

TIP

You can dress up this dish with the simple addition of 1/2 cup (125 mL) diced steamed snow peas or red pepper, or 1/2 cup (125 mL) diced cooked ham.

MAKE AHEAD

Sauce can be made and refrigerated for up to 2 days ahead. Reheat gently, adding more milk to thin.

1. Cook linguine according to package directions or until firm to the bite. Drain and place in serving bowl.

2. Meanwhile, in small saucepan, melt margarine; add flour and cook, stirring, for 30 seconds. Add milk and cook on medium heat, stirring constantly, just until thickened, approximately 3 minutes. Add cheese, nutmeg, and pepper to taste; stir until combined. Pour over pasta and toss well.

PER SERVING

Calories	470
Protein	18 g
Fat	9 g
Carbohydrates	77 g
Sodium	545 mg
Cholesterol	13 mg
Fibre	3 g

MACARONI WITH THREE CHEESES

Serves 4.

TIP

This is a terrific meal for children.

MAKE AHEAD

Make 1 day ahead and refrigerate; reheat, covered, in 350°F (180°C) oven until warm, 20 minutes.

Preheat broiler

1 cup	macaroni	250 mL
1 tbsp	margarine	15 mL
1 tbsp	all-purpose flour	15 mL
1 cup	2% milk	250 mL
1/3 cup	shredded Cheddar cheese	75 mL
1/3 cup	shredded mozzarella cheese	75 mL
2 tbsp	grated Parmesan cheese	25 mL

Topping

1/2 cup	bran cereal*	125 mL
1 tsp	margarine	5 mL
1/2 tsp	crushed garlic	2 mL

* Use a wheat bran breakfast cereal

1. Cook macaroni according to package directions or until firm to the bite. Drain and place in casserole dish.

2. Meanwhile, in saucepan, melt margarine; add flour and cook, stirring, for 1 minute. Add milk and cook, stirring, until thickened, 2 to 3 minutes. Remove from heat. Stir in Cheddar, mozzarella and Parmesan until melted. Pour over macaroni and mix well.

3. Topping: Combine cereal, margarine and garlic in food processor until crushed; sprinkle over macaroni. Broil just until browned, approximately 2 minutes.

PER SERVING

Calories	299
Protein	13 g
Fat	11 g
Carbohydrates	38 g
Sodium	459 mg
Cholesterol	21 mg
Fibre	4 g

• PARSLEY AND BASIL PESTO • • • SPAGHETTINI

Serves 4.

TIP

Try 1 cup (250 mL) basil and omit the parsley for a more intense flavor.

•

Pesto can be made from other leaves such as fresh spinach and coriander.

•

Toast nuts on top of stove in skillet or in 400°F (200°C) oven for 2 minutes.

MAKE AHEAD

Prepare pesto without cheese and freeze up to 6 months or refrigerate for 1 week. Bring pesto to room temperature and add cheese just before tossing with pasta.

PER SERVING

Calories	315
Protein	9 g
Fat	10 g
Carbohydrates	46 g
Sodium	330 mg
Cholesterol	2 mg
Fibre	3 g

8 oz	spaghettini	250 g
1/2 cup	well-packed basil leaves	125 mL
1/2 cup	well-packed parsley leaves	125 mL
1/4 cup	water or chicken stock	50 mL
3/4 tsp	crushed garlic	4 mL
2 tbsp	olive oil	25 mL
2 tbsp	grated Parmesan cheese	25 mL
1 tsp	lemon juice	5 mL
1 tbsp	toasted pine nuts	15 mL

1. Cook pasta according to package directions or until firm to the bite. Drain and place in serving bowl.

2. Meanwhile, in food processor, purée basil, parsley, water, garlic, oil, cheese, lemon juice and pine nuts until smooth. Pour over pasta; mix well.

•••••••••••••••••ROTINI WITH FRESH TOMATOES • AND FETA CHEESE

Serves 4.

TIP

This dish is similar to a Greek pasta salad. Ripe tomatoes are a must.

•

Serve either warm or cold.

MAKE AHEAD

If serving cold, prepare early in day and allow to marinate. Toss well before serving.

8 oz	rotini noodles	250 g
1 1/2 tsp	vegetable oil	7 mL
2 tsp	crushed garlic	10 mL
1/2 cup	chopped onions	125 mL
2 cups	chopped ripe tomatoes	500 mL
1/2 cup	crumbled feta cheese	125 mL
1/4 cup	chopped fresh basil	50 mL
2 tbsp	grated Parmesan cheese	25 mL
1/4 cup	black olives, pitted and sliced	50 mL
	Pepper	

1. Cook pasta according to package directions or until firm to the bite. Drain and place in serving bowl.

2. Meanwhile, in nonstick skillet, heat oil; sauté garlic and onions for 2 minutes. Add tomatoes and cook for 2 minutes, stirring constantly. Add to pasta.

3. Add feta, basil, Parmesan, olives, and pepper to taste; mix well.

PER SERVING

:✗✗✗✗✗✗✗✗✗✗✗✗✗✗:

Calories	333
Protein	12 g
Fat	8 g
Carbohydrates	52 g
Sodium	548 mg
Cholesterol	17 mg
Fibre	3 g

:✗✗✗✗✗✗✗✗✗✗✗✗✗✗:

•••••••••••••••••• FETTUCCINE WITH SCALLOPS ••
AND RED PEPPER SAUCE

Serves 4 to 6.

TIP

Shrimp can replace the
scallops. However, the
sweetness of red pepper
goes well with the flavor
of scallops.

3/4 lb	fettuccine noodles	375 g
1 tbsp	vegetable oil	15 mL
1 tsp	crushed garlic	5 mL
3/4 cup	chopped onion	175 mL
1 1/2 cups	chopped sweet red pepper	375 mL
1/2 cup	chicken stock	125 mL
3/4 lb	raw scallops, sliced in half	375 g
1 tbsp	margarine	15 mL
1/4 cup	chopped fresh dill (or 1 1/2 tsp [7 mL] dried dillweed)	50 mL
3 tbsp	grated Parmesan cheese	45 mL

1. Cook fettuccine according to package directions or just until firm to the bite. Drain and place in serving bowl.

2. Meanwhile, in large nonstick skillet, heat oil; sauté garlic, onion and red pepper until softened, 5 to 8 minutes.

3. Add stock, scallops and margarine; cook for 2 minutes or just until scallops are opaque. Mix in dill. Pour over pasta and toss to combine. Sprinkle with cheese.

PER 1/6TH SERVING

:✕✕✕✕✕✕✕✕✕✕✕✕✕✕:

Calories	329
Protein	22 g
Fat	8 g
Carbohydrates	42 g
Sodium	532 mg
Cholesterol	69 mg
Fibre	4 g

:✕✕✕✕✕✕✕✕✕✕✕✕✕✕:

FETTUCCINE WITH FRESH ... SALMON, DILL AND LEEKS

Serves 4 to 6.

TIP

Here's a wonderful way to use fresh salmon and not have too much protein. Fresh tuna or swordfish is a great substitute.

MAKE AHEAD

The white sauce can be prepared early in day or up to day before, but add a little extra milk when reheating before continuing with recipe.

4 tsp	margarine	20 mL
4 tsp	all-purpose flour	20 mL
2 cups	2% milk	500 mL
1/4 cup	grated Parmesan cheese	50 mL
1/4 cup	white wine	50 mL
2 tbsp	chopped onion	25 mL
1 tsp	crushed garlic	5 mL
2	leeks, washed and sliced in thin rounds	2
12 oz	fresh salmon, boned and cubed	375 g
3 tbsp	chopped fresh dill (or 1 tsp [5 mL] dried dillweed)	45 mL
10 oz	fettuccine noodles	300 g

1. In small saucepan, melt margarine; add flour and cook, stirring, for 30 seconds. Add milk and cook, stirring constantly, until thickened, 4 to 5 minutes. Stir in cheese until melted; set aside.

2. In large skillet, combine wine, onion, garlic and leeks; cook over medium heat for approximately 10 minutes or until leeks are softened. Add white sauce along with salmon. Cook for 2 to 3 minutes or until salmon is almost opaque, stirring gently. Stir in dill.

3. Meanwhile, cook fettuccine according to package directions or until firm to the bite. Drain and place in serving bowl. Toss with sauce.

PER 1/6TH SERVING

Calories	372
Protein	24 g
Fat	9 g
Carbohydrates	45 g
Sodium	358 mg
Cholesterol	30 mg
Fibre	2 g

•••••••••••••••••••••••• LINGUINE WITH SQUID •••••
IN SPICY TOMATO SAUCE

Serves 4 to 5.

TIP

Shrimp or scallops can replace the squid.

•

For a spicier taste, increase capers, anchovies and red pepper flakes.

1 tbsp	olive oil	15 mL
2 tsp	crushed garlic	10 mL
1 tbsp	capers	15 mL
2	anchovies, minced	2
1/3 cup	sliced black olives	75 mL
2 2/3 cups	crushed canned tomatoes	650 mL
2 tsp	dried oregano	10 mL
2 tsp	dried basil	10 mL
	Red pepper flakes	
1 lb	cleaned squid, cut into thin rings	500 g
3/4 lb	linguine noodles	375 g
3 tbsp	grated Parmesan cheese	45 mL
	Chopped fresh parsley	

1. In large nonstick skillet, heat oil; sauté garlic, capers, anchovies and olives for 1 minute. Add tomatoes, oregano, basil, and red pepper flakes to taste; cover and simmer for 15 minutes, stirring occasionally.

2. Add squid and cook just until tender, approximately 3 minutes.

3. Meanwhile, cook linguine according to package directions or just until firm to the bite. Drain and place in serving bowl. Toss with sauce; sprinkle with cheese and garnish with parsley.

PER 1/5TH SERVING

Calories	439
Protein	27 g
Fat	7 g
Carbohydrates	64 g
Sodium	715 mg
Cholesterol	220 mg
Fibre	4 g

•••••••••••••••••••SPAGHETTI WITH ESCARGOTS ••
AND TOMATO SAUCE

Serves 4 to 6.

TIP

If escargots are
unavailable, canned
clams can be used.

•

Linguine can replace the
spaghetti.

1 tbsp	vegetable oil	15 mL
2 tsp	crushed garlic	10 mL
1 cup	chopped onion	250 mL
1	can (19 oz/540 mL) tomatoes (undrained), crushed	1
2 tbsp	chopped fresh basil (or 1 1/2 tsp [7 mL] dried)	25 mL
2 tbsp	chopped fresh oregano (or 1 tsp [5 mL] dried)	25 mL
	Red pepper flakes	
1	small can (200 g) escargots (snails), drained	1
3/4 lb	spaghetti	375 g
1/4 cup	grated Parmesan cheese	50 mL

1. In large nonstick saucepan, heat oil; sauté garlic and onion until softened approximately 5 minutes.

2. Add tomatoes, basil, oregano, and red pepper flakes to taste; simmer, covered, for 10 minutes. Add escargots and cook for 1 minute.

3. Meanwhile, cook spaghetti according to package directions or until firm to the bite. Drain and place in serving bowl. Toss with sauce. Sprinkle Parmesan over top.

PER 1/6TH SERVING

Calories	341
Protein	19 g
Fat	5 g
Carbohydrates	54 g
Sodium	474 mg
Cholesterol	25 mg
Fibre	3 g

·················CANNELLONI SHELLS STUFFED··
WITH CHEESE AND SPINACH

Serves 4 to 6.

TIP

If ricotta cheese is lumpy,
process it in a food
processor.

●

This filling can also be
placed in jumbo pasta
shells.

MAKE AHEAD

Prepare, assemble and
refrigerate up to a day
before, but bake prior to
serving.

Preheat oven to 350°F (180°C)

12	cannelloni shells	12
2 cups	ricotta cheese	500 mL
1/4 cup	chopped drained cooked spinach	50 mL
1	green onion, chopped	1
2 tbsp	chopped fresh parsley	25 mL
3 tbsp	2% milk	45 mL
1/4 cup	grated Parmesan cheese	50 mL
2 cups	tomato sauce	500 mL

1. Cook pasta according to package directions or until firm to the bite. Drain and set aside.

2. In bowl, combine ricotta cheese, spinach, green onion, parsley, milk and all but 1 tbsp (15 mL) Parmesan cheese; mix until smooth.

3. Carefully cut each pasta shell lengthwise on one side, being careful not to cut through other side. Lay shell flat and place 1 tbsp (15 mL) filling over top. Roll up and place in large baking dish. Repeat with remaining shells.

4. Pour tomato sauce over top; sprinkle with reserved cheese. Cover and bake for 15 to 20 minutes or until hot.

PER 1/6TH SERVING

Calories	242
Protein	15 g
Fat	8 g
Carbohydrates	27 g
Sodium	752 mg
Cholesterol	28 mg
Fibre	2 g

·····················LASAGNA WITH ZUCCHINI, ···
RED PEPPER AND MUSHROOMS

Serves 6.

TIP

This rich, filling lasagna is loaded with fresh vegetables. Try other vegetables for a change.

MAKE AHEAD

Prepare and/or bake lasagna up to a day before. The baked lasagna can be reheated in a 350°F (180°C) oven, covered, for 20 minutes.

Preheat oven to 350°F (180°C)
13- x 9-inch (3 L) baking dish sprayed with nonstick vegetable spray

9	lasagna noodles	9
1 tbsp	vegetable oil	15 mL
1 1/2 tsp	crushed garlic	7 mL
1 cup	chopped zucchini	250 mL
1 cup	chopped onion	250 mL
1 cup	diced sweet red pepper	250 mL
1 cup	sliced mushrooms	250 mL
1	can (19 oz [540 mL]) tomatoes, crushed	1
2 cups	tomato sauce	500 mL
1 tsp	dried basil	5 mL
1 tsp	dried oregano	5 mL
1 1/2 cups	2% cottage cheese	375 mL
1/2 cup	2% milk	125 mL
1/2 cup	grated Parmesan cheese	125 mL
8 oz	mozzarella cheese, shredded	250 g

1. Cook lasagna according to package directions or until firm to the bite. Drain and set aside.

2. In large nonstick skillet, heat oil; sauté garlic, zucchini, onion, red pepper and mushrooms until softened, approximately 8 minutes. Add tomatoes, tomato sauce, basil and oregano; cover and simmer for 15 minutes, stirring occasionally.

3. Meanwhile, in food processor, combine cottage cheese, milk and Parmesan cheese. Set aside.

4. To assemble, arrange 3 lasagna noodles in bottom of baking dish. Pour one-third of tomato sauce over top. Pour half of the cottage cheese mixture over top. Repeat layering once. Top with remaining 3 noodles. Pour remaining tomato sauce over top; sprinkle with mozzarella cheese. Bake, uncovered, for 30 minutes or until hot. Let stand for 15 minutes before serving.

PER SERVING

:✗✗✗✗✗✗✗✗✗✗✗✗✗:

Calories	399
Protein	28 g
Fat	13 g
Carbohydrates	42 g
Sodium	1323 mg
Cholesterol	32 mg
Fibre	4 g

:✗✗✗✗✗✗✗✗✗✗✗✗✗:

•••••••••••••••••••••••• ROTINI WITH CHICKEN, ••••
MUSHROOMS AND SUN-DRIED
TOMATOES

Serves 4 to 6.

TIP

If available, wild mushrooms, such as oyster or chanterelle, highlight this pasta.

•

For more fibre, try whole-wheat pasta.

•

Dry sun-dried tomatoes are the most economical to buy. Soak in hot water for 10 minutes before chopping.

3/4 lb	rotini noodles	375 g
8 oz	boneless skinless chicken breast, cubed	250 g
	All-purpose flour	
1 tbsp	vegetable oil	15 mL
2 tsp	crushed garlic	10 mL
1/2 tsp	minced gingerroot	2 mL
1/4 cup	white wine	50 mL
2 tbsp	chopped sun-dried tomatoes	25 mL
2 cups	sliced mushrooms	500 mL
1 cup	chicken stock	250 mL
1 tbsp	cornstarch	15 mL
3 tbsp	grated Parmesan cheese	45 mL
2 tbsp	chopped green onions	25 mL

1. Cook rotini according to package directions or until firm to the bite. Drain and place in serving bowl.

2. Meanwhile, dust chicken with flour. In large nonstick skillet, heat oil; sauté garlic, ginger and chicken just until still slightly pink. Add wine, tomatoes and mushrooms; cook for 2 minutes.

3. Mix stock with cornstarch until dissolved. Add to skillet and cook for 2 minutes or until thickened. Pour over pasta and sprinkle with Parmesan and green onions.

PER 1/6TH SERVING

Calories	554
Protein	30 g
Fat	8 g
Carbohydrates	86 g
Sodium	650 mg
Cholesterol	34 mg
Fibre	5 g

ROTINI WITH STIR-FRIED STEAK • AND CRISP VEGETABLES

Serves 4 or 5.

TIP

This sweet teriyaki sauce goes well with chicken or pork instead of the steak.

MAKE AHEAD

Make sauce early in day and add steak to marinate in refrigerator until cooking time.

1/2 lb	rotini noodles	250 g
1 1/2 tsp	vegetable oil	7 mL
1 cup	diced onions	250 mL
1 cup	chopped broccoli	250 mL
1 cup	snow peas	250 mL
1/2 cup	diced carrots	125 mL
8 oz	steak, sliced thinly	250 g
1/2 cup	sliced water chestnuts	125 mL

Sauce

1/2 cup	hot water	125 mL
1/4 cup	soya sauce	50 mL
2 tbsp	brown sugar	25 mL
2 1/2 tsp	cornstarch	12 mL
1 1/2 tsp	grated gingerroot (or 1/2 tsp [2 mL] ground ginger)	7 mL
1 tsp	crushed garlic	5 mL

1. Sauce: In small bowl, combine water, soya sauce, sugar, cornstarch, ginger and garlic; set aside.

2. Cook rotini according to package directions or until firm to the bite. Drain and place in serving bowl.

3. Meanwhile, in nonstick skillet, heat oil; sauté onions, broccoli, snow peas and carrots almost until tender-crisp, approximately 5 minutes.

4. Add steak and water chestnuts; sauté for 1 minute. Add sauce; cook, stirring, just until beef is cooked, approximately 2 minutes. Pour over pasta and mix well.

PER 1/5TH SERVING

Calories	318
Protein	18 g
Fat	4 g
Carbohydrates	52 g
Sodium	1035 mg
Cholesterol	25 mg
Fibre	4 g

•••••••••••••••••••• WILD RICE, SNOW PEAS •••• AND ALMOND CASSEROLE

Serves 4.

TIP

This is delicious warm or cold.

•

Toast almonds in small skillet on top of stove or in 400°F (200°C) oven for 2 minutes.

•

For a special dinner menu, use 1 cup (250 mL) wild rice and omit the white rice.

MAKE AHEAD

If serving cold, prepare early in day and stir just prior to serving.

2 tsp	margarine	10 mL
1/2 cup	chopped onion	125 mL
1 tsp	crushed garlic	5 mL
1/2 cup	wild rice	125 mL
1/2 cup	white rice	125 mL
3 1/4 cups	chicken stock	800 mL
3/4 cup	chopped snow peas	175 mL
1/4 cup	diced sweet red pepper	50 mL
1/4 cup	toasted sliced almonds	50 mL
1 tbsp	grated Parmesan cheese	15 mL

1. In large nonstick saucepan, melt margarine; sauté onion and garlic until softened. Add wild and white rice; stir for 2 minutes.

2. Add stock; reduce heat, cover and simmer just until rice is tender and liquid is absorbed, 30 to 40 minutes.

3. Add snow peas, red pepper and almonds; cook for 2 minutes. Place in serving bowl and sprinkle with cheese.

PER SERVING

Calories	305
Protein	13 g
Fat	8 g
Carbohydrates	43 g
Sodium	1425 mg
Cholesterol	1 mg
Fibre	3 g

••••••••••••••••••••••••• SAUTÉED RICE WITH ••••
ALMONDS, CURRY AND GINGER

Serves 4.

TIP

Other raw vegetables can replace the red pepper and snow peas. Try chopped broccoli or sliced zucchini.

•

If bok choy or nappa cabbage is unavailable, use sliced romaine or iceberg lettuce. Bok choy and nappa cabbage can be bought at Asian markets or found in the produce section of some supermarkets.

•

Toast almonds in skillet on top of stove or in 400°F (200°C) oven for 2 minutes.

MAKE AHEAD

Prepare and refrigerate early in day. Just prior to serving, reheat on low heat.

PER SERVING

Calories	248
Protein	8 g
Fat	8 g
Carbohydrates	36 g
Sodium	950 mg
Cholesterol	53 mg
Fibre	3 g

1 tbsp	vegetable oil	15 mL
1 tsp	crushed garlic	5 mL
1 1/2 cups	thinly sliced bok choy or nappa cabbage	375 mL
1 cup	snow peas	250 mL
1/2 cup	chopped sweet red pepper	125 mL
1/3 cup	chopped carrot	75 mL
1 tsp	ground ginger	5 mL
1 tsp	curry powder	5 mL
3/4 cup	chicken stock	175 mL
4 tsp	soya sauce	20 mL
1	egg	1
2 cups	cooked rice	500 mL
2 tbsp	toasted chopped almonds	25 mL
2 tbsp	chopped green onion	25 mL

1. In large nonstick skillet, heat oil; sauté garlic, cabbage, snow peas, red pepper and carrot for 3 minutes or just until tender, stirring constantly. Add ginger, curry powder, stock and soya sauce; cook for 1 minute.

2. Add egg and rice; cook for 1 minute or until egg is well incorporated. Place in serving dish and sprinkle with almonds and green onions.

························ WILD RICE WITH FETA ····· CHEESE DRESSING

Serves 4 to 6.

TIP

You can use 1 cup (250 mL) wild rice and omit the white rice to make a very sophisticated salad.

●

Goat cheese instead of feta would also suite this salad.

MAKE AHEAD

Make early in the day and stir well before serving.

PER 1/6TH SERVING

Calories	224
Protein	7 g
Fat	9 g
Carbohydrates	29 g
Sodium	809 mg
Cholesterol	4 mg
Fibre	2 g

3 cups	chicken stock or water	750 mL
1/2 cup	wild rice	125 mL
1/2 cup	white rice	125 mL
3	medium asparagus, chopped	3
1/2 cup	chopped broccoli	125 mL
1	stalk celery, chopped	1
1/3 cup	chopped carrot	75 mL
2	green onions, chopped	2
1/2 cup	chopped sweet red or green pepper	125 mL
3/4 cup	chopped tomato	175 mL

Dressing

1/2 tsp	crushed garlic	2 mL
1 tbsp	lemon juice	15 mL
1 1/2 tsp	red wine vinegar	7 mL
3 tbsp	crumbled feta cheese	45 mL
3/4 tsp	dried oregano (or 1 tbsp [15 mL] chopped fresh)	4 mL
3 tbsp	olive oil	45 mL

1. In saucepan, bring stock to boil; add wild and white rice and reduce heat. Cover and simmer for 25 to 30 minutes or until just tender. Drain, rinse with cold water and place in serving bowl.

2. Blanch asparagus and broccoli in boiling water until still crisp. Drain and rinse with cold water. Add to bowl along with celery, carrot, green onions, red pepper and tomato; mix well.

3. Dressing: In small bowl, whisk together garlic, lemon juice, vinegar, cheese, oregano and oil until well combined. Pour over rice mixture and mix well. Serve at room temperature or chilled.

•••••••••••••••••••• RICE WITH GROUND VEAL ••• AND MUSHROOMS

Serves 4 to 6.

TIP

Ground chicken, pork or beef can also be used.

•

Try wild mushrooms for a change.

MAKE AHEAD

Prepare and refrigerate up to a day ahead, then reheat on low heat.

1 tbsp	margarine	15 mL
1/2 cup	diced sweet red pepper	125 mL
1 cup	chopped onion	250 mL
1 tsp	crushed garlic	5 mL
4 oz	ground veal	125 g
1 cup	sliced mushrooms	250 mL
1 cup	rice	250 mL
3 1/2 cups	beef stock	875 mL
3 tbsp	grated Parmesan cheese	45 mL

1. In nonstick saucepan, melt margarine; sauté red pepper, onion and garlic until softened, approximately 5 minutes. Add veal and sauté until no longer pink, stirring constantly to break up meat.

2. Add mushrooms and cook for 3 minutes or until softened. Add rice and sauté just until browned, approximately 3 minutes.

3. Add stock; cover and simmer for 25 to 30 minutes or until rice is tender and liquid is absorbed. Add cheese.

PER 1/6TH SERVING

Calories	204
Protein	10 g
Fat	4 g
Carbohydrates	31 g
Sodium	822 mg
Cholesterol	15 mg
Fibre	1 g

•••••••••••••••••••••••••• RICE WITH PINE NUTS •••••
AND SPINACH

Serves 4 to 6.

TIP

Instead of fresh spinach,
you can use 1/2 cup
(125 mL) frozen spinach,
cooked and well drained.

•

Freshly grated Parmesan
cheese will make this dish
outstanding.

•

Toast nuts in skillet on
top of stove just until
browned or in 400°F
(200°C) oven for 2
minutes.

MAKE AHEAD

Make and refrigerate up to
a day in advance, then
reheat over low heat.

3 1/2 cups	fresh spinach	875 mL
1 tbsp	vegetable oil	15 mL
1/3 cup	chopped onion	75 mL
1 cup	rice	250 mL
3 cups	chicken stock	750 mL
1 1/2 tsp	margarine	7 mL
1/4 cup	grated Parmesan cheese	50 mL
2 tbsp	toasted pine nuts	25 mL

1. Rinse spinach under cold water and shake off excess water. With just the water clinging to leaves, cook spinach just until wilted. Drain well and squeeze out moisture; chop and set aside.

2. In medium nonstick saucepan, heat oil; sauté onion for 3 minutes. Add rice; sauté until browned, approximately 3 minutes. Add stock; cover and simmer for 15 to 20 minutes or until rice is tender and liquid absorbed.

3. Add spinach, margarine, cheese and pine nuts; mix well.

PER 1/6TH SERVING

Calories	210
Protein	7 g
Fat	7 g
Carbohydrates	29 g
Sodium	852 mg
Cholesterol	3 mg
Fibre	2 g

CREAMY RICE WITH SEAFOOD AND GOAT CHEESE

Serves 4 to 6.

TIP

Serve warm or cold.

●

The seafood can be substituted with 3 oz (100 g) of cooked chicken.

MAKE AHEAD

Prepare up to a day before, then reheat gently so as not to overcook seafood.

1 1/2 tsp	margarine	7 mL
1/2 cup	finely diced onion	125 mL
1 cup	rice	250 mL
3 cups	chicken stock	750 mL
2 oz	goat cheese	50 g
3 oz	cooked seafood, chopped (crabmeat, shrimp or scallops)	75 g
1/3 cup	diced sweet red pepper	75 mL
1/2 tsp	dried basil (or 2 tbsp [25 mL] chopped fresh)	2 mL
1	large green onion, chopped	1

1. In nonstick medium saucepan, melt margarine; sauté onion until softened. Add rice and sauté until golden, 2 to 3 minutes, stirring constantly. Add stock; cover and simmer for 25 to 30 minutes or until rice is tender and liquid absorbed.

2. Add goat cheese, seafood, red pepper and basil; cook for 2 minutes, stirring, until cheese is melted. Garnish with green onion.

PER 1/6TH SERVING

Calories	198
Protein	9 g
Fat	4 g
Carbohydrates	29 g
Sodium	916 mg
Cholesterol	21 mg
Fibre	1 g

SPICY RICE WITH FETA CHEESE AND BLACK OLIVES

Serves 4.

TIP

This can be served either warm or cold.

•

Instead of zucchini, try chopped broccoli.

•

Try goat cheese instead of feta for a change.

MAKE AHEAD

Prepare and refrigerate early in day. Reheat gently until just warm. If serving cold, stir well before serving.

1 tbsp	vegetable oil	15 mL
2 tsp	crushed garlic	10 mL
1/2 cup	chopped onion	125 mL
1/2 cup	chopped zucchini	125 mL
1/4 cup	chopped sweet red pepper	50 mL
1 cup	rice	250 mL
1 1/2 cups	chicken stock	375 mL
1 tsp	dried oregano	5 mL
1 tsp	dried basil	5 mL
1 tsp	chili powder	5 mL
1/4 cup	sliced pitted black olives	50 mL
2 oz	feta cheese, crumbled	50 g

1. In large nonstick saucepan, heat oil; sauté garlic, onion, zucchini and red pepper until softened, approximately 5 minutes. Add rice and brown for 2 minutes, stirring constantly.

2. Add stock, oregano, basil, chili powder and olives; cover and simmer for approximately 20 minutes or until rice is tender. Pour into serving dish and sprinkle with cheese.

PER SERVING

Calories	291
Protein	8 g
Fat	8 g
Carbohydrates	44 g
Sodium	1067 mg
Cholesterol	12 mg
Fibre	2 g

WILD RICE WITH SAUTÉED ORIENTAL VEGETABLES

Serves 4.

TIP

Although wild rice is expensive, it's worth every penny if the occasion is right.

•

Asparagus and yellow pepper are good substitutes for the broccoli and red pepper.

•

Serve warm or cold.

•

Toast almonds in skillet on top of stove until brown or in 400°F (200°C) oven for 2 minutes.

MAKE AHEAD

If serving cold, refrigerate until chilled and stir just before serving. Add almonds and green onions at last minute.

PER SERVING

Calories	217
Protein	8 g
Fat	6 g
Carbohydrates	32 g
Sodium	980 mg
Cholesterol	0 mg
Fibre	3 g

1 tbsp	margarine	15 mL
1/2 cup	chopped onion	125 mL
1 tsp	crushed garlic	5 mL
1/3 cup	wild rice	75 mL
1/3 cup	white rice	75 mL
1 3/4 cups	chicken stock	425 mL
1/2 cup	chopped broccoli	125 mL
1/2 cup	chopped sweet red pepper	125 mL
1 cup	snow peas, cut in half	250 mL
2 tbsp	chicken stock	25 mL
2 1/2 tsp	soya sauce	12 mL
2 tbsp	sliced almonds, toasted	25 mL
1/4 cup	chopped green onions	50 mL

1. In medium nonstick saucepan, melt half of the margarine; sauté onion and garlic for 3 minutes or until softened. Add wild and white rice; sauté just until golden, approximately 3 minutes.

2. Add 1 3/4 cups (425mL) stock; cover and simmer for approximately 40 minutes or just until rice is tender and liquid absorbed, adding more stock if mixture dries out too quickly. Place in serving bowl.

3. In large nonstick skillet, melt remaining margarine; sauté broccoli, red pepper and snow peas just until tender-crisp. Add remaining 2 tbsp (25 mL) stock and soya sauce; cook for 1 minute. Pour over rice and mix well. Sprinkle with almonds and green onions.

COUSCOUS WITH RAISINS, DATES AND CURRY

Serves 4.

TIP

This dish is fine served at room temperature.

●

Try adding 1/4 cup (50 mL) diced carrots to vegetables.

MAKE AHEAD

Prepare up to the day before, then gently reheat over low heat.

1 1/4 cups	chicken stock	300 mL
3/4 cup	couscous	175 mL
1 tbsp	margarine	15 mL
3/4 cup	finely chopped onions	175 mL
1 tsp	crushed garlic	5 mL
1 cup	finely chopped sweet red pepper	250 mL
1/4 cup	raisins	50 mL
1 tsp	curry powder	5 mL
5	dried dates or apricots, chopped	5

1. In small saucepan, bring chicken stock to boil. Stir in couscous and remove from heat. Cover and let stand until liquid is absorbed, 5 to 8 minutes. Place in serving bowl.

2. Meanwhile, in nonstick saucepan, melt margarine; sauté onions, garlic and red pepper until softened, approximately 5 minutes. Add raisins, curry powder and dates; mix until combined. Add to couscous and mix well.

PER SERVING

Calories	243
Protein	6 g
Fat	3 g
Carbohydrates	47 g
Sodium	239 mg
Cholesterol	0 mg
Fibre	3 g

BARLEY WITH SAUTÉED VEGETABLES AND FETA CHEESE

Serves 5 or 6.

TIP

Although barley is rarely used this way, this dish proves how wonderful it is with tomatoes and feta cheese.

•

Try goat cheese, instead of feta, for a change.

MAKE AHEAD

Make early in day and refrigerate; reheat on low to serve. Also delicious at room temperature.

1 tbsp	vegetable oil	15 mL
2 tsp	crushed garlic	10 mL
3/4 cup	chopped sweet green pepper	175 mL
3/4 cup	chopped mushrooms	175 mL
3/4 cup	pot barley	175 mL
1 1/2 cups	crushed canned tomatoes	375 mL
3 cups	chicken stock	750 mL
1 1/2 tsp	dried basil (or 2 tbsp [25 mL] chopped fresh)	7 mL
1/2 tsp	dried oregano	2 mL
3 oz	feta cheese, crumbled	75 g

1. In large nonstick saucepan, heat oil; sauté garlic, green pepper and mushrooms until softened, approximately 5 minutes. Add barley and sauté for 2 minutes, stirring constantly.

2. Add tomatoes, stock, basil and oregano; cover and simmer for approximately 30 minutes or until barley is tender. Pour into serving dish and sprinkle with cheese.

PER 1/6TH SERVING

Calories	185
Protein	8 g
Fat	6 g
Carbohydrates	25 g
Sodium	646 mg
Cholesterol	12 mg
Fibre	4 g

SAUCES, MARINADES AND DRESSINGS

•••••••••••••••••••• SAUCES, MARINADES AND ••• DRESSING TIPS

SAUCES

1. Cook sauce over medium heat, stirring constantly. Stop cooking when the desired consistency is reached. If too thick, add more liquid. Do not allow milk-based sauces to boil.

2. To lessen fat and cholesterol in your old sauce recipes, use 2 percent milk, not cream. Use low-fat cheeses. Use flour as a thickener instead of egg yolks.

DRESSINGS

1. Use 1 to 2 tbsp (15 to 25 mL) per serving of oil-based salad dressings and 2 to 3 tbsp (25 to 45 mL) per serving of yogurt-sour-cream-based salad dressings.

2. Most dressings can be prepared ahead of time and refrigerated in a covered container. Stir well before using.

3. Fresh herbs will always give better flavor than dried.

•HERB VINAIGRETTE • • • • • • •

Makes 1/3 cup (75 mL).

TIP

Serve over a variety of mild-tasting lettuce leaves (Boston, red, leafy).

MAKE AHEAD

Refrigerate for up to 3 weeks.

1 tbsp	red wine vinegar	15 mL
4 tsp	water	20 mL
4 tsp	lemon juice	20 mL
1/2 tsp	Dijon mustard	2 mL
3/4 tsp	crushed garlic	4 mL
2 tbsp	chopped fresh basil (or 1/2 tsp [2 mL] dried)	25 mL
	Salt and pepper	
2 tbsp	vegetable oil	25 mL

1. In small bowl, whisk together vinegar, water, lemon juice, mustard, garlic, basil, and salt and pepper to taste; whisk in oil until combined.

PER TABLESPOON

Calories	51
Protein	0 g
Fat	5 g
Carbohydrates	1 g
Sodium	7 mg
Cholesterol	0 mg
Fibre	0 g

···················· BUTTERMILK DRESSING ·····

Makes 1 cup (250 mL).

TIP

To sour 1/2 cup (125 mL) milk, add 1 tsp (5 mL) lemon juice or vinegar and let stand for 10 minutes before stirring.

•

Serve over a strong-flavored lettuce such as romaine or radicchio.

•

This dressing can also be used as a sauce for grilled fish.

MAKE AHEAD

Refrigerate for up to 2 days. Stir before using.

1/2 cup	buttermilk or soured milk	125 mL
1/4 cup	light sour cream	50 mL
2 tbsp	vegetable oil	25 mL
4 tsp	lemon juice	20 mL
1/2 tsp	Dijon mustard	2 mL
1/2 tsp	crushed garlic	2 mL
2 tbsp	chopped fresh parsley	25 mL

1. In bowl, combine buttermilk, sour cream, oil, lemon juice, mustard, garlic and parsley; mix well.

PER TABLESPOON

Calories	24
Protein	1 g
Fat	2 g
Carbohydrates	1 g
Sodium	14 mg
Cholesterol	2 mg
Fibre	0 g

•••••••••••••••••••••• LEMON DILL VINAIGRETTE •••

Makes 1/2 cup (125 mL).

TIP

If balsamic vinegar is unavailable, substitute red wine vinegar or cider vinegar.

•

Use over soft greens, such as Boston or leafy lettuce.

MAKE AHEAD

Refrigerate for up to 3 weeks.

3 tbsp	balsamic vinegar	45 mL
2 tbsp	lemon juice	25 mL
1 tbsp	water	15 mL
1	large green onion, minced	1
3/4 tsp	crushed garlic	4 mL
2 tbsp	chopped fresh dill (or 1 tsp [5 mL] dried dillweed)	25 mL
3 tbsp	olive oil	45 mL

1. In bowl, whisk together vinegar, lemon juice, water, onion, garlic and dill; whisk in oil until combined.

PER TABLESPOON

Calories	48
Protein	0 g
Fat	5 g
Carbohydrates	1 g
Sodium	2 mg
Cholesterol	0 mg
Fibre	0 g

• • • • • • • • • • • • • • • • • • • LIGHT CREAMY DILL DRESSING •

Makes 1 cup (250 mL).

TIP

Use in a seafood salad, or serve as a tartar sauce with grilled fish.

MAKE AHEAD

Refrigerate for up to 1 day.

1/2 cup	2% yogurt	125 mL
2 tbsp	light mayonnaise	25 mL
3 tbsp	chopped fresh parsley	45 mL
1/4 cup	chopped fresh dill (or 1 1/2 tsp [7 mL] dried dillweed)	50 mL
1 tsp	Dijon mustard	5 mL
3/4 tsp	crushed garlic	4 mL
	Salt and pepper	

1. In bowl, combine yogurt, mayonnaise, parsley, dill, mustard, garlic, and salt and pepper to taste until well mixed.

PER TABLESPOON

Calories	11
Protein	0.5 g
Fat	1 g
Carbohydrates	1 g
Sodium	21 mg
Cholesterol	1 mg
Fibre	0 g

WILD RICE WITH SAUTÉED ORIENTAL VEGETABLES (PAGE 201) ➤

SPICY RICE WITH FETA CHEESE AND BLACK OLIVES (PAGE 200) ➤

·················· CREAMY CHEESE AND ·····
MUSTARD DRESSING

Makes 1/3 cup (75 mL).

TIP

Toss with a salad of romaine and/or radicchio lettuce.

MAKE AHEAD

Refrigerate for up to 2 days.

3 tbsp	light mayonnaise	45 mL
3 tbsp	2% milk	45 mL
1 tbsp	lemon juice	15 mL
1 tsp	white wine vinegar	5 mL
1/2 tsp	Dijon mustard	2 mL
1 tbsp	grated Parmesan cheese	15 mL
	Salt and pepper	

1. In small bowl, whisk together mayonnaise, milk, lemon juice, vinegar, mustard, Parmesan, and salt and pepper to taste until well combined.

PER TABLESPOON

Calories	37
Protein	1 g
Fat	3 g
Carbohydrates	1 g
Sodium	80 mg
Cholesterol	3 mg
Fibre	0 g

◄ ROTINI WITH TOMATOES, BLACK OLIVES AND GOAT CHEESE (PAGE 178)

• • • • • • • • • • • • • • • • • HONEY POPPY SEED DRESSING • •

Makes 1/3 cup (75 mL).

TIP

Serve over a light leafy lettuce salad.

MAKE AHEAD

Refrigerate for up to 3 weeks.

2 tbsp	lemon juice	25 mL
2 tbsp	vegetable oil	25 mL
2 tsp	honey	10 mL
1 1/2 tsp	white wine vinegar	7 mL
3/4 tsp	Dijon mustard	4 mL
1 tsp	poppy seeds	5 mL

1. In small bowl, whisk together lemon juice, oil, honey, vinegar, mustard and poppy seeds until well combined.

PER TABLESPOON

Calories	60
Protein	0 g
Fat	5 g
Carbohydrates	3 g
Sodium	10 mg
Cholesterol	0 mg
Fibre	0 g

•••••••••••••••••••••••••• BLUE CHEESE CREAMY ••••• DRESSING

Makes 1/2 cup (125 mL).

TIP

Serve as a dressing for a
tossed salad
or as a light dip for
vegetables.

MAKE AHEAD

Refrigerate for up to 2
days.

2 oz	blue cheese	50 g
1/3 cup	light sour cream	75 mL
1/4 tsp	crushed garlic	1 mL
2 tbsp	2% yogurt	25 mL

1. In food processor, combine cheese, sour cream, garlic and yogurt; process until smooth. (If chunky consistency is desired, crumble cheese and mix by hand.)

PER TABLESPOON

Calories	41
Protein	2 g
Fat	2 g
Carbohydrates	2 g
Sodium	112 mg
Cholesterol	9 mg
Fibre	0 g

•••••••••••••••••• CREAMY GARLIC DRESSING ••

Makes 3/4 cup (175 mL).

TIP

Use over a salad of romaine lettuce or a variety of lettuces. Sprinkle with a little extra cheese.

MAKE AHEAD

Refrigerate for up to 2 days. Stir before serving.

1/3 cup	2% cottage cheese	75 mL
1 tsp	crushed garlic	5 mL
3 tbsp	lemon juice	45 mL
2 tbsp	vegetable oil	25 mL
2 tbsp	water	25 mL
2 tbsp	light mayonnaise	25 mL
2 tbsp	grated Parmesan cheese	25 mL

1. In food processor, combine cottage cheese, garlic, lemon juice, oil, water, mayonnaise and Parmesan; process until smooth.

PER TABLESPOON

Calories	38
Protein	1 g
Fat	3 g
Carbohydrates	1 g
Sodium	57 mg
Cholesterol	2 mg
Fibre	0 g

•••••••••••••••••••• TOMATO FRENCH DRESSING ••

Makes 2/3 cup (150 mL).

TIP

Toss with salad or pour over sliced tomatoes and cucumbers.

MAKE AHEAD

Refrigerate for up to 2 days.

1/3 cup	2% cottage cheese	75 mL
4 tsp	tomato paste	20 mL
2 tbsp	vegetable oil	25 mL
2 tbsp	water	25 mL
2 tbsp	lemon juice	25 mL
3/4 tsp	crushed garlic	4 mL

1. In food processor, combine cottage cheese, tomato paste, oil, water, lemon juice and garlic; process until very smooth.

PER TABLESPOON

Calories	34
Protein	1 g
Fat	3 g
Carbohydrates	1 g
Sodium	48 mg
Cholesterol	0.6 mg
Fibre	0 g

•••••••••••••••••LEMON MUSTARD VINAIGRETTE •

Makes 1/3 cup (75 mL).

TIP

Use over a variety of mild-tasting lettuce leaves.

2 tbsp	lemon juice	25 mL
2 tbsp	water	25 mL
1 tsp	Dijon mustard	5 mL
	Salt and pepper	
1/2 tsp	crushed garlic	2 mL
1 tsp	honey	5 mL
2 tbsp	vegetable oil	25 mL

1. In small bowl, mix together lemon juice, water, mustard, salt and pepper to taste, garlic and honey; whisk in oil until combined.

PER TABLESPOON

Calories	55
Protein	0 g
Fat	5 g
Carbohydrates	2 g
Sodium	14 mg
Cholesterol	0 mg
Fibre	0 g

···················· ORANGE DRESSING ······

Makes 2/3 cup (150 mL).

TIP

Serve over a spinach salad with mandarin oranges.

MAKE AHEAD

Refrigerate for up to 1 day.

2 tsp	grated orange rind	10 mL
1/4 cup	orange juice	50 mL
1 tbsp	frozen orange juice concentrate, thawed	15 mL
2 tbsp	light mayonnaise	25 mL
3 tbsp	vegetable oil	45 mL
1 tbsp	chopped fresh tarragon (or 1 tsp [5 mL] dried)	15 mL
1/2 tsp	crushed garlic	2 mL

1. In small bowl, combine orange rind and juice, orange juice concentrate, mayonnaise, oil, tarragon and garlic until well mixed.

PER TABLESPOON

Calories	48
Protein	0 g
Fat	5 g
Carbohydrates	1 g
Sodium	18 mg
Cholesterol	1 mg
Fibre	0 g

RED PEPPER DRESSING

Makes 1/3 cup (75 mL).

TIP

Use with a tossed salad or bean salad.

•

Brush over fish or chicken before cooking.

•

Serve as a side sauce to cooked fish or chicken.

MAKE AHEAD

Refrigerate for up to 2 days.

2 tbsp	olive oil	25 mL
2 tbsp	chopped red onion	25 mL
1/4 cup	chopped sweet red pepper	50 mL
2 tsp	red wine vinegar	10 mL
2 tsp	lemon juice	10 mL
1/2 tsp	crushed garlic	2 mL
1/2 tsp	Dijon mustard	2 mL
2 tbsp	chopped fresh parsley	25 mL
	Salt and pepper	

1. In food processor, combine oil, onion, red pepper, vinegar, lemon juice, garlic, mustard, parsley, and salt and pepper to taste; process until smooth.

PER TABLESPOON

Calories	52
Protein	0 g
Fat	5 g
Carbohydrates	1 g
Sodium	8 mg
Cholesterol	0 mg
Fibre	0 g

•••••••••••••••••••••••••••• CAESAR DRESSING •••••••

Makes 1/2 cup (125 mL).

TIP

Toss with romaine lettuce or use over cooked asparagus or broccoli.

MAKE AHEAD

Refrigerate for up to 1 day.

1	egg	1
1 tsp	crushed garlic	5 mL
1	anchovy, minced	1
4 tsp	lemon juice	20 mL
1 tbsp	red wine vinegar	15 mL
1 tsp	Dijon mustard	5 mL
1 tbsp	grated Parmesan cheese	15 mL
3 tbsp	olive oil	45 mL

1. In small bowl, whisk together egg, garlic, anchovy, lemon juice, vinegar, mustard and cheese; whisk in oil until thickened.

PER TABLESPOON

Calories	60
Protein	1 g
Fat	6 g
Carbohydrates	1 g
Sodium	46 mg
Cholesterol	27 mg
Fibre	0 g

• • • • • • • • • • • • • • • • • • • CREAMY TARRAGON DRESSING •

Makes 3/4 cup (175 mL).

TIP

Use over a mixed vegetable salad or serve alongside grilled fish.

MAKE AHEAD

Refrigerate for up to 1 day.

1/2 cup	2% yogurt	125 mL
2 tbsp	lemon juice	25 mL
2 tbsp	light mayonnaise	25 mL
3/4 tsp	crushed garlic	4 mL
1 tsp	Dijon mustard	5 mL
1/4 cup	chopped fresh parsley	50 mL
2 tsp	dried tarragon (or 3 tbsp [45 mL] fresh)	10 mL
	Salt and pepper	

1. In bowl, combine yogurt, lemon juice, mayonnaise, garlic, mustard, parsley, tarragon, and salt and pepper to taste until well mixed.

PER TABLESPOON

Calories	15
Protein	1 g
Fat	1 g
Carbohydrates	1 g
Sodium	28 mg
Cholesterol	1 mg
Fibre	0 g

Ginger Soya Dressing

Makes 1/3 cup (75 mL).

TIP

Serve over spinach or Bibb lettuce.

MAKE AHEAD

Refrigerate for up to 3 days.

1 1/2 tsp	soya sauce	7 mL
2 tbsp	light sour cream	25 mL
3/4 tsp	crushed garlic	4 mL
1 tsp	minced gingerroot (or 1/4 tsp [1 mL] ground ginger)	5 mL
1 tsp	granulated sugar	5 mL
1 tbsp	rice wine vinegar or white wine vinegar	15 mL

1. In small bowl, combine soya sauce, sour cream, garlic, ginger, sugar and vinegar; mix well.

PER TABLESPOON

Calories	14
Protein	0.3 g
Fat	0.3 g
Carbohydrates	1 g
Sodium	100 mg
Cholesterol	1 mg
Fibre	0 g

•••••••••••••••••• ORIENTAL SESAME DRESSING ••

Makes 1/3 cup (75 mL).

TIP

Serve over spinach leaves.

MAKE AHEAD

Refrigerate for up to 2 weeks.

4 tsp	rice wine vinegar or white wine vinegar	20 mL
1 tbsp	soya sauce	15 mL
1 tbsp	lemon juice	15 mL
1 tsp	sesame seeds	5 mL
1/2 tsp	Dijon mustard	2 mL
4 tsp	vegetable oil	20 mL
1 1/2 tsp	sesame oil	7 mL

1. In small bowl, combine vinegar, soya sauce, lemon juice, sesame seeds and mustard; whisk in vegetable and sesame oils until well combined.

PER TABLESPOON

Calories	40
Protein	0.2 g
Fat	3 g
Carbohydrates	0.5 g
Sodium	200 mg
Cholesterol	0 mg
Fibre	0 g

···················· PEANUT DRESSING ·······

Makes 1/2 cup (125 mL).

TIP

Try other nuts such as pecans, cashews or macadamias.

●

Use over pasta salad or brush over fish, meat or chicken before grilling.

MAKE AHEAD

Refrigerate for up to 2 weeks.

3 tbsp	unsalted peanuts	45 mL
1 tsp	minced gingerroot (or 1/4 tsp [1 mL] ground)	5 mL
2 tbsp	water	25 mL
2 tbsp	lemon juice	25 mL
1 tbsp	soya sauce	15 mL
1 tbsp	honey	15 mL
4 tsp	vegetable oil	20 mL
1 1/2 tsp	sesame oil	7 mL
1 tsp	crushed garlic	5 mL

1. In food processor, combine peanuts, gingerroot, water, lemon juice, soya sauce, honey, vegetable and sesame oils and garlic; process until smooth.

PER TABLESPOON

Calories	58
Protein	1 g
Fat	4 g
Carbohydrates	3 g
Sodium	130 mg
Cholesterol	0 mg
Fibre	0.3 g

•••••••••••••••••••••••RED PEPPER SAUCE •••••••

Makes 1 cup (250 mL).

TIP

For a change, try yellow pepper.

•

Serve over cooked vegetables and fish.

MAKE AHEAD

Refrigerate for up to 1 day.

1 1/2 tsp	margarine	7 mL
1/2 tsp	crushed garlic	2 mL
1/4 cup	chopped onion	50 mL
1	sweet red pepper, diced	1
1/2 cup	chicken stock	125 mL
1 1/2 tsp	vegetable oil	7 mL

1. In small nonstick saucepan, melt margarine; sauté garlic and onion for 2 minutes. Add red pepper and chicken stock; simmer for 5 minutes.

2. Pour into food processor; add oil and pureé until smooth.

PER TABLESPOON

Calories	17
Protein	0.2 g
Fat	1 g
Carbohydrates	0.6 g
Sodium	39 mg
Cholesterol	0 mg
Fibre	0 g

•••••••••••••••••••• Sun-Dried Tomato Sauce ••

Makes 1 1/3 cups (325 mL).
Serves 8.

TIP

Toss with pasta or serve
over cooked fish or
chicken.

•

If sauce is too thick, add a
little water to thin.

•

This sauce makes enough
for 1 1/2 lb (750 g) pasta.

4 oz	sun-dried tomatoes	125 g
1 tsp	crushed garlic	5 mL
3/4 cup	water or chicken stock	175 mL
1/2 cup	chopped fresh parsley	125 mL
2 tbsp	olive oil	25 mL
2 tbsp	toasted pine nuts	25 mL
1 tbsp	grated Parmesan cheese	15 mL

1. In bowl, pour enough boiling water over tomatoes to cover; let sit for 15 minutes or until soft enough to cut. Cut into smaller pieces.

2. In food processor, combine tomatoes, garlic, water, parsley, oil, pine nuts and cheese; process until well blended.

PER SERVING

Calories	80
Protein	1 g
Fat	4 g
Carbohydrates	4 g
Sodium	95 mg
Cholesterol	0 mg
Fibre	1 g

•••••••••••••••••••••••• MUSHROOM SAUCE •••••••

Makes 1 1/2 cups (375 mL).

TIP

If they're available, use wild mushrooms, such as chanterelle or oyster.

•

Serve over cooked beef, chicken or pork.

MAKE AHEAD

Prepare and refrigerate up to a day before, then gently reheat.

1 tbsp	margarine	15 mL
1 1/2 cups	sliced mushrooms	375 mL
2 tbsp	all-purpose flour	25 mL
1/2 cup	chicken or beef stock	125 mL
1/2 cup	2% milk	125 mL
1 tbsp	sherry (optional)	15 mL

1. In small nonstick saucepan, melt margarine; sauté mushrooms until tender, approximately 3 minutes. Add flour and stir until combined.

2. Add stock and milk; cook on low heat, stirring constantly, until thickened, 4 to 5 minutes. Add sherry (if using). If too thick add more milk.

PER 1/4 CUP (50 ML)

Calories	43
Protein	2 g
Fat	2 g
Carbohydrates	3 g
Sodium	101 mg
Cholesterol	1 mg
Fibre	0.3 g

•••••••••••••••••••••••••••••••• THICK AND RICH ••••••••
TOMATO SAUCE

Makes 3 cups (750 mL).

TIP

If a meat sauce is
desired, cook 1/2 lb
(250 g) lean ground beef,
veal or chicken,
breaking up meat, until
no longer pink.
Pour off fat and add to
sauce before simmering for
30 minutes.

•

Serve over any kind of
pasta.

MAKE AHEAD

Refrigerate the day before
or freeze for up to 6 weeks.
If too thin when
reheated, add 2 tbsp
(25 mL) tomato paste.

1 tbsp	vegetable oil	15 mL
2 tsp	crushed garlic	10 mL
1/2 cup	chopped onion	125 mL
1/2 cup	chopped sweet green pepper	125 mL
1/2 cup	chopped carrots	125 mL
1 can	(28 oz [796 mL]) canned tomatoes crushed	1
1/4 cup	red wine	50 mL
2 tbsp	tomato paste	25 mL
1	bay leaf	1
1 tsp	dried oregano	5 mL
1 tsp	dried basil	5 mL

1. In large nonstick saucepan, heat oil; sauté garlic, onion, green pepper and carrots until softened, approximately 10 minutes.

2. Add tomatoes, wine, tomato paste, bay leaf, oregano and basil; cover and simmer for approximately 30 minutes, stirring occasionally. Discard bay leaf. Purée if desired.

PER 1/3 CUP (75 ML)

Calories	66
Protein	2 g
Fat	3 g
Carbohydrates	10 g
Sodium	210 mg
Cholesterol	0 mg
Fibre	3 g

•••••••••••••••••• BASIC QUICK TOMATO SAUCE •

Makes 2 1/2 cups (625 mL).

TIP

Other finely diced vegetables can be added, as well as Italian seasonings such as basil and oregano.

•

Serve over 1 lb (500 g) pasta.

•

Add 2 tbsp (25 mL) tomato paste for a thicker sauce.

MAKE AHEAD

Refrigerate for up to 2 days, or freeze for up to 6 weeks. After defrosting, add 2 tbsp (25 mL) tomato paste to thicken.

1 tbsp	olive oil	15 mL
1	small onion, finely chopped	1
2 tsp	crushed garlic	10 mL
1	can (28 oz [796 mL]) plum tomatoes, crushed	1

1. In large nonstick saucepan, heat oil; sauté onion and garlic for 5 minutes, stirring often.

2. Add tomatoes and cook on medium heat for 15 to 20 minutes, stirring occasionally, or until reduced slightly.

PER 1/3 CUP (75 ML)

Calories	60
Protein	1 g
Fat	2 g
Carbohydrates	7 g
Sodium	250 mg
Cholesterol	0 mg
Fibre	2 g

PESTO SAUCE

Makes 3/4 cup (175 mL).

1/2 cup	well-packed chopped fresh parsley	125 mL
1/2 cup	well-packed chopped fresh basil	125 mL
1/4 cup	water or chicken stock	50 mL
1 tbsp	toasted pine nuts	15 mL
2 tbsp	grated Parmesan cheese	25 mL
3 tbsp	olive oil	45 mL
3/4 tsp	crushed garlic	4 mL

1. In food processor, combine parsley, basil, water, pine nuts, Parmesan, oil and garlic; process until smooth.

PER TABLESPOON

Calories	39
Protein	1 g
Fat	4 g
Carbohydrates	1 g
Sodium	17 mg
Cholesterol	1 mg
Fibre	0.3 g

• Basic White Sauce • • • • • •

Makes 1 cup (250 mL).

1 tbsp	margarine	15 mL
1 tbsp	all-purpose flour	15 mL
1 cup	2% milk	250 mL
	Salt and pepper	

TIP

Chili powder or cayenne pepper can be added for extra zing.

•

Pour over vegetables, chicken, meat or fish.

MAKE AHEAD

Prepare and refrigerate up to a day in advance. Thin with a little more milk when reheating.

1. In nonstick saucepan, melt margarine; add flour and cook, stirring, for 1 minute. Slowly add milk, stirring constantly; season with salt and pepper to taste. Simmer for 3 to 5 minutes or until sauce thickens, stirring constantly.

Variation – Cheese Sauce

Stir 1/3 cup (75 mL) shredded Cheddar cheese into thickened sauce until melted.

PER TABLESPOON

Calories	25
Protein	1 g
Fat	2 g
Carbohydrates	1 g
Sodium	32 mg
Cholesterol	4 mg
Fibre	0 g

BARBECUE SAUCE

Makes 1 cup (250 mL).

TIP

Other finely diced vegetables can be added.

•

Brush over chicken or beef while barbecuing.

MAKE AHEAD

Prepare up to 2 days in advance and refrigerate.

1/2 cup	ketchup	125 mL
1/4 cup	minced onion	50 mL
2 tbsp	chili sauce	25 mL
2 tbsp	brown sugar	25 mL
2 tbsp	vegetable oil	25 mL
1 tbsp	lemon juice	15 mL
1 tbsp	red wine vinegar	15 mL

1. In medium saucepan, combine ketchup, onion, chili sauce, sugar, oil, lemon juice and vinegar; bring to boil and cook for 2 minutes.

PER TABLESPOON

Calories	33
Protein	0 g
Fat	1 g
Carbohydrates	4 g
Sodium	112 mg
Cholesterol	0 mg
Fibre	0 g

•••••••••••••••••••• ORIENTAL PEANUT SAUCE •••

Makes 2/3 cup (150 mL).

TIP

Use over meat, fish or chicken when cooking or barbecuing.

MAKE AHEAD

Prepare up to 2 days in advance.

2 tbsp	vegetable oil	25 mL
2 tbsp	rice wine vinegar	25 mL
2 tbsp	water	25 mL
1 tbsp	soya sauce	15 mL
1 tbsp	lemon juice	15 mL
1 tbsp	red wine vinegar	15 mL
4 tsp	peanut butter	20 mL
1 tbsp	hoisin sauce	15 mL
2 tsp	sesame oil	10 mL

1. In small saucepan, combine vegetable oil, rice wine vinegar, water, soya sauce, lemon juice, red wine vinegar, peanut butter, hoisin sauce and sesame oil; bring to boil and remove immediately.

PER TABLESPOON

Calories	63
Protein	1 g
Fat	6 g
Carbohydrates	1 g
Sodium	213 mg
Cholesterol	0 mg
Fibre	0 g

• ORANGE SAUCE • • • • • • • • •

Makes 3/4 cup (175 mL).

TIP

Use over cooked chicken, turkey or Cornish hens.

•

Try substituting fruit nectar for the orange juice.

MAKE AHEAD

Make and refrigerate early in day. Reheat, adding a little more juice to thin.

1 1/2 tsp	margarine	7 mL
1 1/2 tsp	all-purpose flour	7 mL
3/4 cup	orange juice	175 mL
1/2 tsp	grated orange rind	2 mL

1. In small saucepan, melt margarine; stir in flour and cook, stirring, for 1 minute. Add orange juice and rind; cook, stirring, until thickened.

PER TABLESPOON

Calories	13
Protein	0 g
Fat	0.5 g
Carbohydrates	2 g
Sodium	7 mg
Cholesterol	0 mg
Fibre	0 g

•••••••••••••••••••••••• TERIYAKI MARINADE ••••••

Makes 1/2 cup (125 mL).

TIP

Use to marinate
1 lb (500 g) beef, poultry,
fish or veal for at least
30 minutes.

MAKE AHEAD

Prepare marinade up to
a day before.

3 tbsp	rice wine vinegar or white wine vinegar	45 mL
2 tbsp	soya sauce	25 mL
2 tbsp	water	25 mL
2 tbsp	brown sugar	25 mL
1 tbsp	vegetable oil	15 mL
1 tsp	minced gingerroot (or 1/4 tsp [1 mL] ground ginger)	5 mL
1 tsp	sesame oil	5 mL
1/2 tsp	crushed garlic	2 mL

1. In small bowl, combine vinegar, soya sauce, water, sugar, vegetable oil, ginger, sesame oil and garlic; mix well.

PER TABLESPOON
▪▪▪▪▪▪▪▪▪▪▪▪▪▪

Calories	37
Protein	0.3 g
Fat	2 g
Carbohydrates	4 g
Sodium	259 mg
Cholesterol	0 mg
Fibre	0 g

HOISIN MARINADE

Makes 1/2 cup (125 mL).

When stir-frying vegetables, add this sauce after the vegetables are slightly sautéed. Cook 2 more minutes.

•

Use to marinate chicken, beef, veal or lamb.

MAKE AHEAD

Prepare marinade up to the day before.

2 tbsp	soya sauce	25 mL
2 tbsp	hoisin sauce	25 mL
2 tbsp	rice wine vinegar	25 mL
1 tbsp	brown sugar	15 mL
1 tbsp	vegetable oil	15 mL
1/2 tsp	minced gingerroot (or 1/4 tsp [1 mL] ground ginger)	2 mL
1/2 tsp	crushed garlic	2 mL

1. In bowl, combine soya sauce, hoisin sauce, vinegar, sugar, oil, ginger and garlic; mix well.

PER TABLESPOON

Calories	33
Protein	0.6 g
Fat	2 g
Carbohydrates	4 g
Sodium	428 mg
Cholesterol	0 mg
Fibre	0 g

•••••••••••••••••• GINGER LEMON MARINADE ••

Makes 1/2 cup (125 mL).

TIP

Use to marinate chicken, fish or veal. Remove meat and boil marinade for 3 to 5 minutes until thickened. Brush over meat before cooking.

MAKE AHEAD

Prepare up to 2 days in advance and refrigerate.

3 tbsp	lemon juice	45 mL
2 tbsp	water	25 mL
1 tbsp	vegetable oil	15 mL
1 1/2 tsp	red wine vinegar	7 mL
4 tsp	brown sugar	20 mL
2 tsp	sesame oil	10 mL
1 tsp	minced gingerroot (or 1/4 tsp [1 mL] ground ginger)	5 mL
1/2 tsp	ground coriander	2 mL
1/2 tsp	ground fennel seeds (optional)	2 mL

1. In small bowl, combine lemon juice, water, vegetable oil, vinegar, sugar, sesame oil, ginger, coriander, and fennel seeds (if using); mix well.

PER TABLESPOON

Calories	27
Protein	0 g
Fat	3 g
Carbohydrates	0.5 g
Sodium	1 mg
Cholesterol	0 mg
Fibre	0 g

CHOCOLATE SAUCE

Makes 1/3 cup (75 mL).

TIP

Serve over frozen yogurt or use it to dress up a plain cake. Pierce top of a cake with holes and pour sauce over top.

MAKE AHEAD

Prepare up to a day before. Reheat gently, stirring until smooth and adding a little more milk if too thick.

1/3 cup	granulated sugar	75 mL
1/4 cup	2% milk	50 mL
2 tbsp	sifted unsweetened cocoa powder	25 mL

1. In small saucepan, combine sugar, milk and cocoa; simmer for 5 minutes, stirring often.

PER TABLESPOON

Calories	52
Protein	1 g
Fat	1 g
Carbohydrates	15 g
Sodium	7 mg
Cholesterol	1 mg
Fibre	1 g

•••••••••••••••••••• STRAWBERRY OR RASPBERRY ••
SAUCE

Makes 1 cup (250 mL).

TIP

Instead of water, use fruit liqueur, such as kirsch, peach liqueur or orange liqueur.

•

Serve alongside cheesecakes, fruit or over frozen vanilla yogurt. Excellent over chocolate desserts.

MAKE AHEAD

Prepare up to 2 days in advance or freeze for up to 6 weeks.

8 oz	fresh or frozen (thawed) strawberries or raspberries	250 g
2 tbsp	water	25 mL
	Icing sugar (optional)	

1. In blender or food processor, purée berries and water until smooth. If using raspberries, add 2 tbsp (25 mL) icing sugar if too tart.

PER TABLESPOON
:■■■■■■■■■■■■■■:

Calories	8
Protein	0 g
Fat	0 g
Carbohydrates	2 g
Sodium	0 mg
Cholesterol	0 mg
Fibre	0.2 g

:■■■■■■■■■■■■■■:

ITALIAN SEASONED BREAD CRUMBS

Makes 1 1/2 cups (375 mL).

TIP

Use other spices of your choice and other types of breads, such as English muffins, tortillas and bagels.

●

Use to bread fish, meat or chicken before sautéeing or baking.

●

Sprinkle over casseroles before browning.

MAKE AHEAD

Prepare in advance and keep in airtight container.

Preheat broiler

4	slices whole wheat bread	4
1/4 tsp	dried basil (1 tbsp [15 mL] chopped fresh)	1 mL
1/4 tsp	dried oregano	1 mL
1 tbsp	grated Parmesan cheese	15 mL
1/4 tsp	crushed garlic	1 mL

1. Place bread on baking sheet; broil until browned on both sides, 4 to 5 minutes. Let cool. In food processor, combine bread, basil, oregano, cheese and garlic; process until in crumbs.

PER TABLESPOON

Calories	13
Protein	1 g
Fat	0.2 g
Carbohydrates	2 g
Sodium	29 mg
Cholesterol	0.3 mg
Fibre	0.3 g

············CROUTONS ············

Makes 1 3/4 cups (425 mL).

TIP

Use spices and breads of your choice.

MAKE AHEAD

Prepare in advance and keep in airtight container.

Preheat broiler

2 tsp	margarine, melted	10 mL
1/2 tsp	crushed garlic	2 mL
1 1/2 tsp	grated Parmesan cheese	7 mL
1/4 tsp	dried basil	1 mL
2	slices whole wheat bread	2

1. In small bowl, combine margarine, garlic, cheese and basil. Brush over both sides of bread.

2. Place bread on baking sheet; broil until browned on both sides. Cut into small cubes.

PER TABLESPOON

Calories	8
Protein	0.3 g
Fat	0.3 g
Carbohydrates	1 g
Sodium	16 mg
Cholesterol	0.1 mg
Fibre	0.1 g

DESSERTS

• DESSERT TIPS • • • • • • • • • •

1. Ovens and utensils can affect baking times. Five or ten minutes before the baking time is up, check the cakes, muffins and loafs. Stick a toothpick in several different points in the cake. If it comes out wet, continue baking. Brownies are the exception; their centre should be wet when ready.

2. When adding liquid and dry ingredients for a cake batter, blend just until incorporated. Do not overmix.

3. Cheesecakes should appear a little loose before removing from oven to ensure moistness. Do not bake until set or cheesecake can dry out.

4. Cookies can be baked longer to achieve a crispy texture. Less time gives a softer, chewier cookie. Cookie dough can be frozen and used frozen on cookie sheets. Bake a few minutes longer.

5. Cakes, cheesecakes, brownies, muffins and loaves can be frozen for up to 3 months if wrapped tightly. Do not freeze cakes with fruit garnishes. Add the garnish before serving.

6. Whole-wheat flour can replace up to half the flour in a recipe. Do not add more or the cake will be heavy and dense.

7. Substitute yogurt or light sour cream for milk in the batter of cakes, muffins or loaf recipes.

8. Sliced fresh fruit is a beautiful garnish for desserts. Brush with a glaze of 2 tbsp (25 mL) melted apple or red currant jelly to give a shiny appearance.

9. Sifted icing sugar and cocoa can be sprinkled over cake tops for decoration. For a patterned effect, place a doily over the cake before sprinking, then carefully remove it.

10. Desserts are delicious and look great with puréed fruit sauce over top or alongside. Purée fresh or frozen strawberries or raspberries until smooth. Add a little water for desired consistency. (Raspberries may need a little icing sugar added.)

11. Muffins and loaf recipes can be interchanged. Check baking times carefully.

12. Use nonstick vegetable spray to coat baking pans.

CHOCOLATE CHEESECAKE WITH SOUR CREAM TOPPING (PAGE 244) ➤

••••••••••••••••••••• STRAWBERRY AND KIWI ••••
CHEESECAKE

Makes 12 servings.

TIP

This cake can be made without a crust if you are in a hurry.

•

To glaze the cake, brush fruit with 2 tbsp (25 mL) melted strawberry or red currant jam.

•

Substitute any fresh fruit for the kiwi and strawberries.

MAKE AHEAD

Prepare the day before. Or prepare without garnish and freeze for up to 6 weeks.

PER SERVING

Calories	172
Protein	6 g
Fat	4 g
Carbohydrates	26 g
Sodium	192 mg
Cholesterol	26 mg
Fibre	1 g

Preheat oven to 350°F (180°C)
8-inch (2 L) springform pan

8 oz	ricotta cheese	250 g
8 oz	2% cottage cheese	250 g
2/3 cup	granulated sugar	150 mL
1	large egg	1
1/4 cup	light sour cream	50 mL
2 tbsp	all-purpose flour	25 mL
1 tbsp	lemon juice	15 mL
1 tsp	lemon rind	5 mL

Crust

1 1/2 cups	graham wafer crumbs	375 mL
2 tbsp	granulated sugar	25 mL
1 tbsp	margarine, melted	15 mL
2 tbsp	water	25 mL

Garnish

2	kiwifruit, sliced	2
1 cup	sliced strawberries	250 mL

1. **Crust:** In bowl, combine graham crumbs, sugar, margarine and water; mix well. Pat onto sides and bottom of cake pan; refrigerate.

2. In food processor, combine ricotta and cottage cheeses, sugar and egg; process until completely smooth. Add sour cream, flour, lemon juice and rind; process until well combined. Pour into pan and bake for 35 minutes or until set around edge but still slightly loose in centre. Let cool; refrigerate until well chilled.

3. Garnish cake decoratively with kiwifruit and strawberries.

◄ LEMON POPPY SEED LOAF (PAGE 245)

• • • • • • • • • • • • • • • • • • • CHOCOLATE CHEESECAKE • • • WITH SOUR CREAM TOPPING

Makes 12 servings.

TIP

Garnish with fresh berries or sifted cocoa.

•

Serve with puréed Strawberry or Raspberry sauce (page 238).

•

Cooking with cocoa rather than chocolate has a major advantage. One ounce of semisweet chocolate has 140 calories and 9 g of fat. One ounce of cocoa has 90 calories and 3 g of fat.

MAKE AHEAD

Prepare a day before or freeze for up to 3 weeks.

PER SERVING

:■■■■■■■■■■■■■■■:

Calories	209
Protein	8 g
Fat	5 g
Carbohydrates	32 g
Sodium	206 mg
Cholesterol	32 mg
Fibre	1 g

:■■■■■■■■■■■■■■■:

Preheat oven to 350°F (180°)
8-inch (2 L) springform pan sprayed with nonstick vegetable spray

8 oz	ricotta cheese	250 g
8 oz	2% cottage cheese	250 g
1 cup	granulated sugar	250 mL
1	large egg	1
1 tsp	vanilla	5 mL
1/4 cup	sifted unsweetened cocoa powder	50 mL
1 tbsp	all-purpose flour	15 mL

Crust

1 1/2 cups	graham or chocolate wafer crumbs	375 mL
2 tbsp	water	25 mL
1 tbsp	margarine, melted	15 mL

Topping

1 cup	light sour cream	250 mL
2 tbsp	granulated sugar	25 mL
1 tsp	vanilla	5 mL

1. **Crust:** In bowl, combine crumbs, water and margarine; mix well. Pat onto bottom and sides of springform pan. Refrigerate.

2. In food processor, combine ricotta and cottage cheeses, sugar, egg and vanilla; process until smooth. Add cocoa and flour; process just until combined. Pour into pan and bake for 30 minutes or until set around edge but still slightly loose in centre.

3. **Topping:** Meanwhile, stir together sour cream, sugar and vanilla; pour over cheesecake. Bake for 10 more minutes. (Topping will be loose.) Let cool and refrigerate for at least 3 hours or until set.

· · · · · · · · · · · · · · · · · · LEMON POPPY SEED LOAF · · ·

Makes 20 half slices.

TIP

You can also make muffins by pouring batter into 12 cups and baking in 375ºF (190ºC) oven for 15 to 20 minutes.

●

If you like a strong lemon taste, use 1 tsp (5 mL) more lemon rind.

MAKE AHEAD

Bake a day before or freeze for up to 6 weeks.

Preheat oven to 350ºF (180ºC)
9- x 5- inch (2 L) loaf pan sprayed with nonstick vegetable spray

3/4 cup	granulated sugar	175 mL
1/3 cup	soft margarine	75 mL
1	egg	1
2 tsp	grated lemon rind	10 mL
3 tbsp	lemon juice	45 mL
1/3 cup	2% milk	75 mL
1 1/4 cups	all-purpose flour	300 mL
1 tbsp	poppy seeds	15 mL
1 tsp	baking powder	5 mL
1/2 tsp	baking soda	2 mL
1/3 cup	2% yogurt or light sour cream	75 mL

Glaze

1/4 cup	icing sugar	50 mL
2 tbsp	lemon juice	25 mL

1. In large bowl or food processor, beat together sugar, margarine, egg, lemon rind and juice, mixing well. Add milk, mixing well.

2. Combine flour, poppy seeds, baking powder and baking soda; add to bowl alternately with yogurt, mixing just until incorporated. Do not overmix. Pour into pan and bake for 35 to 40 minutes or until tester inserted into centre comes out dry.

3. Glaze: Prick holes in top of loaf with fork. Combine icing sugar with lemon juice; pour over loaf.

PER HALF SLICE

Calories	101
Protein	1 g
Fat	3 g
Carbohydrates	15 g
Sodium	89 mg
Cholesterol	11 mg
Fibre	0.5 g

• • • • • • • • • • • • • • • • • • • BANANA NUT RAISIN LOAF • •

Makes 20 half slices.

TIP

You can also make muffins by pouring batter into 12 cups and baking for 15 to 20 minutes.

•

Raisins can be replaced with chopped dates or apricots.

•

Buy firm, plump bananas which are green at the stem. Ripen them in a bowl at room temperature, then refrigerate. The skin will turn brown, but the fruit will be unaffected.

MAKE AHEAD

Bake up to 2 days in advance or freeze for up to 6 weeks.

PER HALF SLICE

Calories	108
Protein	2 g
Fat	5 g
Carbohydrates	15 g
Sodium	78 mg
Cholesterol	10 mg
Fibre	1 g

Preheat oven to 375°F (190°C)
9- x 5-inch (2 L) loaf pan sprayed with
nonstick vegetable spray

2	large ripe bananas	2
1/3 cup	soft margarine	75 mL
1/2 cup	granulated sugar	125 mL
1	egg	1
1	egg white	1
1/4 cup	hot water	50 mL
1 1/3 cups	whole wheat flour	325 mL
3/4 tsp	baking soda	4 mL
1/4 cup	raisins	50 mL
1/3 cup	chopped pecans or walnuts	75 mL

1. In bowl or food processor, beat bananas and margarine; beat in sugar, egg, egg white and water until smooth.

2. Combine flour and baking soda; stir into batter along with raisins and all but a few of the pecans, mixing just until blended. Do not overmix. Pour into pan; arrange reserved nuts down middle of mixture. Bake for 35 to 45 minutes or until tester inserted into centre comes out dry.

CARROT PINEAPPLE ZUCCHINI LOAF

Makes 20 slices.

TIP

If you like muffins, fill 12 muffin cups and bake approximately 20 minutes or until tops are firm to the touch.

MAKE AHEAD

Make up to 2 days in advance or freeze for up to 2 months.

Preheat oven to 350°F (180°C)
9- x 5-inch (2 L) loaf pan sprayed with nonstick vegetable spray

1/4 cup	margarine	50 mL
1 cup	granulated sugar	250 mL
1	egg	1
1	egg white	1
2 tsp	cinnamon	10 mL
1 1/2 tsp	vanilla	7 mL
1/4 tsp	nutmeg	1 mL
3/4 cup	grated carrot	175 mL
3/4 cup	grated zucchini	175 mL
1/2 cup	drained crushed pineapple	125 mL
1/3 cup	raisins	75 mL
1 1/4 cups	all-purpose flour	300 mL
1/2 cup	whole wheat flour	125 mL
1 tsp	baking powder	5 mL
1 tsp	baking soda	5 mL

1. In large bowl or food processor, cream margarine with sugar. Add egg, egg white, cinnamon, vanilla and nutmeg; beat well. Stir in carrot, zucchini, pineapple and raisins, blending until well combined.

2. Combine all-purpose and whole wheat flours, baking powder and soda; add to bowl and mix just until combined. Pour into loaf pan and bake for 35 to 45 minutes or until tester inserted into centre comes out dry.

PER SLICE

Calories	117
Protein	2 g
Fat	3 g
Carbohydrates	22 g
Sodium	99 mg
Cholesterol	11 mg
Fibre	1 g

• GLAZED ESPRESSO • • • • • • • CHOCOLATE CAKE

Preheat oven to 350°F (180°C)
8-inch (2 L) springform pan sprayed with
nonstick vegetable spray

1/2 cup	brown sugar	125 mL
1/2 cup	granulated sugar	125 mL
1/3 cup	margarine	75 mL
2	eggs	2
1 tsp	vanilla	5 mL
1/4 cup	unsweetened cocoa powder	50 mL
1 cup	all-purpose flour	250 mL
1 tsp	baking soda	5 mL
1 tsp	baking powder	5 mL
1/2 cup	hot strong coffee	125 mL
1/3 cup	low-fat yogurt or buttermilk	75 mL

Glaze

1 cup	icing sugar	250 mL
2 tbsp	strong coffee	25 mL
	Unsweetened cocoa powder	

1. In large bowl or food processor, beat together brown and granulated sugars, margarine, eggs and vanilla until well blended. Add cocoa and mix until well incorporated.

2. Combine flour, baking soda and baking powder; add to bowl along with coffee and yogurt. Mix just until combined, being careful not to overmix. Pour into pan; bake for 35 to 40 minutes or until tester inserted into centre comes out dry. Let cool completely.

3. Glaze: In small bowl, mix icing sugar with coffee until smooth, adding more coffee if too thick. Spread over cake, smoothing with knife. Sift cocoa over top to decorate.

• BLUEBERRY PEACH CAKE • • • •

Makes 16 slices.

TIP

If using frozen blueberries, thaw first; then drain off the excess liquid.

●

Apples or pears are good substitutes for the peaches.

MAKE AHEAD

Bake a day before or freeze for up to 6 weeks.

Preheat oven to 350°F (180°C)

9-inch (3 L) Bundt pan sprayed with nonstick vegetable spray

1 cup	granulated sugar	250 mL
3/4 cup	applesauce	175 mL
1/4 cup	vegetable oil	50 mL
2	eggs	2
1 tsp	vanilla	5 mL
1 1/2 cups	all-purpose flour	375 mL
1/2 cup	whole wheat flour	125 mL
2 tsp	cinnamon	10 mL
1 1/2 tsp	baking powder	7 mL
1 tsp	baking soda	5 mL
1/2 cup	2% yogurt	125 mL
1 cup	sliced peeled peaches	250 mL
1 cup	blueberries	250 mL
	Icing sugar	

1. In large bowl, beat together sugar, applesauce, oil, eggs and vanilla, mixing well.

2. Combine all-purpose and whole wheat flours, cinnamon, baking powder and baking soda; stir into bowl just until blended. Stir in yogurt; fold in peaches and blueberries. Pour into pan.

3. Bake for 40 to 45 minutes or until cake tester inserted into centre comes out clean. Let cool; dust with icing sugar.

PER SLICE

Calories	171
Protein	3 g
Fat	4 g
Carbohydrates	31 g
Sodium	102 mg
Cholesterol	27 mg
Fibre	1 g

CHOCOLATE MARBLE COFFEE CAKE

Makes 16 slices.

TIP

One ounce of unsweetened cocoa has 3 g of fat compared to 1 oz of semi-sweet chocolate which has 9 g of fat.

•

Sift icing sugar over top of cooled cake to decorate.

MAKE AHEAD

Bake a day before or freeze for up to 6 weeks.

Preheat oven to 350°F (180°C)
8-inch (2 L) square cake pan sprayed with
nonstick vegetable spray

1/4 cup	margarine	50 mL
3/4 cup	granulated sugar	175 mL
1	egg	1
1	egg white	1
1 1/2 tsp	vanilla	7 mL
1 1/4 cups	all-purpose flour	300 mL
1 1/2 tsp	baking powder	7 mL
1 tsp	cinnamon	5 mL
1/2 tsp	baking soda	2 mL
1 cup	2% yogurt	250 mL

Chocolate Marble

1/4 cup	granulated sugar	50 mL
3 tbsp	sifted unsweetened cocoa powder	45 mL
3 tbsp	2% milk	45 mL

1. In large bowl or food processor, cream together margarine and sugar. Beat in egg, egg white and vanilla.

2. Combine flour, baking powder, cinnamon and baking soda; add to bowl alternately with yogurt, mixing just until blended. Do not overmix. Pour all but 1 cup (250 mL) into cake pan.

3. Chocolate Marble: In small bowl, stir together sugar, cocoa and milk until blended. Add to reserved batter, mixing well. Pour over batter in pan; draw knife through mixture to create marbled effect. Bake for 35 to 40 minutes or until cake tester inserted into centre comes out clean.

PER SLICE

Calories	130
Protein	3 g
Fat	3 g
Carbohydrates	22 g
Sodium	119 mg
Cholesterol	14 mg
Fibre	1 g

ORANGE-GLAZED COFFEE CAKE

Makes 16 slices.

TIP

If you pierce the cake with a fork when warm and pour glaze over top, the icing will filter through the cake.

•

You can serve this cake without the glaze.

MAKE AHEAD

Bake a day before, or freeze for up to 6 weeks.

Preheat oven to 350°F (180°C)
9-inch (3 L) Bundt pan sprayed with nonstick vegetable spray

1/4 cup	soft margarine	50 mL
1 cup	granulated sugar	250 mL
2	eggs	2
1	egg white	1
1 1/2 cups	orange juice	375 mL
1 1/2 tsp	grated orange rind	7 mL
1 cup	whole wheat flour	250 mL
1 cup	all-purpose flour	250 mL
1 tsp	cinnamon	5 mL
1 tsp	baking powder	5 mL
1 tsp	baking soda	5 mL

Glaze

1/2 cup	icing sugar	125 mL
4 tsp	frozen orange juice concentrate, thawed	20 mL

PER SLICE

Calories	166
Protein	3 g
Fat	4 g
Carbohydrates	31 g
Sodium	125 mg
Cholesterol	26 mg
Fibre	1 g

1. In large bowl or food processor, cream together margarine and sugar. Beat in eggs, egg white, orange juice and rind until well blended.

2. Combine whole wheat and all-purpose flours, cinnamon, baking powder and baking soda; add to creamed mixture and mix until well blended. Pour into pan. Bake for 35 to 40 minutes or until cake tester inserted into centre comes out clean. Let cool.

3. Glaze: Mix icing sugar with orange juice concentrate; pour over cake, allowing to drip down sides.

•••••••••••••••••••••••••••••BANANA MARBLE ••••••••
CHOCOLATE CAKE

Makes 16 slices.

TIP

This can also be made in a 9-inch (2.5 L) square cake pan. Test cake at 40 minutes for doneness.

•

Use ripe bananas for the best flavor.

MAKE AHEAD

Bake a day before, or freeze for up to 6 weeks.

Preheat oven to 350°F (180°C)
9-inch (3 L) Bundt pan sprayed with
nonstick vegetable spray

1/4 cup	soft margarine	50 mL
1 cup	granulated sugar	250 mL
2	eggs	2
2	large bananas, mashed	2
1 tsp	vanilla	5 mL
1 3/4 cups	all-purpose flour	425 mL
1 1/2 tsp	baking powder	7 mL
1 tsp	baking soda	5 mL
3/4 cup	2% yogurt	175 mL

Marble

2 tbsp	granulated sugar	25 mL
4 tsp	sifted unsweetened cocoa powder	20 mL
4 tsp	2% milk	20 mL

1. In large bowl or food processor, cream together margarine and sugar. Beat in eggs, bananas and vanilla until well mixed.

2. Combine flour, baking powder and baking soda; add to bowl alternately with yogurt, mixing just until blended. Pour all but 1/2 cup (125 mL) batter into cake pan.

3. Marble: Combine sugar, cocoa and milk; add to reserved batter, blending well. Pour over batter in pan; draw knife through mixture to create marbled effect. Bake for 45 to 55 minutes or until cake tester inserted into centre comes out clean.

PER SLICE

Calories	163
Protein	3 g
Fat	4 g
Carbohydrates	30 g
Sodium	130 mg
Cholesterol	27 mg
Fibre	1 g

• • • • • • • • • • • • • • • • • APPLE PECAN STREUSEL CAKE • •

Makes 16 slices.

TIP

Try substituting pears for the apples and chopped dates for the raisins.

•

When measuring flour, fill a dry measure to overflowing, then level off with a knife.

MAKE AHEAD

Bake a day before or freeze for up to 6 weeks.

Preheat oven to 350°F (180°C)
9-inch (3 L) Bundt pan sprayed with nonstick vegetable spray

1/4 cup	soft margarine	50 mL
1 cup	brown sugar	250 mL
2	eggs	2
2 tsp	vanilla	10 mL
1 1/4 cups	all-purpose flour	300 mL
3/4 cup	whole wheat flour	175 mL
2 1/2 tsp	cinnamon	12 mL
1 1/2 tsp	baking powder	7 mL
1 tsp	baking soda	5 mL
1 cup	2% yogurt or light sour cream	250 mL
2 3/4 cups	diced peeled apples	675 mL
1/4 cup	raisins	50 mL

<u>Topping</u>

1/4 cup	chopped pecans	50 mL
1/4 cup	all-purpose flour	50 mL
3 tbsp	brown sugar	45 mL
1 tbsp	margarine, melted	15 mL
1 1/2 tsp	cinnamon	7 mL

PER SLICE

Calories	207
Protein	4 g
Fat	6 g
Carbohydrates	36 g
Sodium	161 mg
Cholesterol	27 mg
Fibre	2 g

1. Topping: In small bowl, combine pecans, flour, sugar, margarine and cinnamon until crumbly. Set aside.

2. In large bowl or food processor, cream together margarine and sugar. Beat in eggs and vanilla until well blended.

3. Combine all-purpose and whole wheat flours, cinnamon, baking powder and baking soda; add to bowl alternately with yogurt, mixing just until blended. Fold in apples and raisins. Pour into pan.

4. Sprinkle with topping; bake for 40 to 45 minutes or until cake tester inserted into centre comes out clean.

BANANA DATE CAKE

Makes 25 squares.

TIP

For easier preparation, use scissors to cut dates.

•

Be sure to buy pitted dates.

MAKE AHEAD

Prepare up to 2 days in advance or freeze for up to 6 weeks.

Preheat oven to 350°F (180°C)
9-inch (2.5 L) square cake pan sprayed with nonstick vegetable spray

1 tsp	baking soda	5 mL
1 cup	boiling water	250 mL
2 cups	chopped dates	500 mL
	(about 10 oz [280 g])	
1/2 cup	brown sugar	125 mL
3 tbsp	margarine	45 mL
1	egg	1
1	ripe banana, mashed	1
1 1/2 cups	all-purpose flour	375 mL
1 cup	bran cereal*	250 mL
1/3 cup	chopped pecans or walnuts	75 mL
2 tsp	cinnamon	10 mL

Use a wheat bran breakfast cereal.

1. In bowl, stir baking soda into water; add dates and let stand for 10 minutes.

2. In large bowl or food processor, beat together sugar, margarine, egg and banana until well blended.

3. Combine flour, cereal, pecans and cinnamon; add to banana mixture alternately with soaked dates, mixing well. Pour into cake pan; bake for 25 to 30 minutes or until cake tester comes out dry.

PER SQUARE

Calories	121
Protein	2 g
Fat	3 g
Carbohydrates	24 g
Sodium	87 mg
Cholesterol	8 mg
Fibre	2 g

Apricot Date Streusel Cake

Makes 16 slices.

Preheat oven to 350°F (180°C)
9-inch (3 L) Bundt pan sprayed with nonstick vegetable spray

3 tbsp	margarine	45 mL
3/4 cup	granulated sugar	175 mL
1	egg	1
2	egg whites	2
3 tbsp	lemon juice	45 mL
1 tsp	vanilla	5 mL
1 3/4 cups	all-purpose flour	425 mL
1/2 cup	wheat bran breakfast cereal	125 mL
1 tsp	cinnamon	5 mL
1 tsp	baking powder	5 mL
1 tsp	baking soda	5 mL
1 1/3 cups	2% yogurt	325 mL
1/3 cup	finely chopped dates	75 mL
1/3 cup	finely chopped dried apricots	75 mL

Topping

1/4 cup	brown sugar	50 mL
2 tbsp	all-purpose flour	25 mL
2 tbsp	wheat bran cereal, crushed	25 mL
1 tsp	cinnamon	5 mL
1 tbsp	margarine	15 mL

PER SLICE

Calories	173
Protein	4 g
Fat	4 g
Carbohydrates	32 g
Sodium	171 mg
Cholesterol	14 mg
Fibre	2 g

1. Topping: In small bowl, combine sugar, flour, cereal and cinnamon; cut in margarine until crumbly. Set aside.

2. In large bowl or food processor, cream together margarine and sugar; beat in egg, egg whites, lemon juice and vanilla until well mixed.

3. Combine flour, cereal, cinnamon, baking powder and baking soda; stir into bowl just until incorporated. Stir in yogurt; fold in dates and apricots.

4. Pour half of batter into pan. Sprinkle with half of topping. Pour remaining batter over top; sprinkle with remaining topping. Bake for 35 to 45 minutes or until tester inserted into centre comes out clean.

• STREUSEL APPLE AND • • • • • • RAISIN MUFFINS

Makes 12 muffins.

TIP

For a change, bake in 9- x 5-inch (2 L) loaf pan. Check loaf at 15 minutes for doneness.

•

Use unsweetened applesauce.

MAKE AHEAD

Prepare up to a day before. Freeze for up to 6 weeks.

Preheat oven to 375°F (190°C)
12 muffin cups sprayed with nonstick vegetable spray

1/2 cup	brown sugar	125 mL
1/2 cup	applesauce	125 mL
1/4 cup	vegetable oil	50 mL
1	egg	1
1 tsp	vanilla	5 mL
1 cup	all-purpose flour	250 mL
1 tsp	baking soda	5 mL
1 tsp	baking powder	5 mL
1/2 tsp	cinnamon	2 mL
3/4 cup	diced peeled apple	175 mL
1/4 cup	raisins	50 mL

Topping

2 tbsp	brown sugar	25 mL
2 tsp	all-purpose flour	10 mL
1/2 tsp	cinnamon	2 mL
1 tsp	margarine	5 mL

PER MUFFIN

Calories	141
Protein	1 g
Fat	5 g
Carbohydrates	22 g
Sodium	114 mg
Cholesterol	17 mg
Fibre	1 g

1. In large bowl, combine sugar, applesauce, oil, egg and vanilla until well mixed. Combine flour, baking soda, baking powder and cinnamon; stir into bowl just until incorporated. Stir in apple and raisins. Pour into muffin cups, filling two-thirds full.

2. Topping: In small bowl, combine sugar, flour and cinnamon; cut in margarine until crumbly. Sprinkle evenly over muffins. Bake for 20 minutes or until tops are firm to the touch.

• • • • • • • • • • • • • • • • • • BLUEBERRY BANANA MUFFINS •

Makes 12 muffins.

TIP

A 9- x 5-inch (2 L) loaf pan can also be used; bake for 30 to 40 minutes or until tester comes out dry.

•

Use the ripest bananas possible for the best flavor.

MAKE AHEAD

Bake a day before or freeze for up to 6 weeks.

Preheat oven to 375°F (190°C)
12 muffin cups sprayed with nonstick vegetable spray

3/4 cup	puréed bananas (about 1 1/2 bananas)	175 mL
1/2 cup	granulated sugar	125 mL
1/3 cup	vegetable oil	75 mL
1	egg	1
1 tsp	vanilla	5 mL
1 cup	all-purpose flour	250 mL
1 tsp	baking powder	5 mL
1 tsp	baking soda	5 mL
1/4 cup	2% yogurt or light sour cream	50 mL
1/2 cup	blueberries	125 mL

1. In large bowl, beat together bananas, sugar, oil, egg and vanilla until well mixed.

2. Combine flour, baking powder and baking soda; stir into bowl. Stir in yogurt; fold in blueberries.

3. Pour batter into muffin cups; bake for approximately 20 minutes or until tops are firm to the touch.

PER MUFFIN

Calories	150
Protein	2 g
Fat	6 g
Carbohydrates	21 g
Sodium	110 mg
Cholesterol	18 mg
Fibre	1 g

• YOGURT BRAN MUFFINS • • • •

Makes 12 muffins.

TIP

Muffin batter should remain a little lumpy; if it is overmixed, the muffins will become tough and dry.

•

Substitute raisins with chopped dates, prunes or apricots.

MAKE AHEAD

Prepare a day before or freeze for up to 6 weeks.

Preheat oven to 375°F (190°C)
12 muffin cups sprayed with nonstick vegetable spray

1/2 cup	brown sugar	125 mL
1/4 cup	margarine	50 mL
1 tbsp	molasses	15 mL
1	egg	1
1 tsp	vanilla	5 mL
3/4 cup	bran cereal*	175 mL
1/2 cup	all-purpose flour	125 mL
1/3 cup	whole wheat flour	75 mL
3/4 tsp	baking powder	4 mL
1/2 tsp	baking soda	2 mL
1/2 cup	2% yogurt	125 mL
1/3 cup	raisins	75 mL

* Use a wheat bran breakfast cereal

1. In large bowl, combine sugar, margarine, molasses, egg and vanilla until well blended.

2. Combine cereal, all-purpose and whole wheat flours, baking powder and baking soda; add to bowl alternately with yogurt. Stir in raisins. Pour into muffin cups; bake for 15 to 18 minutes or until tops are firm to the touch.

PER MUFFIN

Calories	157
Protein	3 g
Fat	4 g
Carbohydrates	28 g
Sodium	177 mg
Cholesterol	18 mg
Fibre	2 g

•••••••••••••••••••••• Sour Cream Apple Pie ••••

Makes 16 slices.

TIP

A similar recipe in my "Manhattan Dessert" book had triple the amount of whole-fat sour cream. This version is just as delicious with a quarter the calories.

●

For an attractive presentation, sprinkle a little icing sugar over top.

●

Substitute vanilla wafer crumbs for the graham crumbs for a change.

MAKE AHEAD

Prepare early in the day and warm slightly before serving. Or freeze for up to 2 weeks.

PER SLICE

Calories	153
Protein	2 g
Fat	4 g
Carbohydrates	28 g
Sodium	98 mg
Cholesterol	17 mg
Fibre	1 g

Preheat oven to 350°F (180°C)
8-inch (2 L) springform pan

5 1/2 cups	sliced peeled apples (5 to 6 apples)	1.375 L
1/2 cup	granulated sugar	125 mL
1/2 cup	2% yogurt	125 mL
1/2 cup	light sour cream	125 mL
1/4 cup	raisins	50 mL
2 tbsp	all-purpose flour	25 mL
1 tsp	cinnamon	5 mL
1	egg, lightly beaten	1
1 tsp	vanilla	5 mL

Crust

1 1/2 cups	graham wafer crumbs	375 mL
2 tbsp	margarine, melted	25 mL
1 tbsp	brown sugar	15 mL
1 tbsp	water	15 mL

Topping

1/4 cup	brown sugar	50 mL
3 tbsp	all-purpose flour	45 mL
2 tbsp	rolled oats	25 mL
1/2 tsp	cinnamon	2 mL
1 tbsp	margarine	15 mL

1. **Crust:** In bowl, combine graham crumbs, margarine, sugar and water; pat onto bottom and sides of pan. Refrigerate.

2. In large bowl, combine apples, sugar, yogurt, sour cream, raisins, flour cinnamon, egg and vanilla; toss together until well mixed. Pour over crust.

3. **Topping:** In small bowl, combine sugar, flour, rolled oats and cinnamon; cut in margarine until crumbly. Sprinkle over pie; bake for 30 to 40 minutes or until topping is browned and apples are tender.

•••••••••••••••••••••••••• TROPICAL FRUIT TART •••••

Makes 12 servings.

TIP

For a change, try lemon juice and rind instead of orange.

•

If desired, brush fruit with 2 tbsp (25 mL) melted apple jelly for a glaze.

MAKE AHEAD

Prepare a day before.

Preheat oven to 400°F (200°C)
9-inch (2 L) tart or springform pan sprayed with nonstick vegetable spray

1 3/4 cups	2% yogurt	425 mL
2/3 cup	granulated sugar	150 mL
1/2 cup	light sour cream	125 mL
3 tbsp	frozen orange juice concentrate, thawed	45 mL
2 tbsp	all-purpose flour	25 mL
1 1/2 tsp	orange rind	7 mL

<u>Crust</u>

1 1/4 cups	all-purpose flour	300 mL
1/4 cup	icing sugar	50 mL
1/3 cup	margarine	75 mL
3 tbsp	(approx) cold water	45 mL

<u>Topping</u>

3 cups	sliced fruit (kiwifruit, mangos, papayas, star fruit)	750 mL

PER SERVING

■■■■■■■■■■■■■■■

Calories	221
Protein	4 g
Fat	6 g
Carbohydrates	37 g
Sodium	103 mg
Cholesterol	5 mg
Fibre	2 g

■■■■■■■■■■■■■■■

1. **Crust:** In bowl, combine flour with sugar; cut in margarine until crumbly. With fork, gradually stir in water, adding 1 tbsp (15 mL) more if necessary to make dough hold together. Pat into pan and bake for 15 minutes or until browned. Reduce heat to 375°F (190°C).

2. Meanwhile, in bowl, combine yogurt, sugar, sour cream, orange juice concentrate, flour and orange rind; mix well and pour over crust. Bake for 35 to 45 minutes or until filling is set. Let cool and refrigerate until chilled.

3. **Topping:** Decoratively arrange sliced fruit over filling.

PEAR, APPLE AND RAISIN STRUDEL

Makes 12 slices.

TIP

Sprinkle with icing sugar for a finishing touch.

•

Serve with Frozen Vanilla Yogurt (page 275).

•

Ripen pears at room temperature in a bowl or paper bag.

MAKE AHEAD

Filling can be prepared a couple of hours before baking. Keep covered. Do not assemble strudel until ready to bake.

PER SLICE

Calories	114
Protein	1 g
Fat	2 g
Carbohydrates	23 g
Sodium	65 mg
Cholesterol	0 mg
Fibre	2 g

Preheat oven to 350°F (180°C)
Baking sheet sprayed with nonstick vegetable spray

2 2/3 cups	chopped peeled apples	650 mL
2 2/3 cups	chopped peeled pears	650 mL
1/3 cup	raisins	75 mL
2 tbsp	chopped pecans or walnuts	25 mL
2 tbsp	brown sugar	25 mL
1 tbsp	lemon juice	15 mL
1 tbsp	honey	15 mL
1 tsp	cinnamon	5 mL
6	phyllo sheets	6
4 tsp	margarine, melted	20 mL

1. In bowl, combine apples, pears, raisins, pecans, sugar, lemon juice, honey and cinnamon; mix well.

2. Lay out 2 sheets of phyllo; brush with some margarine. Place 2 more sheets over top; brush with margarine again. Top with remaining 2 sheets phyllo.

3. Spread filling over phyllo, leaving 1-inch (2.5 cm) border uncovered. Roll up like jelly roll and place seam down on baking sheet. Brush with remaining margarine. Bake for 40 to 50 minutes or until golden and fruit is tender.

• BAKLAVA WITH RAISINS • • • • AND CINNAMON

Makes 12 pieces.

TIP

For a change, use pistachio nuts instead of walnuts, and chopped dates instead of raisins.

•

While working with phyllo, keep it covered with damp tea towel to prevent it drying out.

MAKE AHEAD

Filling can be prepared early in day and covered. Do not assemble baklava until ready to bake.

Preheat oven to 350°F (180°C)
8-inch (2 L) square cake pan sprayed with nonstick vegetable spray

8	sheets (each 8-inch [20 cm] square) phyllo pastry	8
2 1/2 tsp	margarine, melted	12
1 tbsp	lemon juice	15 mL
4 tsp	honey	20 mL

Filling

1/2 cup	raisins	125 mL
1/2 cup	chopped walnuts or pecans	125 mL
2 tbsp	brown sugar	25 mL
1/2 tsp	cinnamon	2 mL

1. Filling: In food processor, combine raisins, nuts, brown sugar and cinnamon; process just until crumbly. Set aside.

2. Fit 2 phyllo sheets into cake pan; brush with some margarine. Place 2 more sheets over top and brush with margarine again. Pour raisin filling over top. Repeat with remaining phyllo, brushing every other one with margarine.

3. With sharp knife, cut through top layers to make 12 squares. Bake for 20 to 30 minutes or until golden.

4. Combine lemon juice and honey; pour over baklava and bake for 5 minutes. Let cool. Cut carefully through to bottom of squares to serve.

PER PIECE

Calories	117
Protein	2 g
Fat	4 g
Carbohydrates	19 g
Sodium	63 mg
Cholesterol	0 mg
Fibre	1 g

• • • • • • • • • • • • • • • • • • # COCOA ROLL WITH • • • •
CREAMY CHEESE AND BERRIES

Makes 10 slices.

TIP

Decorate roll with fresh berries or pour Chocolate sauce over top (page 237).

•

Substitute other fresh berries of your choice.

MAKE AHEAD

Prepare cake early in day and keep covered until ready to roll with filling.

Preheat oven to 325°F (160°C)
Jelly roll pan lined with parchment paper and sprayed with nonstick vegetable spray

5	egg whites	5
1/8 tsp	cream of tartar	0.5 mL
2/3 cup	granulated sugar	150 mL
1/2 cup	cake-and-pastry flour	125 mL
4 tsp	unsweetened cocoa powder	20 mL
1 1/2 tsp	vanilla	7 mL
	Icing sugar	

Filling

1 1/4 cups	ricotta cheese	300 mL
1/4 cup	light sour cream	50 mL
3 tbsp	icing sugar	45 mL
1 1/4 cups	sliced strawberries and/or blueberries	300 mL

1. In medium bowl, beat egg whites and cream of tartar until soft peaks form. Gradually beat in 1/3 cup (75 mL) of sugar until stiff peaks form.

2. Sift together remaining sugar, flour and cocoa; sift over egg whites and fold in gently along with vanilla. Do not overmix. Pour onto baking sheet and spread evenly. Bake for 15 to 20 minutes or until top springs back when lightly touched.

3. Filling: In bowl or food processor, mix together cheese, sour cream and sugar until smooth. Fold in berries. Set aside.

4. Sprinkle cake lightly with icing sugar. Carefully invert onto surface sprinkled with icing sugar. Carefully remove parchment paper. Spread filling over cake and roll up. Place on serving dish. Sprinkle with icing sugar.

PER SLICE

Calories	152
Protein	6 g
Fat	3 g
Carbohydrates	25 g
Sodium	72 mg
Cholesterol	11 mg
Fibre	1 g

• • • • • • • • • • • • • • • • • • •PEACH AND BLUEBERRY CRISP • •

Serves 6 to 8.

TIP

Blueberries should be removed from their carton and placed in a moistureproof container in the refrigerator. Do not wash until just before using.

•

Other fresh, ripe fruit such as apples and pears are excellent variations.

MAKE AHEAD

Although best straight from the oven, crisp can be prepared early in day and reheated slightly before serving.

Preheat oven to 350°F (180°C)
9-inch (2.5 L) square cake pan

1/2 cup	granulated sugar	125 mL
2 tbsp	all-purpose flour	25 mL
2 tsp	lemon juice	10 mL
1 tsp	grated lemon rind	5 mL
1 tsp	cinnamon	5 mL
3 cups	sliced peeled ripe peaches	750 mL
2 cups	blueberries	500 mL

Topping

1/2 cup	rolled oats	125 mL
1/3 cup	all-purpose flour	75 mL
3 tbsp	brown sugar	45 mL
1/2 tsp	cinnamon	2 mL
3 tbsp	soft margarine	45 mL

1. In large bowl, combine sugar, flour, lemon juice, rind and cinnamon; stir in peaches and blueberries until well mixed. Spread in cake pan.

2. Topping: In small bowl, combine rolled oats, flour, sugar and cinnamon; cut in margarine until crumbly. Sprinkle over fruit. Bake for 30 to 35 minutes or until topping is browned and fruit is tender. Serve warm.

PER 1/8TH SERVING

Calories	199
Protein	2 g
Fat	5 g
Carbohydrates	38 g
Sodium	60 mg
Cholesterol	0 mg
Fibre	2 g

• SOUR CREAM BROWNIES • • • •

Makes 16 squares.

TIP

If desired, sprinkle
2 tbsp (25 mL) chopped
nuts over the batter
before baking.

•

Garnish with a sprinkling
of icing sugar after baking.

MAKE AHEAD

Bake a day before or freeze
for up to 6 weeks.

Preheat oven to 350°F (180°C)
8-inch (2 L) square cake pan sprayed with
nonstick vegetable spray

2/3 cup	granulated sugar	150 mL
1/3 cup	soft margarine	75 mL
1	egg	1
1 tsp	vanilla	5 mL
1/3 cup	unsweetened cocoa powder	75 mL
1/3 cup	all-purpose flour	75 mL
1 tsp	baking powder	5 mL
1/4 cup	light sour cream	50 mL

1. In bowl, beat together sugar and margarine until smooth. Beat in egg and vanilla, mixing well.

2. Combine cocoa, flour and baking powder; stir into bowl just until blended. Stir in sour cream. Pour into pan.

3. Bake for 15 to 20 minutes or until edges start to pull away from pan and centre is still slightly soft.

PER SQUARE

Calories	90
Protein	1 g
Fat	4 g
Carbohydrates	12 g
Sodium	83 mg
Cholesterol	14 mg
Fibre	1 g

•••••••••••••••••••• DATE OATMEAL SQUARES •••

Makes 16 squares.

TIP

Use scissors to cut the dates for easier preparation.

•

Try half dates and half pitted, chopped prunes for a change.

MAKE AHEAD

Bake up to 2 days in advance or freeze for up to 6 weeks.

Preheat oven to 350°F (180°C)
8-inch (2 L) square cake pan sprayed with nonstick vegetable spray

1/2 lb	pitted dates, chopped	250 g
1 cup	water or orange juice	250 mL
3/4 cup	all-purpose flour	175 mL
1 cup	rolled oats	250 mL
2/3 cup	brown sugar	150 mL
1/2 cup	bran cereal*	125 mL
1/2 tsp	baking powder	2 mL
1/2 tsp	baking soda	2 mL
1/2 cup	soft margarine	125 mL

* Use a wheat bran breakfast cereal.

1. In saucepan, cover and cook dates and water over low heat, stirring often, for approximately 15 minutes or until dates are soft and liquid absorbed. Set aside.

2. In bowl, combine flour, rolled oats, sugar, cereal, baking powder and baking soda; cut in margarine until crumbly.

3. Pat half onto bottom of cake pan; spoon date mixture over top. Pat remaining crumb mixture over date mixture. Bake for 20 to 25 minutes or until golden.

PER SQUARE

Calories	187
Protein	2 g
Fat	6 g
Carbohydrates	32 g
Sodium	142 mg
Cholesterol	0 mg
Fibre	2 g

PEANUT BUTTER CHOCOLATE • CHIP COOKIES

Makes 40 cookies.

TIP

The longer they bake, the crispier the cookie.

•

Nuts can replace the raisins.

•

Use natural peanut butter made from only peanuts.

MAKE AHEAD

Dough can be frozen up to 2 weeks. Bake just before eating for best flavor.

Preheat oven to 350°F (180°C)
Baking sheets sprayed with nonstick vegetable spray

1/2 cup	brown sugar	125 mL
1/3 cup	granulated sugar	75 mL
1/3 cup	peanut butter	75 mL
1/3 cup	2% milk	75 mL
1/4 cup	soft margarine	50 mL
1	egg	1
1 tsp	vanilla	5 mL
3/4 cup	all-purpose flour	175 mL
1/3 cup	whole wheat flour	75 mL
1 tsp	baking soda	5 mL
1/3 cup	chocolate chips	75 mL
1/4 cup	raisins	50 mL

1. In large bowl or food processor, beat together brown and granulated sugars, peanut butter, milk, margarine, egg and vanilla until well blended.

2. Combine all-purpose and whole wheat flours and baking soda; add to bowl and mix just until incorporated. Do not overmix. Stir in chocolate chips and raisins.

3. Drop by heaping teaspoonfuls (5 mL) 2 inches (5 cm) apart onto baking sheets. Bake for 12 to 15 minutes or until browned.

PER COOKIE

Calories	61
Protein	1 g
Fat	3 g
Carbohydrates	8 g
Sodium	50 mg
Cholesterol	5 mg
Fibre	0.5 g

DOUBLE CHOCOLATE RAISIN COOKIES

Makes 40 cookies.

TIP

Try white chocolate or peanut butter chips for a change.

MAKE AHEAD

Dough can be frozen for up to 2 weeks.

Preheat oven to 350°F (180°C)
Baking sheets sprayed with nonstick vegetable spray

1/4 cup	soft margarine	50 mL
3/4 cup	granulated sugar	175 mL
1	egg	1
1 tsp	vanilla	5 mL
3 tbsp	unsweetened cocoa powder	45 mL
1/2 tsp	baking soda	2 mL
1/2 tsp	baking powder	2 mL
1/3 cup	whole wheat flour	75 mL
2/3 cup	all-purpose flour	150 mL
1/4 cup	chocolate chips	50 mL
1/4 cup	raisins	50 mL

1. In large bowl or food processor, beat together margarine, sugar, egg and vanilla until well blended.

2. Combine cocoa, baking soda, baking powder, whole wheat and all-purpose flours; add to bowl and mix until just combined. Stir in chocolate chips and raisins.

3. Drop by heaping teaspoonfuls (5 mL) 2 inches (5 cm) apart onto baking sheets. Bake for 12 to 15 minutes or until browned.

PER COOKIE

Calories	49
Protein	1 g
Fat	1 g
Carbohydrates	8 g
Sodium	32 mg
Cholesterol	5 mg
Fibre	0.5 g

OATMEAL RAISIN PECAN COOKIES

Makes 30 cookies.

TIP

These cookies are soft and chewy if baked for a shorter time; crisp if baked longer.

●

If wheat germ is unavailable, substitute another 1/4 cup (50 mL) rolled oats.

MAKE AHEAD

Dough can be frozen for up to 2 weeks.

Preheat oven to 350°F (180°C)
Baking sheets sprayed with nonstick vegetable spray

1/2 cup	brown sugar	125 mL
1/4 cup	soft margarine	50 mL
1	egg	1
1 tsp	vanilla	5 mL
1/2 cup	rolled oats	125 mL
1/4 cup	whole wheat flour	50 mL
1/4 cup	wheat germ	50 mL
1/4 cup	pecan pieces	50 mL
1/4 cup	raisins	50 mL
1/2 tsp	baking powder	2 mL

1. In large bowl or food processor, beat together sugar, margarine, egg and vanilla until well blended.

2. Add rolled oats, flour, wheat germ, pecans, raisins and baking powder; mix just until incorporated.

3. Drop by heaping teaspoonfuls (5 mL) 2 inches (5 cm) apart onto baking sheets. Bake for 12 to 15 minutes or until browned

PER COOKIE

Calories	55
Protein	1 g
Fat	3 g
Carbohydrates	7 g
Sodium	31 mg
Cholesterol	7 mg
Fibre	0.5 g

• • • • • • • • • • • • • • • • • • CINNAMON GINGER COOKIES •

Makes 30 cookies.

TIP

This cookie dough can be chilled, then rolled out and cut into various patterns.

MAKE AHEAD

Dough can be frozen for up to 2 weeks.

Preheat oven to 350°F (180°C)
Baking sheet sprayed with nonstick vegetable spray

1/4 cup	brown sugar	50 mL
3 tbsp	margarine, melted	45 mL
2 tbsp	molasses	25 mL
2 tbsp	2% yogurt	25 mL
1 tsp	vanilla	5 mL
1 cup	all-purpose flour	250 mL
1/2 tsp	baking soda	2 mL
1/2 tsp	ginger	2 mL
1/2 tsp	cinnamon	2 mL
Pinch	nutmeg	Pinch
1 1/2 tsp	brown sugar	7 mL

1. In bowl, combine 1/4 cup (50 mL) brown sugar, margarine, molasses, yogurt and vanilla until well mixed.

2. Combine flour, baking soda, ginger, cinnamon and nutmeg; stir into bowl just until combined.

3. Using teaspoon, form dough into small balls and place on baking sheet. Press flat with fork; sprinkle with 1 1/2 tsp (7 mL) brown sugar. Bake for 10 to 12 minutes or until golden.

PER COOKIE

Calories	38
Protein	0.5 g
Fat	1 g
Carbohydrates	6 g
Sodium	31 mg
Cholesterol	0 mg
Fibre	0 g

• # PECAN BISCOTTI • • • • • • •

Makes 45 cookies.

TIP

Use almonds, hazelnuts, pine nuts or a combination.

MAKE AHEAD

Store in an airtight container up to 2 weeks, or freeze for up to 1 month.

Preheat oven to 350°F (180°C)
Baking sheet sprayed with nonstick vegetable spray

2	eggs	2
3/4 cup	granulated sugar	175 mL
1/3 cup	margarine	75 mL
1/4 cup	water	50 mL
2 tsp	vanilla	10 mL
1 tsp	almond extract	5 mL
2 3/4 cups	all-purpose flour	675 mL
1/2 cup	chopped pecans	125 mL
2 1/4 tsp	baking powder	11 mL

1. In large bowl, blend eggs with sugar; beat in margarine, water, vanilla and almond extract until smooth.

2. Add flour, pecans and baking powder; mix until dough forms ball. Divide dough in half; shape each portion into 12-inch (30 cm) long log and place on baking sheet. Bake for 20 minutes. Let cool for 5 minutes.

3. Cut logs on angle into 1/2-inch (1 cm) thick slices. Place slices on sides on baking sheet; bake for 20 minutes or until lightly browned.

PER COOKIE

Calories	60
Protein	1 g
Fat	2 g
Carbohydrates	8 g
Sodium	40 mg
Cholesterol	9 mg
Fibre	0.5 g

• RASPBERRY CREAM SORBET • • •

Serves 4 to 6.

TIP

Soften slightly in refrigerator for 15 to 20 minutes before serving.

MAKE AHEAD

Prepare a day before and allow to soften slightly before serving.

1/2 cup	granulated sugar	125 mL
1/2 cup	water	125 mL
1 1/2 cups	frozen or fresh raspberries	375 mL
1	medium egg white	1

1. In saucepan, heat sugar and water on medium heat; cook, stirring constantly, until mixture sticks to back of spoon, approximately 2 to 4 minutes. Let cool.

2. In food processor or blender, purée raspberries. Add sugar mixture and egg white; blend well. Freeze in ice-cream machine according to manufacturer's directions. (Or pour into cake pan and freeze until nearly solid. Chop into chunks and beat with electric mixer or process in food processor until smooth. Freeze until solid.)

PER 1/6TH SERVING

Calories	82
Protein	1 g
Fat	0 g
Carbohydrates	20 g
Sodium	9 mg
Cholesterol	0 mg
Fibre	1 g

• Fresh Fruit Sorbet • • • • • •

Serves 4 to 6.

TIP

Try a combination of fresh fruits.

MAKE AHEAD

Best if served immediately. If refreezing, purée again before serving.

| 2 1/2 cups | chopped peeled soft fresh fruit (bananas, peaches, strawberries, etc.) | 625 mL |

1. Spread fruit on baking sheet and freeze. Purée frozen fruit in food processor and serve immediately.

PER 1/6TH SERVING

:■■■■■■■■■■■■■:

Calories	40
Protein	0 g
Fat	0 g
Carbohydrates	10 g
Sodium	0 mg
Cholesterol	0 mg
Fibre	1 g

:■■■■■■■■■■■■■:

• STRAWBERRY ORANGE • • • • • BUTTERMILK SORBET

Serves 3 or 4.

TIP

To make soured milk, place 2 tsp (10 mL) lemon juice or vinegar in measuring cup; pour in milk to 1 cup (250 mL) level and let stand for 10 minutes, then stir.

•

Substitute raspberries for strawberries; increase honey to 1/3 cup (75 mL).

MAKE AHEAD

Although sorbets are best prepared just before eating so they do not crystallize, they can be prepared up to 2 days in advance.

1 cup	buttermilk or soured milk	250 mL
1/2 cup	puréed strawberries	125 mL
1/4 cup	water	50 mL
1/4 cup	honey	50 mL
1/2 tsp	grated orange rind	2 mL
1 tbsp	orange juice	15 mL

1. In bowl, mix together buttermilk, strawberries, water, honey, orange rind and juice.

2. Freeze in ice-cream machine according to manufacturer's directions. (Or pour into cake pan and freeze until nearly solid. Chop into chunks and beat with electric mixer or process in food processor until smooth. Freeze again until solid.)

PER 1/4TH SERVING
:✗✗✗✗✗✗✗✗✗✗✗✗✗:

Calories	103
Protein	2 g
Fat	1 g
Carbohydrates	22 g
Sodium	65 mg
Cholesterol	3 mg
Fibre	0.5 g

:✗✗✗✗✗✗✗✗✗✗✗✗✗:

··················· Frozen Vanilla Yogurt ···

Serves 4 to 6.

TIP

Add 1 tsp (5 mL) each lemon extract and grated lemon rind to make lemon yogurt.

•

Serve with Chocolate sauce (page 237).

MAKE AHEAD

This dessert can be prepared up to 2 days in advance, but it is best if served right after freezing.

1	egg	1
1/3 cup	brown sugar	75 mL
1/2 cup	2% milk	125 mL
1 1/2 cups	2% yogurt	375 mL
1 1/2 tsp	vanilla	7 mL

1. In bowl, beat egg with sugar until combined; set aside. In saucepan, heat milk just until bubbles appear around side of pan. Stir a little into egg mixture, then pour back into saucepan. Cook over low heat, stirring, just until thickened, 2 to 4 minutes. (Do not let boil or egg will curdle.) Remove from heat and let cool completely.

2. Beat yogurt and vanilla into cooled mixture. Freeze in ice-cream machine according to manufacturer's directions. (Or pour into cake pan and freeze until nearly solid. Chop into chunks and beat with electric mixer or process in food processor until smooth. Freeze again until solid.)

PER 1/6TH SERVING

Calories	109
Protein	5 g
Fat	2 g
Carbohydrates	17 g
Sodium	68 mg
Cholesterol	40 mg
Fibre	0 g

• MOCHA ICE CREAM • • • • • •

Serves 4.

Omit coffee if desired.

MAKE AHEAD

Prepare and freeze up to 2 days in advance, but allow to soften slightly before serving.

2 cups	2% milk	500 mL
1	egg	1
1/2 cup	granulated sugar	125 mL
2 tbsp	sifted unsweetened cocoa powder	25 mL
1 tsp	instant coffee granules	5 mL

1. In saucepan, heat 1 cup (250 mL) of the milk just until bubbles form around edge of pan.

2. Meanwhile, in small bowl, beat egg with sugar until combined; stir in half of the warm milk. Pour egg mixture back into saucepan; stir in cocoa and coffee granules. Cook, stirring, on low heat for 4 minutes or until slightly thickened. (Do not let boil or egg will curdle.) Let cool completely.

3. Stir in remaining milk. Pour into ice-cream machine and freeze according to manufacturer's instructions. (Or pour into cake pan and freeze until nearly solid. Chop into chunks and beat with electric mixer or process in food processor until smooth. Freeze again until solid.)

PER SERVING

Calories	183
Protein	6 g
Fat	4 g
Carbohydrates	32 g
Sodium	78 mg
Cholesterol	62 mg
Fibre	1 g

Healthy and Delicious Eating Out

It would be much easier to eat well if we always did the cooking ourselves. But we can't always do that — and most of us wouldn't want to. We often dine in restaurants, in other homes, and in fast food establishments.

Here are some simple rules to follow in these situations. They will allow you to enjoy your meal and still eat healthy foods. If occasionally you want to indulge, by all means do so — but do it infrequently.

RESTAURANTS

Select restaurants with a varied menu.

●

Ask for dressing, sauces or marinades to be served alongside, rather than overtop. Avoid ready-mixed salads such as Caesar.

●

Avoid cream-based soups. Choose those that are tomato or stock-based.

●

Enjoy your bread, use butter and margarine sparingly.
As a main meal, select chicken, fish, meat, or pasta in a tomato-based sauce. Avoid quiche, lasagna, ribs and macaroni and cheese. These all contain hidden fat and calories.

●

Ask for your entrée to be broiled, steamed, poached or baked, not fried.

●

Ask for plain rice, baked or boiled potatoes or steamed or lightly sautéed vegetables. Avoid french fries, batter-dipped vegetables and added sour cream or butter.

●

If the main entrée is a large portion (more than 8 oz [250g]), do not finish it. If you are still hungry, eat extra salad and vegetables.

●

Avoid ice-cream, cakes or pies. For dessert ask for a fruit cup, frozen yogurt or sorbet.

FAST-FOOD OUTLETS

Select a small portion. For example, instead of a deluxe hamburger with the works, order a basic hamburger and add lettuce, tomatoes, onions and cucumbers.

•

Order juice, milk or water instead of a milkshake or pop.

•

Avoid french fries which have a lot of fat in them.

Menu Planning

The more than 240 recipes in this book offer enough choices to satisfy most people's tastes and enough variety to suite any occasion, from simple weekday meals to more sophisticated weekend dishes and festive buffets to serve a crowd. But deciding which foods go together is not simple. In the final analysis, you should choose whatever appeals to you personally.

I have suggested several menu plans for a variety of occasions. You can either follow them exactly or experiment with your own choices.

WEEKDAY FAMILY DINNERS
Potato Corn Chowder
Meatloaf Topped with Sautéed Vegetables and Tomato Sauce
Linguini Alfredo

•

Pita or Tortilla Pizzas
Beef, Macaroni and Cheese Casserole
Fresh fruit

•

Greek Salad
Tortellini with Creamy Tomato Sauce
Asparagus with Lemon and Garlic
Fruit sorbet

DINNER PARTY MENUS READY IN AN HOUR
Caesar Salad with Baby Shrimp
Sautéed Veal with Lemon Garlic Sauce
Tortellini with Creamy Tomato Sauce
Fresh strawberries

•

Goat Cheese and Sun Dried Tomato Salad
Cod with Almonds and Lemon Sauce
Fettucini Alfredo with Red Pepper and Snow Peas
Fruit sorbet

•

Chinese Scallop and Shrimp Broth with Snow Peas
Chicken, Red Pepper and Snow Pea Stir-Fry
White rice
Pear, Apple and Raisin Strudel
(*Make dessert first*)

WEEKDAY MEALS THAT CAN BE REHEATED AND SERVED MORE THAN ONCE

Chicken Tetrazzini

Lemon Chicken with Nutty Coating

Chili Bean Stew

Vegetable and Bean Minestrone

Cheesy Ratatouille Bean Casserole

Beef, Macaroni and Cheese Casserole

Curried Lamb Casserole with Sweet Potatoes

Veal Stew in a Chunky Tomato Sauce

Meatloaf Topped with Sautéed Vegetables and Tomato Sauce

Lasagna with Zucchini, Red Pepper and Mushrooms

Serve any of these with a large green salad and any of the dressings listed.

WINTER DINNER PARTY

Sautéed Mushrooms on Toast Rounds
Broccoli and Lentil Soup
Roasted Leg of Lamb with Crunchy Garlic Topping
Snow Peas with Sesame Seeds
Rice with Pine Nuts and Spinach
Chocolate Cheesecake with Sour Cream Topping

FALL DINNER MENU

Bruschetta with Basil and Oregano
Curried Pumpkin and Sweet Potato Soup
Roasted Chicken Stuffed with Apple and Raisins
Roasted Garlic Sweet Pepper Strips
Sour Cream Apple Pie

LIGHT AFTER THEATRE SUPPER

Caesar Salad with Baby Shrimp
Rotini with Fresh Tomatoes and Feta Cheese
Chocolate Marble Coffee Cake

LIGHT LUNCH MENUS

Gazpacho with Baby Shrimp
Rotini with Tomatoes Black Olives and Goat Cheese
Orange-glazed Coffee Cake

•

Spinach Salad with Oriental Sesame Dressing
Lake Trout with Red Pepper Sauce
Carrot Pineapple Zucchini Loaf

Pita or Tortilla Pizzas
Chicken Kabob with Ginger Lemon Marinade
Fruit sorbet

VEGETARIAN DINNERS

Vegetable and Bean Minestrone
Sautéed Rice with Almonds, Curry and Ginger*
Banana Date Cake

•

Broccoli, Snow Pea, Baby Corn Salad with Orange Dressing
Rotini with Fresh Tomatoes and Feta Cheese
Lemon Poppy Seed Loaf

•

Dill Carrot Soup
Cheese and Vegetable Stuffed Tortillas
Tropical Fruit Tart

* *Make these recipes with vegetable stock, not chicken or beef*

BARBECUE SUMMER DINNERS

Avocado, Tomato and Chili Guacamole
Hamburgers Stuffed with Cheese and Onions
Baked French Wedge Potatoes
Strawberry and Kiwi Cheesecake

•

Greek Salad
Seafood Kabobs with Snow Peas and Red Pepper
Linguini Alfredo
Peach and Blueberry Crisp

•

Sweet Pepper Salad with Red Pepper Dressing
Steak Kabobs with Honey Garlic Marinade
Couscous with Raisins, Dates and Curry
Frozen Yogurt

INEXPERIENCED COOK'S DINNERS

Bagel Garlic Bread
Caesar Salad with Baby Shrimp
Lemon Chicken with Nutty Coating
Sour Cream Brownies

•

Chinese Scallop and Shrimp Broth with Snow Peas
Chinese Beef with Crisp Vegetables
White rice
Cinnamon Ginger Cookies

"FAST FOOD" AT HOME

More delicious and better for your family

Beef, Macaroni and Cheese Casserole
Tortillas stuffed with Sautéed Vegetable, Beans and Beef
Pita or Tortilla Pizza
Cheese and Vegetable Stuffed Tortillas
Macaroni and Three Cheeses
Lasagna with Zucchini, Red Pepper and Mushrooms
Hamburgers stuffed with Cheese and Onions

CHILDREN'S AND TEENAGERS' MEALS

Pita or Tortilla Pizza
(use toppings your children like)

Pasta with Basic Quick Tomato Sauce
Oatmeal Raisin Pecan Cookies

•

Beef, Macaroni and Cheese Casserole
Peanut Butter Chocolate Chip Cookies

•

Macaroni and Three Cheeses
Date Oatmeal Squares

•

Tortillas Stuffed with Sautéed Vegetables, Beans and Beef
Yogurt Bran Muffins

•

Hamburgers Stuffed with Cheese and Onions
(Use a mild cheese for children and eliminate onions if desired.)
Baked French Wedge Potatoes

•

Chili with Veal and Kidney Beans
Double Chocolate Raisin Cookies

CHILDRENS PARTY

Serve a selection of the following:

Pita or Tortilla Pizza
(Add children's choice of topping.)

Pasta with Basic Quick Tomato Sauce
Beef, Macaroni and Cheese Casserole
Macaroni and Three Cheeses
Baked French Potato Wedges
Sour Cream Brownies
Peanut Butter Chocolate Chip Cookies
Double Chocolate Raisin Cookies

BEFORE THEATRE DINNERS

Salade Niçoise
Cannelloni Shells Stuffed with Cheese and Spinach
Apple Pecan Streusel Cake

•

Onion Soup with Mozzarella
Fresh Salmon and Leafy Lettuce Salad with Creamy Dill Dressing
Peach and Blueberry Crisp

SUMMER SALAD BUFFET
(Serves 8)

Appetizers
Fresh Mussels with Tomato Salsa
Ricotta and Smoked Salmon Tortilla Bites
Crab Celery Sticks

Salads
Sweet Pepper Salad with Red Pepper Dressing
Tabbouleh Greek Style

Entrée
Seafood Kabobs with Snow Peas and Red Pepper
Barbecued Veal and Vegetable Kabobs

Side Dishes
Wild Rice with Feta Cheese Dressing
Chilled Penne Salad with Fresh Tomatoes, Yellow Pepper and Basil

Desserts
Strawberry and Kiwi Cheesecake
Chocolate Marble Coffee Cake

INDOOR BUFFET DINNER
(Fall, Winter Or Spring — Serves 8)

Appetizers
Hummus with Tortilla Bread or Pita Crackers
Warm Cherry Tomatoes Stuffed with Garlic and Cheese

Salads
Greek Salad
Caesar Salad with Baby Shrimp

Entrées
Seafood with Rice, Mushrooms and Tomatoes
Lasagna with Zucchini, Red Pepper and Mushrooms

Side Dishes
Green Beans and Diced Tomatoes
Asparagus with Lemon and Garlic

Desserts
Chocolate Cheesecake with Sour Cream Topping
Apricot Date Streusel Cake

AFTER SPORTS DINNER

Bruschetta with Basil and Oregano
Caesar Salad with Baby Shrimp
Chili with Veal and Kidney Beans
Cheese and Vegetable Stuffed Tortillas
Peach and Blueberry Crisp

PICNIC LUNCHES
(Serves 6)

Spinach and Ricotta Dip
(served with crackers)

Potato Salad with Crispy Fresh Vegetables
Rotini with Fresh Tomatoes and Feta Cheese
(served cold)

Cinnamon Ginger Cookies
Banana Date Cake

•

Spicy Mexican Dip
(served with crackers)
Creamy Coleslaw with Apples and Raisins
Chicken Salad with Tarragon and Pecans
Chilled Penne Salad with Fresh Tomatoes, Yellow Pepper and Basil
Sour Cream Brownies
Oatmeal Raisin Pecan Cookies

A FESTIVE DINNER

Large green salad with choice of dressing
Bruschetta with Basil and Oregano
Potato Corn Chowder
Roasted Chicken with Asian Glaze and Fruit Sauce
Sweet Potato Apple and Raisin Casserole
Sour Cream Apple Pie

COCKTAIL PARTY

(Appetizers and Hors d'oeurves — 6 to 8 pieces per person)
Oriental Chicken Wrapped Mushrooms
Pita or Tortilla Pizzas
Salmon Swiss Cheese English Muffins
Ricotta and Smoked Salmon Tortilla Bites
Avocado, Tomato and Chili Guacamole
Crab Celery Sticks
Snow Peas Wrapped Around Shrimp

GLOSSARY

Al dente The texture of properly cooked pasta — slightly underdone or chewy to the tooth.

Bake To cook in an oven with dry circulating air. Heat the oven before baking. Do not crowd food or uneven cooking will result.

Barbecue To cook meats or poultry on a rack over charcoal, gas or open pit fire.

Baste To brush food during cooking with drippings, marinade or glaze to keep it moist.

Beat To mix ingredients quickly, allowing air to be incorporated, to achieve a smooth, lump-free mixture.

Bind To add an ingredient such as an egg or bread crumbs, to hold food together.

Blanch To place raw vegetables into boiling water for 2 to 3 minutes to slightly cook, bring out odor or loosen skin. To stop cooking, rinse immediately under cold water.

Blend To mix ingredients together until well combined.

Boil To heat liquids until surface is covered with bubbles.

Braise To brown meat over high heat with a little fat, then place in baking dish with a small amount of liquid; cover and cook slowly in oven. Ideal for tougher cuts of meat.

Brochette Meat, poultry, fish or vegetables placed on a barbecue skewer, then barbecued, baked or broiled.

Broil To cook under intense direct heat. This method of cooking sears the outside and keeps the food tender by sealing in the natural juices.

Brown To cook food quickly over a high heat to brown the outside and retain natural juices within food.

Chowder A thick and chunky soup made from seafood and chopped vegetables.

Cream To mix a soft ingredient with other ingredients until very soft and well blended. Usually refers to the process of creaming butter or margarine with sugar.

Cube To cut food into cube-shaped pieces, usually ranging from 1/4 inch to 1 inch (5mm to 2.5 cm).

Curdle The separation of ingredients mixed together. This situation, which is usually seen when adding citrus juice to milk products or if egg and creamed-based foods are cooked too quickly, should be avoided.

Deglaze To add a liquid such as broth or wine to the dish in which meat or poultry has been cooked to dissolve browned pieces from the bottom of the skillet. This liquid is cooked down until it has reached the desired consistency.

Devein To clean out the intestinal tract of shrimp. After shrimp has been shelled, make a slit down the back with a sharp knife and remove vein. Rinse with cold water.

Dice To cut into small, equal pieces, usually 1/4 inch by 1/2 inch (5 mm by 10 mm).

Drain To remove liquid from food by use of a strainer.

Dredge To coat meat, fish or vegetables lightly with flour or bread crumbs. It can be done in a bowl or plastic bag. Shake off excess before cooking.

Drizzle To pour a thin stream of liquid slowly over food.

Dust To sprinkle food lightly with flour, sugar or cocoa.

Fillet A portion of chicken, fish or meat removed from the bone.

Flake When fish is cooked properly, the meat should flake, or separate easily with a fork.

Fold To add one ingredient, usually beaten egg whites, to another by lifting gently from underneath with a wooden spoon or rubber spatula. Do not stir or beat.

Garnish Decoration of food just before serving. Fresh herbs, vegetables or fruit are commonly used.

Grate To shred a solid food finely. Lemon, orange and lime rinds, as well as cheeses and vegetables, are grated.

Gratin Food that has a topping of bread crumbs or grated cheese and is browned under a broil.

Grill To cook under a direct intense heat or on a rack over hot coals.

Grind To cut food into small, fine pieces with the aid of a food processor or mill.

Hors d'oeuvres Small bite-size pieces of prepared food served warm or cold before dinner.

Julienne To cut foods (specifically vegetables) into long thin strips of equal length.

Line To cover the surface of a baking pan with parchment paper, foil or waxed paper to keep food from sticking.

Marinate To place meat, fish or chicken in seasoned liquid to flavor and tenderize it.

Mince To cut food into very fine morsels.

Parboil To cook partially in boiling water or stock. Vegetables can be parboiled before sautéeing to shorten cooking time.

Phyllo Thin sheet of dough used for pastries, vegetable and main dish entrées.

Poach To cook food in simmering - not boiling - liquid until just cooked. Ideal for fish or chicken.

Pound To flatten food by hitting it with a mallet or rolling pin. Boneless chicken breasts and veal scallopini are first placed between sheets of waxed paper, then pounded.

Purée To mash or grind food until smooth and free of lumps. A food processor is ideal for this use.

Roast To cook with dry heat. A higher heat is usually used to seal in juices, then a lower heat to finish cooking.

Sauté To cook food in fat in a skillet until just browned.

Sift To pass dry ingredients through a fine mesh strainer to remove lumps.

Simmer To cook liquid alone or with other food over a low heat. Do not allow to boil.

Steam To cook food over a small amount of boiling water, keeping covered. Typically used with vegetables to retain color, nutrients and taste. An excellent low-fat cooking method.

Stew To cook meats and vegetables in a covered pan with more than enough liquid to cover. Can be done on top of stove or in oven.

Stir fry To sauté meat, fish or vegetables quickly so as to retain color and taste. A wok is the best utensil to use.

Stock Broth made from the bones and/or meat of beef, fish, poultry or vegetables. Spices and herbs are added for flavor. Simmer, covered 1 1/2 to 2 1/2 hours for best taste. Strain before using.

Strain To remove solid food particles from liquids by pouring through a colander.

Toast To brown over a stove or in a hot oven (400°F/200°C).

Toss To mix ingredients together quickly and gently.

Zest The outermost colored peel of oranges, lemons or limes. When removing it, be sure not to include the white skin underneath, which is bitter.

Index

NOTES

NOTES

Notes

NOTES

NOTES

NOTES

NOTES